A HISTORY of SWEDEN

Lars O. Lagerqvist

A HISTORY *of* SWEDEN

THE SWEDISH INSTITUTE

Lars O. Lagerqvist was born in
1929. He worked as a museum
curator for many years and was
head of the Royal Coin Cabinet.
He is the author of a large number of books and articles on historical, cultural, numismatic and
gastronomical subjects.

The author is solely responsible
for the opinions presented in this
book.

Cover picture:

Count Magnus Gabriel De la Gardie
(1622-86), in the aristocratic fashion
of the day, with his wife, Maria Eufrosyne of the Palatinate, who is
placed one step above her husband
because she has a higher rank. An illustrious representative of the period
when Sweden was a Great Power, De
la Gardie long enjoyed the highest
office, including Chancellor of the
Realm and Regent for Karl XI, but he
was brought low by the ransacking of
the regency and the Reduction. As a
patron of culture and a builder of
palaces, and as Chancellor of Uppsala
University, he made an indelible contribution to the Swedish cultural her-
itage. In 1666, thanks to De la Gardie,
Sweden enacted its first law relating to
ancient monuments.

Painting by H. Münnichhoven, 1653.

Editor: Ulla von Schultz
Translation: Hugh Rodwell
Design and picture editor: Inga Britt Liljeroth
Maps: Stig Söderlind
Paper: G-Print, Colorit, Invercote Creato
First reprint
Printed in Sweden by Fälth & Hässler AB,
Värnamo, 2005
ISBN 91-520-0609-3

CONTENTS

7 · PREHISTORIC SWEDEN
7 · The Ice Age and hunter-gatherer cultures
9 · The New Stone Age – Agriculture
11 · The Bronze Age
12 · The Iron Age
14 · The Early Middle Ages – the Vendel
Period in Sweden
16 · The Viking Age
20 · Old and new religions

23 · THE SWEDISH MIDDLE AGES
23 · Civil war and the founding of the nation
25 · The High Middle Ages –
the Age of the Folkungs
33 · The Kalmar Union 1397–1521

41 · THE EARLY MODERN AGE
41 · The early Vasa period
43 · The Diet of Västerås
44 · Out of debt!
44 · Farms, estates and castles
45 · The sons of the Vasa dynasty
50 · War, expenses, inflation
52 · The struggle for power
53 · Karl IX – a national monarchy
55 · Commerce and society

57 · SWEDEN AS A GREAT POWER 1611–1718
58 · Reforms
60 · Peace and the second Älvsborg ransom
61 · War, peace, armistice
62 · The Thirty Years War
64 · The regency and the continuation of the war
66 · War with Denmark

67 · The Peace of Westphalia, 1648
67 · The succession
69 · Immigrants, trade and commerce, colonies
and finance
70 · The abdication
70 · The conqueror takes power
73 · The regency
75 · The king comes of age and war breaks out
77 · Absolutism and Reduction
79 · The death of the king
79 · A teenage king
80 · The Great Northern War and the end of Sweden
as a Great Power
82 · The defeat at Poltava
83 · The kalabalik of Bender
83 · The king's return and his death
85 · The seventeenth century – glory and poverty

87 · THE AGE OF FREEDOM 1719–72
87 · A queen on a leash – the fall of absolutism
88 · The peace treaties of 1719–21
90 · The abdication of Ulrika Eleonora
90 · Rule by Parliament and Council.
The Age of Arvid Horn
92 · Commerce and industry
94 · The fall of Arvid Horn and the Hats in power
95 · The war with Russia 1741–43
96 · The Peace of Åbo. The rebellion in Dalarna
and the election of the successor to the throne
99 · A north German dynasty
101 · A failed coup. The Seven Years War
102 · The bankruptcy of commercial policy
102 · The Caps take power

104 · The government and fall of the Caps
105 · The final government of the Hats.
        The death of the king
106 · The Age of Freedom – a summary

107 · THE GUSTAVIAN AGE 1772–1809
107 · The end of the Age of Freedom and
        the overturn of the Constitution
109 · The Constitution of 1772
109 · Opinions of the Age of Freedom
110 · The personality and family life of Gustav III
113 · The Gustavian reforms
114 · The parliament of 1778–79
114 · Foreign policy before 1785
115 · Domestic policy before 1788 and
        the parliament of 1786
116 · The attack on Russia and the war of 1788–90
118 · The parliament of 1789.
        The fall of the nobility
119 · The peace of 1790. Gustav III's final years
121 · The assassination of the king, 1792
122 · The regency government of 1792–96
124 · The reign of Gustav IV Adolf
124 · Foreign policy and war. The king is deposed

127 · FROM A LAND OF PEASANT FARMERS
        TO AN INDUSTRIAL NATION
127 · The Constitution of 1809
128 · The election of a successor. The peaces
129 · The murder of Axel von Fersen
130 · The Örebro parliament of 1810.
        The election of Bernadotte
132 · One-man rule
133 · Sweden's last wars. The Union with Norway
134 · Swedish neutrality
137 · "No one has had a career like mine"
137 · Defence, the national finances and
        domestic policy
139 · The opposition
141 · Liberalism
142 · Emigration and gradual industrialization
143 · Foreign policy
144 · The government takes charge
144 · Reforms
146 · The parliamentary reform of 1866

149 · Foreign policy. The bankruptcy of
        Scandinavianism
150 · Monetary policy

151 · INDUSTRIALIZATION AND
        SLOW PROGRESS
151 · A new king and the gold standard
152 · Parliament and the military question
152 · Financial crisis and protectionism
154 · Military reform and the franchise
156 · A new foreign policy
157 · Norway's secession from the Union
158 · Preparing for parliamentary democracy
159 · Reforms and the military question
160 · The growth of Swedish industry
162 · Living standards
164 · The popular mass movements
165 · The labour movement
167 · The women's movement
167 · The First World War and
        the victory of parliamentary democracy

171 · DEMOCRACY AND
        THE "PEOPLE'S HOME"
171 · The Åland question
172 · A period of weak governments
174 · The Social-Democrats in government
175 · Foreign policy
176 · Sweden during the Second World War
179 · Swedish concessions to Germany
180 · The final stages of the war
181 · Domestic policy 1939–45
182 · The immediate postwar period
183 · International undertakings
185 · Modern Sweden
187 · A new Constitution
188 · Alternating governments
192 · The EU, the EMU and the euro
194 · Embarking on a new millennium

196 · Sweden's kings and regents from AD 1000
197 · Sweden's wars and peace treaties after
        the dissolution of the Kalmar Union in 1523
198 · Prime ministers and parties in power from 1876
199 · Political parties
200 · Index

P PREHISTORIC SWEDEN

THE ICE AGE AND HUNTER-GATHERER CULTURES ∾ The part of northern Europe that was to become Sweden was completely covered by ice some 40,000 years ago, when the most recent Ice Age reached its peak. The ice covered parts of northern Germany, while the Scandinavian peninsula and Denmark were covered by a layer of ice several kilometres thick; only in the far west, in Norway, were there a few small areas that were unaffected, but this was in all probability only the case when the cold period was coming to an end. A lot of oceanic water was held frozen in the ice and the sea level sank between 100 and 175 metres. But the weight of the ice also pressed the land mass far below its current level.

With a certain degree of regularity the climate on our planet gets milder and the ice melts. This process got under way some 15,000-20,000 years ago, and a few thousand years later Denmark was free of ice and the southernmost part of Sweden – which much later came to be known as Skåne – could be reached on foot by a landbridge across the Sound linking the peninsula-to-be with the Continent, or rather Zealand. Migrating hunters were met by tundra, and what was to become the Baltic was an inland lake, now known as the Baltic Ice Lake. This migration must have taken place around 12,000 years before our era, and the oldest settlement yet dated is from exactly that period. It was found at Mölleröd by Finja Lake in Skåne. A newly discovered settlement in northern Småland is a little more recent. These hunters probably kept close to the edge of the melting ice. A second wave of migration left many settlement remains in western Sweden. The whole of this period, from about 12000 to 9000 BC, is known as the Late Paleolithic or Late Glacial era. Who were these people? We do not know for certain, but currently a number of researchers tend to think they were probably the ancestors of the present-day Sami of Lapland. Which wave of migration brought the Indo-Europeans, who at least linguistically have long made up the majority of the Swedish population? This again we cannot determine with any certainty. Perhaps they came with agriculture (around 4000 BC). In any case, by 2000 BC many of them must have been speaking an Indo-European language – but well-mixed with the earliest inhabitants. It all seems to have happened quite peacefully.

Somewhat before 9000 BC the edge of the ice had retreated to central Sweden, and now the water broke through, forming a large sound, and the ice lake was united with the present-day North Sea and replaced by the Yoldia Sea. The name is derived from a salt-water mussel common in its waters, which had become salt after mixing with the inflowing ocean. But now a new factor made its presence felt – the rising of the land mass. About 8000 BC the Yoldia Sea was replaced by the inland Ancylus Lake, named after a snail that only thrives in fresh water. The ice-sheet which had planed away most of the surface from periods preceding the Ice Age disappeared from the north of Sweden, too. The land elevation continued, and is still in progress today. The gravel ridges, moraine and clay soils and layers of sand which had formed became hosts to various kinds of vegetation and to the animals the people used as food and whose skins and furs they made into clothes and other necessities. The forest migrated from the south – first dwarf birch and related species, then alder, willow, the common birch, a pine or two and then, at the time of the formation of the Ancylus Lake, lime and oak. Eventually the spruce came down from the north, but by then a later period had already begun.

From about 9000 to around 4000 BC historians speak of the Mesolithic period, or the Middle Stone Age. From about 7500 BC people are known to have settled central and northern Sweden. They lived by hunting, fishing and gathering, and many tools of bone and horn have been preserved where the settlements were in boggy locations. Otherwise the remains are predominantly flints in the south and quartz and other minerals in the north of Sweden. The great extent of Sweden and the fact that it has many climatic zones, from the fertile Skåne in the south to regions north of the Arctic Circle with long, dark winters, was already proving to be a significant factor. Warm periods have also been succeeded by several centuries of cooler conditions which made survival difficult. It is no coincidence that the hunting communities continued their traditional way of life

This unusually well-preserved skeleton was found at Bäckaskog in Skåne, southern Sweden. It was initially believed to be male, but "he" was later shown to have given birth to several children and the skeleton is now referred to as the "Bäckaskog woman". Modern methods have specified a date for the skeleton between 7000 and 6000 BC, during the hunting-gathering period.

8

much longer in the northern regions than elsewhere.

Around 4500 BC the sea returned, or more correctly, Lake Ancylus broke out. The Belts and the Sound were formed and the land links between southern Sweden and Denmark were broken. Initially there was a great inflow of salt water, and the Baltic of the period is known as the Littorina Sea, after yet another mollusc, a snail. After another 1,500 years, the Baltic and the lands around it had taken on a shape not unlike today's, even if the coast was still under water – Lake Mälaren was an inlet of the Baltic until the twelfth century AD, and salt waves lapped the beaches just east of present-day Enköping.

New cultures arose, named after the places where the archaeologists have made their most important finds. There were large settlements near the coast in southern Sweden – one of them was recently excavated in connection with the construction of the approach roads to the bridge over the Sound south of Malmö and surprised even the specialists by its extent.

The natural resources of the place, not least the plentiful fish, induced people to settle there more or less permanently. The dog was still the only domestic animal. Far to the north, in Norrland, where the stone-age village of Vuollerim has been shown to be at least 6,000 years old, more use was being made of slate in tools by inhabitants who appear to have penetrated here from both east and west. But new times were approaching. That great revolution in human history, agriculture and animal husbandry, was about to sweep into these latitudes, or at least the most southerly of them.

THE NEW STONE AGE – AGRICULTURE (4000-1800 BC) ❧ Farming societies developed along a path from south to north. The process began about 4000 BC. The Beaker culture got its name from the pottery of the period. Domesticated cattle and small-scale agriculture were introduced in the southern and central parts of the country, and considerably more slowly in the coastal areas of the north. Throughout the world, this type of society was a precondition for the development of a new kind of civilization, with time to spare for reflection, invention and planning for the future. Agriculture made it possible to systematically store food and thus obtain more free time for other activities.

The cereals introduced and used during the New Stone Age, or Neolithic period, were barley and wheat. Then as now, certain soils were more suitable than others for grain cultivation, but in general it is probably fair to say that cattle breeding was more important and remained so for many centuries. Those whose main occupation was agriculture regularly saw their land lose its vigour and had to move after one or two generations. But settlements became more and more permanent and this must have been due to improved technologies, such as the use of manure on the fields. As late as the Viking era (800-1050 AD), food was primarily lacto-animal in character, that is, it was based on milk products and meat and fish, supplemented by porridge, simple (unleavened) bread and certain herbs and vegetables such as peas and broad beans. The domesticated cow had been developed from the aurochs, the pig from the wild boar; and there were also sheep and even-

Neolithic passage graves are found in many places in southern and central Sweden, but nowhere in such profusion as in Västergötland. They were family graves, in which several generations were buried. In Karleby in Västergötland the farms still lie on one side of the road, and the passage graves on the other.

tually a few goats. And all the while, of course, hunting and fishing were of great importance. During the middle of the New Stone Age (around 3300-2200 BC) there was a new climatic reversal, leading to the abandonment of agriculture in central Sweden for a period. There are clear indications of eastern influences.

In their permanent settlements, people did not just erect buildings but also devoted a good deal of energy to preparing their graves. The early New Stone Age is known for its large dolmens and passage graves from around 3700 BC onwards. These required much labour to construct and functioned as family graves for many generations. Towards the end of the period, a new culture appears.

Nothing has been so controversial among researchers specializing in the early history of Europe than problems concerning mass migration and the languages of ethnic groups (and thus eventually of nations). How many waves of migration, how many ethnic or linguistic shifts has any given country been exposed to? When did the Indo-European languages arrive? Did they come with agriculture or were they later? Is Basque an aboriginal language of Europe? Or Etruscan? And where do those speaking Finno-Ugric languages, including the Sami, fit in? When did the Sami come to what was to become Sweden? Is it an aboriginal population, as seems to be the case? And how do all the various theories fare in the light of the most recent DNA research?

Around 2800 BC, a new culture moved into southern Scandinavia from the Continent – known as the Boat-axe or Battle-axe culture, named for their elegant shaft-holed axe-heads, which imitated bronze models. Communal graves fell into disuse and were replaced by individual graves. The new grave culture extended to Uppland, but little further. This culture covered the whole of Europe otherwise, with the exception of the Balkans. Towards the end of this period, metal-working reached Scandinavia. Curiously enough there are a few isolated, early finds of copper objects datable to between 4000-2700 BC. The evidence points to gold, copper or bronze primarily being used as measures of value and as ornaments. But what were the dimensions of the migration involved – great or small? Did the Battle-axe people give rise not just to a new culture, a new religion and social divisions, but also to a new language? We cannot tell, but it is possible that they did.

The rock carvings and rock paintings of Norrland (and Finland) are probably associated with the end of the New Stone Age and the beginning of the next period. Their motives are magical and associated principally with elk-hunting and fishing. These monuments are more difficult to date than the rock carvings of southern and central Sweden, with which we shall deal in the next period, the Bronze Age, when the climate was milder once more.

T HE BRONZE AGE (1800-500 BC) ❧ Trading in flints from mines mainly located in Skåne took place as early as the New Stone Age. Depots have been found along the coast of Norrland and even to the north of Skellefteå. By way of trade – that is, imports – the soft metal copper (and gold, too) became known to the northerners, although to begin with it was only regarded as an item of pure luxury. No copper lodes were known here until the Viking Age or the period just preceding it. Some two or three hundred years later bronze, the harder alloy of copper and tin, made its appearance. It must also have been imported. The nearest tin mines were in England and copper was mined in Austria and other places. For everyday work, stone implements still had to be used.

The culture that arose during the Bronze Age in southern and central Sweden was highly developed. This is the period to which we owe the remarkable rock carvings that can be encountered by the coast or along (ancient) waterways. By no means all of them have been discovered yet! They bear exciting testimony

The rock carvings of Bohuslän have been dated to the Bronze Age. The figures symbolize fertility, ships, arms and many other things. This ancient rock carving, created in Södra Ödsmål 3,000 years ago, depicts fishing from a boat with a line and hook.

A sensational find of Bronze Age shields was made in Fröslunda in Västergötland in 1985. They are from the eighth century BC and were evidently for ritual use – the bronze plating is too thin to afford any protection in battle.

to the religion of the Swedes three thousand years ago or more. Their links with an agricultural form of culture are self-evident – the cult depicted is associated with fertility, but also with trade (ploughing, erotic couples, ships). There are also pictures of ceremonial axes, horns and swords which have made it easier to date these carvings.

Social divisions emerge more clearly than in the preceding period. Luxury goods like beautiful spiral jewellery, gilded razors, bowls, etc., were naturally not the property of everyman (or everywoman). The great Bronze Age mounds were raised over chieftains of whose jurisdiction we know nothing. The remarkable Kivik grave in Skåne is from this period, with its carved grave slabs, but so too is the large, earthcovered "royal mound" at Håga near Uppsala, which was excavated in 1902 and yielded rich finds such as a gold-inlaid bronze sword, but also bore traces of human sacrifice. The dead chieftain had been burnt. Cremation had first appeared during the older Bronze Age and was becoming more common, although burials with graves containing skeletons are known from the whole of the prehistoric period. Sometimes the dead were laid in an oak chest, and in a few cases this in conjunction with suitable soil has preserved the clothing (although

this only applies to finds in Denmark; a mantle found at Gerum in the province of Västergötland has now been dated to the early Iron Age). Wool was woven.

New foods included oats and millet. Salting was used, although the usual methods of conservation were drying, smoking and fermenting. Towards the end of the Bronze Age, the climate again grew colder. This meant more work for peasants collecting stores and hay. Houses were more solidly built and barns were built for the cattle.

THE IRON AGE (500 BC-1050 AD) ∾ Historical times were now approaching, but it would still be some time before ancient historians first mentioned Scandinavia and the tribes living there. However, archaeological finds show that people here had learned to use and to make iron objects, initially mostly of what is known as bog-iron ore from lake bottoms or the red earth in ore-rich areas. Southern and western Sweden were still in constant contact with the Continent, especially with the Celtic La Tène culture. For a couple of centuries after 500 BC the climate was still cold and there are few finds. The peasants gathered in villages and presumably the farming community had begun to assume the form it retained until modern times.

From around the time of Christ's birth to AD 350, historians speak of the Roman Iron Age. The influence of the Roman Empire extended to Scandinavia. At the same time or a little earlier, Germanic tribes had pushed further into Europe and the influence of the Celts had diminished. The Gauls and some Britons were subdued by Rome. Renewed trading exchanges gave rise to rich hoards of Roman silver coins and objects, some of which were luxuries. And now the first written sources made their appearance. In about AD 100, the Roman author Tacitus mentions Scandinavia and a tribe he calls the Suiones in his work *De Germania*. In this and later works, Scandinavia is reported to have many tribes, all ruled by chieftains.

After the conflicts and galloping inflation of the third century AD had weakened Rome's world dominion, a period of great turbulence set in around 350 that was to last into the sixth century. German tribes were on the move and the period has become known as the Age of the Great Migrations. New states took shape on the ruins of the collapsing Western Roman Empire, but the Eastern Roman Empire and its capital Constantinople were to survive for many centuries yet. During the Age of the Great Migrations, contacts between Scandinavia and the Continent were still close. Some soldiers became mercenaries as guards in the service of the Byzantine emperors. Gold took the place of silver as the favoured import of value. This period gave rise to some of the most exquisite gold ornaments ever produced in Sweden, such as the three surviving gold necklets. For the most part gold was imported in the form of Western and Eastern Roman *solidus* coins, many of which have been found on the islands of Öland and Gotland and in the Mälaren basin.

Notable among the German tribes ravaging Europe were the Ostrogoths and the Visigoths, who at various times established kingdoms in Spain and northern Italy. Their relationship with the Geats of Götaland and the Gotlanders

and the claim of a Roman chronicler that they were thought to come from Scandinavia encouraged in early modern times the Great Swedish notion that it was none other than emigrants from Gotland and Öster- and Västergötland respectively that had brought about the downfall of the Roman Empire. There is no incontrovertible historical evidence for these old tales, however, even if we are able to establish that the links among related branches of the various tribes were quite intimate. In addition, the proto-Germanic languages were very closely related.

The Age of the Great Migrations was a turbulent period, and saw the construction of fortresses offering shelter to the population. Farms were destroyed or abandoned, not least in Gotland and Öland. In eastern Sweden in particular the changes may well have regional-economic explanations, or even political ones. The plague was rife in large parts of Europe and may also have ravaged Sweden.

One of the large gold necklets from the Age of the Great Migrations, made by highly skilled local goldsmiths. The gold came from late Roman coins known as *solidi*. Two such necklets have been found in Västergötland and one in Öland. This many-ringed necklet from Möne in Västergötland may have decorated the statue of a god, or was perhaps worn by a person of high rank.

A helmet and sword from one of the graves at Vendel in Uppland. The Vendel Period – the seventh and eighth centuries – is named after these finds. These splendid objects – the height of luxury in their age – have been conserved and partially restored.

This period also saw the erection of the three great royal burial mounds at Old Uppsala. A rich web of traditional tales has been woven around these monuments. Two of them have been excavated. According to recent studies a fourteen-year-old and a woman were buried in the eastern mound, not Ane the Old, who lived to be two hundred according to the Icelandic sagas (written eight hundred years later!). The western mound holds a middle-aged man. The funeral rites involved cremation.

THE EARLY MIDDLE AGES – THE VENDEL PERIOD IN SWEDEN (CA 550-800) ❧ In central and southern Europe, where written documents were already being produced in ancient times, the Middle Ages are usually considered to start with the fall of the Western Roman Empire, just before AD 500. This view has not often been shared by Nordic historians, however. Here we shall use the customary Nordic periodization, but also wish to indicate (as in the heading) that the period in question is that of the early European Middle Ages.

The period immediately preceding the Viking Age is usually known as the Vendel Period after the large, richly equipped shipgraves at Vendel in northern Uppland, where the dead chieftains were buried unburnt. With them they took to the next life possessions that were luxuries rather than of any practical use in war. Some of the equipment has close parallels with Byzantine objects and the finds at the great burial site of Sutton Hoo in England. Similar graves have since been found in places like Valsgärde and Tuna. Few finds of this type have yet

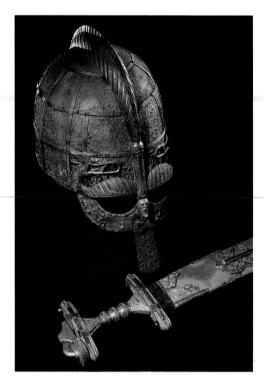

been made outside the province of Uppland. In Västmanland, women have been found buried in ships. One thing these finds teach us is that there were powerful chieftains and a rich society with connections far beyond their own immediate boundaries. Places like Helgö in Lake Mälaren, which was discovered by chance in the 1950s, show us that even before Birka (see below) there were important trading settlements where a number of handicrafts were also practised.

Most of the remarkable pictorial stones from Gotland belong to the Vendel Period, too, at least the most detailed and impressive of them. The religious myths of the time may be studied

14

on these stones. Some, however, remain uninterpreted. This is because the Icelandic sagas, that were written down much later, provide our key to the iconography of the stones and it is not likely that all the sagas of the gods that were current in Gotland were still being retold in distant Iceland many centuries later. Furthermore, historians are not in complete agreement concerning these interpretations.

The writing of the German peoples, the runes, originated with the Goths as early as the Roman Iron Age and the oldest inscriptions are found in Gotland – the Kylver stone, an ornament and an arrowhead. They are usually dated to shortly after AD 200. Subsequently the use of runes became more commonplace, even if most of our finds are from the Viking Age and the early (Nordic) Middle Ages, particularly the late rune stones from the eleventh century.

At this time a proto-Germanic language had long been spoken in Scandinavia. This is shown both by research into the origin of place names and words we possess thanks to foreign documents or runic inscriptions. It is hardly possible to trace any differences between Danish, Norwegian or Swedish before the eleventh century, except possibly with respect to pronunciation. What differences there were were quite insignificant. Modern Icelandic is still very close to Primitive Norse, both in grammar and vocabulary (though its pronunciation has changed), and as a result speakers of Danish, Norwegian and Swedish, which have adopted many loanwords and radically simplified their grammatical forms, are no longer able to understand Icelandic, although they usually are able to understand one another.

The Sami are another ethnic group which perhaps came to Sweden from a number of directions (see above) and used to live much further south in prehistoric times. The Stone Age in Norrland, which in part developed directly into the Iron Age, is better known today than it used to be thanks to comprehensive excavations. The coastal areas of the far north were inhabited early on, and agriculture and animal husbandry were introduced from the south by

Gotland is the home of great pictorial stones, most of which date from the seventh and eighth centuries. This stone from Ardre parish depicts an episode from a gory prehistoric saga known to us from later Icelandic versions.

Model of Birka. Most scholars are now convinced that ancient Birka was located on the island of Björkö in Lake Mälaren, where the nearby royal demesne at Adelsö afforded protection. The first archaeological excavations took place in the seventeenth century. In the late twentieth century the settlement and harbour areas were excavated.

the people who migrated here. In the interior, hunters and fishers were still living. They were most probably Sami. They can at least be distinguished as Sami at a fairly early period, preceding the Iron Age. They adopted reindeer herding much later. The Sami language is related to Finnish and belongs to the Finno-Ugric group. The question of the migration of the Finns and the development of the two languages has also been the subject of much discussion. The first mention of the Sami (by foreign authors) in the sixth century AD refers to them as *skridfinnar*, or gliding Finns, from their use of skis. The Finns proper refer to their own language as *suomi* and the Sami language as *saame*, both words coming from the same stem. The word *Lapland* and the name *Lapps* are mediaeval loans from Finnish and have never been used by the Sami themselves.

THE VIKING AGE (800-1050) ❧ There is probably no period in Scandinavian history that has been as fascinating to people of other countries as the Viking Age. There are few historical sources for the period and over the centuries they have been interpreted in very different ways. Since the nineteenth century, however, archaeology has provided more and more material for us to learn from. The written sources are scarce and of varying reliability.

16

Foreign chroniclers occasionally mention the peoples, rulers and chieftains of Scandinavia, as do the much later works of Icelandic literature or brief notes in mediaeval manuscripts such as the catalogue of kings in the Old Law of Västergötland. Contemporary testimony is found in inscriptions on rune stones and coins. Among the relatively reliable sources we may include the chronicler Rimbert, who wrote of Ansgar's journeys to Sweden and Birka in the ninth century to preach Christianity, and Adam of Bremen, who wrote the history of the archdiocese of Hamburg and Bremen in the 1070s and deals with the Scandinavian countries that formed part of its jurisdiction. Adam never visited Sweden. His source was King Sven Estridsen of Denmark, who had lived in exile at the court of the Swedish King Anund Jakob for a number of years. One recent researcher considers Adam's book to be a partisan contribution to the ecclesiastical disputes of his day (a very natural interpretation) and this of course hardly improves its value as an impartial source. And from all these fragments, we are obliged to construct a history of the Viking Age – not an easy task!

When was Sweden unified? There is no research consensus on this, but it would seem that the nation, which did not include the southern or the northern parts of present-day Sweden, had a single king some time towards the end of the tenth century, either Erik the Victorious or his son Olof Skötkonung. It was a kind of federation, very loosely articulated, whose head had certain functions, such as leading the levied forces of the navy and the army in war and officiating at sacrificial ceremonies in Old Uppsala.

This latter function ceased when the king converted to Christianity, a move which did little to strengthen his hold on power. From laws put into written form much later we learn that the Thing assemblies in the various provinces had considerable power, and that the new king had to be accepted by them all. He had to undertake an *eriksgata*, a progress through the realm in the course of which he presented himself in each province, whereupon he would be led to the Thing and there acclaimed and shown homage. But it is an open question whether Sweden was an elective kingdom in the Viking Age – perhaps the ceremony in which the king was "taken" and shown homage at Mora Stone in Uppland took on a new aspect in later phases of the Middle Ages.

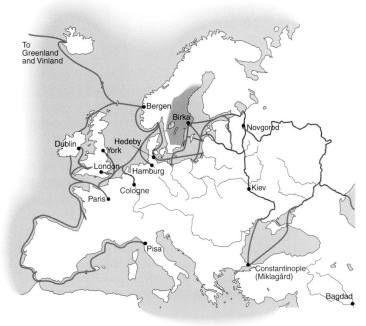

Map of the main Viking routes 800-1050. Most Swedish Vikings travelled the eastern routes, but some from what is today southern and western Sweden also participated in western campaigns. Expeditions to America (Vinland) set out from Iceland and Greenland.

At this time there were no taxes. The king's revenues came from a number of estates which belonged to the Crown from at least the end of the Viking Age. Such a royal demesne was known as a *husaby* ("household estate"). Most such places are found in Svealand, but there are some in Götaland. Perhaps the best known of them is Husaby near Kinnekulle ridge in Västergötland, where there is a sacred spring and a church whose oldest parts perhaps date back to the end of the eleventh century.

Where did the expansive force originate that powered the deeds of the Northern peoples during the Viking Age? Why did they embark on these Viking expeditions, this colonization both of virtually uninhabited regions (such as Iceland, Greenland and Vinland) and of rich and populated lands (such as Normandy and the Danelaw), and these long trading voyages that even took them to the Great Caliphate in the East? The trading centres that were now emerging in Scandinavia – Hedeby in (what was then) Denmark, Ribe in Zealand, Birka in Lake Mälaren, Kaupang in Norway, and others – can be shown to have been established by the end of the eighth century (Ribe even earlier). But the first known pillaging raid by Nordic Vikings

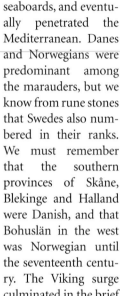

A Viking sword had to be made from the finest steel to serve its purpose as a weapon. It was no luxury, even though the hilts could be richly decorated.

was recorded when they plundered the monastery of Lindisfarne on Holy Island off the English coast in 793.

The Viking expeditions in the West are the best known. They soon spread to Germany, France and the Portuguese and Spanish seaboards, and eventually penetrated the Mediterranean. Danes and Norwegians were predominant among the marauders, but we know from rune stones that Swedes also numbered in their ranks. We must remember that the southern provinces of Skåne, Blekinge and Halland were Danish, and that Bohuslän in the west was Norwegian until the seventeenth century. The Viking surge culminated in the brief but extensive Danish realm of Sweyn Forkbeard (d. 1014) and Canute the Great (d. 1035), which also included England and Norway. Many regions of England had already been under Viking dominion, most notably the Danelaw with York as its capital. The Isle of Man was also a Nordic "kingdom". The Norwegian kingdom of Dublin flourished in Ireland. And in the early tenth century, Rollo (Rolf the Ganger – who was said to be too tall to sit on a horse) became duke of Normandy and a vassal of the king of France. Charles the Simple had become exasperated by the Viking raids, especially when they didn't shrink from besieging Paris, and he calculated that Rollo the Vassal would be more accommodating than Rollo the Raider. Rollo's successor, William the Conqueror, would invade England in 1066 and

order to the land. The impulse for these lucrative expeditions, according to certain historians, was provided by Islam and the Caliphate, which began their expansion with the death of Mohammed in 632 and were only brought to a halt one hundred years later in France. Trade

The great silver hoard of Lummelunda parish in Gotland caused a sensation when it was discovered in 1969. It mainly consists of Viking Age coins from the Caliphate, Germany and England. The silver ingots are ancient Russian "grivna" with Old Slavic inscriptions. Several of the coins were previously unknown.

make himself king of the island nation.

In the East, Swedish Vikings predominated. Their expeditions were launched from the Mälaren region and Gotland and reached Miklagård (Constantinople) and the Black Sea by way of the great Russian rivers. According to the Chronicle of Nestor, written in the twelfth century, Swedes – the "rus", perhaps from the Roslagen region north-east of Stockholm – actually founded the Russian kingdom when the tribes living there summoned a man named Rurik and his followers to rule them and bring

between western Europe and the Near East was cut off and replaced by the Russian trade routes, in which Scandinavians played a significant part. Towards the end of the tenth century we can see that imports from and trade with the eastern countries started to diminish. After 1013, no more Islamic silver coins reached the Nordic countries. Trade in the Mediterranean was resumed. This is an important – but far from the only – factor explaining the Viking successes and their subsequent decline.

The remarkable island of Gotland has a spe-

Equestrian figures in a collection of chess pieces discovered in the Hebrides and dated to the twelfth century. Note that the helmets had no horns! Horned Viking helmets are a recent and unhistorical fabrication.

Pictorial stones and jewellery tell us how the women of the Viking Age used to dress. This is a small silver figure from Birka.

cial position with its rich and widely-travelled peasants, whose wealth arose from both farming and Viking expeditions. For the period between 800 and 1140, there is no place on earth that has yielded so many finds of silver treasure. Various explanations have been given for why so much silver has remained in the soil here, and so little elsewhere. Since most of the silver was hidden in dwelling houses, it was probably a matter of laying aside a reserve that was not needed for everyday purposes. Gotland represents more than 65 per cent of all finds of precious metals (almost exclusively silver) from the Viking Age in what is now Sweden. In 1999, two early Viking treasures were found in close proximity, and they are almost eight times as big as the Burge treasure from Lummelunda which weighs over 10 kilos and was buried around 1140, the most recent date to be verified for a Viking treasure. In the finds, by far the most numerous coins are Islamic, although there are a few Persian Sassanid coins from the seventh century, in spite of the fact that such

coins were hardly imported before the end of the eighth century. During the tenth century, silver dirhams are found less and less frequently, and cease altogether at the beginning of the eleventh. At that time they had been replaced for some decades by German, Anglo-Saxon and Byzantine coins. The silver pennies that came in large quantities from England most likely originate in the large-scale Danegeld payments being squeezed by Viking kings out of the nation they plundered and eventually conquered. In the decades preceding 1100, this import diminishes and finally stops altogether, last of all in Gotland.

OLD AND NEW RELIGIONS ❧ The most reliable monuments of the old religion in Sweden are to be found in a number of place names (Frösåker, Odensvi, Torslunda, etc.) and in pre-Christian rune stones and objects that were linked to religious practices. We have reason to be grateful to Icelandic literature for many things, but it was written down in a Christian society and we have to treat its statements with some caution. The old world view with Odin (creation and wisdom), Thor (thunder), Frigg (Odin's wife), Tyr (war), Frey (fertility) and Baldur (sweetness and light) was in all likelihood much more primitive than depicted in the sagas, especially in everyday peasant households. At home, simple magic was practised and various nature spirits were propitiated – this is the origin of the fairies, wood nymphs, trolls and goblins of folk lore. The custom of anointing bowl-shaped pits with fat and of making sacrifices at springs had very ancient roots.

There were communal sites for worshipping these divinities and they were mainly in the open air. The famous temple at Uppsala described by Adam of Bremen in the 1070s (but which he had never seen) was probably an exception – if indeed it ever existed. Archaeolo-

Mediaeval legends tell of Saint Sigfrid preaching Christianity in Sweden in the early eleventh century. He is said to have baptized Olof Skötkonung at Husaby in Västergötland. Historical painting by J. Z. Blackstadius, 1866.

gists have found no reliable traces of it in Old Uppsala. Perhaps it was situated in Östra Aros, near the present cathedral, as some of the old chroniclers thought. This was where the king of the Swedes would officiate at sacrificial rites – until he became Christian.

The first known Christian mission to Sweden was described in Rimbert's chronicle, mentioned above, which is considered to be fairly reliable. It was led by the "Apostle of the North", Ansgar, who was born in France but came to Birka on the island of Björkö in Lake Mälaren in 830 and obtained the king's permission to preach. Despite a return visit in 852, his work and that of others at the same period had little lasting effect and the small Christian congregation found it difficult to maintain contact with its southern coreligionists. When Birka was abandoned some time in the 970s, Christianity had probably suffered a temporary defeat. It was not until the end of this same century that missionary work began in earnest. At Sigtuna in Svealand, founded in the 970s, it was not long before a church was built, but the most notable successes of the early missionaries were in southern Sweden, in Götaland. German and Anglo-Saxon missionaries vied with each other in spreading the faith. Olof Skötkonung (who ruled from ca 995 to 1022) had himself baptized early in his reign, and started the nation's first mint in Sigtuna, shortly after 995. The first coins had English pennies as their model.

But Swedish Christianity was nothing like the European variety. The priests were appointed by chieftains or peasant communities and the thralls remained in bondage. Initially, therefore, the Church had no independence.

Christianity was eventually introduced with little controversy. The majority of the eleven-century rune stones in Uppland were carved and erected by Christians. The heathen cult was still being practised in Uppsala in 1070, if Adam of Bremen is to be believed, but by then the old royal dynasty had passed away with a son of king Olof.

A small, early tenth century silver crucifix from a woman's grave in Birka.

THE SWEDISH MIDDLE AGES

CIVIL WAR AND THE FOUNDING OF THE NATION (1060-1250) ∾ Should the Middle Ages really be considered to start with a change of dynasty? From a political perspective, the Viking Age actually came to an end earlier. The expansive surge had ebbed and trade with the East had practically ceased. The final flourish, Ingvar's expedition, well-attested thanks to the many rune stones in the Mälaren basin commm-memorating its victims, took place in the 1040s and was a fiasco in which most of its participants, including Ingvar, died in an epidemic. Economically speaking, at least according to the testimony of imported coins, the Viking Age lasted a few more decades, until the early years of the twelfth century, and even longer in Gotland. Historically speaking, the period after 1060 is even more obscure, at least until around 1130, than the final years of the Viking Age. Royal power was weak, the provinces with their Things, law-speakers (prominent figures who memorized and transmitted the law in the old oral tradition) and Jarls were more important than the distant ruler. For more than 200 years, Swedish historians have had to go to the few available sources and weigh probabilities. Every chronicle, every fragment of a document and every find bearing an inscription has been turned inside out, been interpreted and reinterpreted, time and time again.

After the death of Emund the Old in 1060, a prominent Christian chieftain called Stenkil was elected king. This was to be followed by 200 years of internecine struggles between dynasties and pretenders to the throne. At the same time the population was increasing and so were the new agricultural settlements. The climate was in fact rather favourable until the end of the thirteenth century, when what is known as the "minor Ice Age" began. During this period it is believed that the population tripled. The number of thralls decreased as some received their liberty,

The round church in Bromma near Stockholm. Swedish round churches are usually from the late twelfth century and served a dual function – for church services and for defence.

and it was often probably these freed thralls who broke the ground for new settlements. Towns appeared, but they were still few and insignificant, the houses were of wood and only the churches were built of stone. Trade increased, at least from the twelfth century onwards. The Pope turned his thoughts to this distant country and wrote one or two letters, whose drafts are still preserved, in the 1070s. Fifty years later, there were dioceses in Skara, Linköping, Eskilstuna, Strängnäs, Västerås and Sigtuna. In the mid-twelfth century, the bishop moved from Sigtuna to Old Uppsala, where a church had been built.

The male line of the Stenkil dynasty had expired in the early 1120s. The struggles for succession continued, and for a hundred years two clans alternated on the throne. These were the Sverkers and the Eriks, named after their founders Sverker (ca 1130-1156) and Erik, later known as Saint Erik, who only reigned briefly before being killed in 1160. The weakness of the monarchy benefited powerful local chieftains in southern and central Sweden, and increased the autonomy of the provinces.

Two synods were crucial in bringing the Swedish Church more power and wealth. The first took place in Linköping in 1153. The Papal legate was Nicholas of Albano, who would later himself become Pope. He managed to persuade the Swedes to accept a tax to Rome that was known as Peter's pence. He noted that conditions in the country were turbulent and that the Swedes were not yet ready for an archbishop of their own. However, king Karl Sverkersson was able to obtain this privilege in 1164, when Stefan, an English-born monk from the Alvastra monastery in Östergötland, was ordained archbishop in Old Uppsala. This made him the head of the Swedish Church, although he was still subordinate to the Danish archdiocese of Lund. The second synod was convened at Skänninge in 1248, with William of Sabina as the Papal legate. This synod removed most of the exceptional provisions regarding Sweden. The peasants were no longer able to elect their priests, and these were not allowed to be married. A cathedral chapter was instituted. A few decades later Church property was exempted from taxation, thus creating a privileged religious nobility.

Monasteries, most of them Cistercian, had already been established, the first of them in Götaland at Vreta, Alvastra and other places in the early twelfth century. These were soon followed by a number of monasteries in Svealand. During the thirteenth century the mendicant orders made their appearance and set themselves up in the towns. These were the Franciscans, known as the greyfriars, and the Dominicans, known as the blackfriars, from the colour of their robes. The monasteries occupied themselves with caring for the sick, bringing new land under cultivation, laying out gardens and teaching the Swedes how to make bricks. The cultural impact on Sweden, a country hitherto very marginal to Europe, was felt in every field: architecture, art, handicrafts, legal notions and names. Some Swedes travelled abroad to study at universities such as the Sorbonne in Paris.

The royal power – if power it was – long had its centre of gravity in Götaland. Both the rival clans had their principal estates there, and Östergötland, the province of the Sverkers, was of especial importance to the kings. But since the twelfth century the powerful figure of the Jarl had been a fixture alongside the king. Many Jarls had come from the clan later known as the Folkungs, whose base was the Bjälbo estate in Östergötland. An historically verifiable clan patriarch who flourished around 1100 was a certain prominent chieftain called Folke the Stout, who was married to the daughter of a Danish king. In 1248, Folke's great-grandson Birger became the last and most powerful of the Jarls. He filled the post until his death in 1266 and was the real regent of Sweden. Soon after Birger became Jarl, the last of the Erik clan, Erik Eriksson the Lisping and Lame – not a vigorous monarch – died in 1250. The Sverker dynasty had expired in 1222. A royal election was due!

THE HIGH MIDDLE AGES – THE AGE OF THE FOLKUNGS (1250-1389)

The elections for the king were duly held in 1250, and we are told of these in a number of sources, particularly in the Chronicle of Erik, written in the 1320s. The son of Birger Jarl, the child Valdemar, became king, but the Jarl was to rule until his death. He brutally put down a rebellion. He introduced legislation covering the whole of the realm – the so-called "oath-penny" laws. This was not as trivial as it might seem, since

In the thirteenth century, the chivalric system reached Sweden, although the country never developed into a fully-fledged feudal state. Knights were exempt from ordinary taxes, but were obliged to provide men, expensive armour and equipment, and horses in the event of war. The knight in the illustration is from a seal used to authorize documents recording transactions such as a sale of land. Signatures were not used – many knights were unable to write.

25

The stone head in the centre is from Varnhem's monastic church in Västergötland and depicts Birger Jarl, who ruled Sweden from 1250 to 1266. He is flanked by casts of stone heads of his sons, ca 1270 from Skara Cathedral, painted in accordance with preserved fragments of colour. Left, king Valdemar (1250-75), and right, Magnus the Barn-Lock (1275-90) in a ducal crown before he became king.

the king received a share of the fines exacted for such crimes as violations of the sanctity of the hearth, the Thing and the church. Crimes of this nature were seen as a violation of the king's sworn oath, hence the name. Military and other feudal levies were soon transformed into a money tax. And it may have been Birger who introduced the stipulation allowing women to inherit property, but only half of what fell to male heirs. Towns were founded, including Stockholm. Two trade agreements were concluded with Lübeck and one with Hamburg, and German influence increased noticeably. The Hanse, a confederation of mainly German cities with Lübeck predominant among them, became the principal actor in Baltic affairs, and its high-prowed ships were seen everywhere. The traditionally oral laws of the provinces were put into writing, although this mostly took place after Birger's death.

The country now known as Finland slowly began to be integrated with Sweden. Swedish migration to the coastal areas had already occurred in prehistoric times, and military expe-

ditions are mentioned in the Icelandic sagas. But now crusades took place. The first is a rather apocryphal affair led by Saint Erik to southeastern Finland in the 1150s. He left the English-born bishop Henrik there, who would soon be martyred and eventually became the patron saint of Finland. The next crusade was Birger Jarl's. According to the Chronicle of Erik it took place in 1250, but modern research dates it to 1239. Its objective was the province of Tavastland (Häme). The third and final crusade targeted Karelia in 1293, and it is doubtful that there were by now many "heathens" left to convert. It is probably better to call them campaigns of conquest than crusades. After these expeditions a large part of what is now Finland belonged to the Swedish realm. This expansion generated new problems in relation to the Grand Prince of Moscow and the eastern border.

Only now did Sweden become a realm in the full sense of the word, even though the provinces retained a not inconsiderable degree of influence and were the seats of local judicial authority. They also still had the right of approving the new king at the Thing. This was an obsolescent form of government that was about to lose its meaning, however. Now there were tax revenues and a Council of the Realm whose members were taken from the lords temporal, that is to say, the nobility. The Earl Marshal (*marsk*), the Lord Chief Justice (*drots*), and the Chancellor (*kansler*) were the high officials responsible for military affairs, the judiciary and the administration respectively. An organization was created of more or less fixed fiefdoms or counties directly under the king, and fortresses were built. At the Alsnö Diet of 1279, king Magnus the Barn-Lock (*Ladulås*), who four years earlier had deposed his brother Valdemar, promulgated a statute instituting the temporal nobility. Their privileges included freedom from regular taxation, although in return the nobles had the duty of providing the king with military service, equipment and provisions when needed. The laws protecting the

Saint Erik is said to have been martyred at Uppsala in 1160. This picture from Länna church in Uppland, now in the Museum of National Antiquities, is from the 1450s and shows the saintly king and Saint Henrik setting sail to convert the Finns. They are dressed in typical fifteenth century fashion!

sanctity of the hearth, the Thing and the church were reaffirmed. In 1281, the Church, as the spiritual nobility, had its exemption from taxation renewed.

Construction work on cathedrals and other spiritual refuges was initiated under the Folkungs, although the pace of completion was leisurely. Uppsala Cathedral was one of these buildings, as was Greyfriars Church in Stockholm, now better known as Riddarholmen Church, where Magnus the Barn-Lock was laid to rest (as later Gustav II Adolf and all Swedish monarchs after him).

When Magnus died, his son Birger (who had already been elected king) was a child of eleven. The Council became a kind of regency, and real power was wielded by the forceful Earl Marshal Torgils Knutsson. The final "crusade", mentioned above, conquered further extensive areas of Finland. Viborg was founded, and the Neva formed the south-eastern border. In 1298, Birger was married off to a daughter of the Danish king, and in 1302 his brother, duke Erik, was betrothed to the one-year-old daughter of the king of Norway. But the powerful position of the Earl Marshal was brought into question and his anti-clerical policies were a cause of irritation.

When Birger was crowned king in 1302, his brothers Erik and Valdemar took the reins of power in their respective duchies. After a number of disputes with the Earl Marshal the dukes fled and started a war in Västergötland, with the help of the king of Norway. A reconciliation between the brothers in 1305 proved fateful for Torgils Knutsson. He was imprisoned and taken to Stockholm, where his head was cut off.

The subsequent events are well known. A tragic civil war followed, a struggle for power which was to lead to brutal and ugly deaths. The best known historical source for these events is the Chronicle of Erik, which must be considered partial, however. It was written in doggerel verse in the 1320s by someone in the circle of the murdered duke Erik. It was not long before king Birger came to realize that the Earl Marshal would have been a better support than his brothers. They attacked and captured him at the royal estate of Håtuna in Uppland (an episode known as the Games of Håtuna). After a period of imprisonment south of Stockholm at the fortress of Nyköpingshus he was compelled to hand over large areas of the realm to them. This arrangement gave rise to several years of struggle and Birger lost even more of his power and his kingdom. Duke Erik now ruled a large part of western Sweden and married Ingeborg, the daughter of the king of Norway, who was next in line to the Norwegian throne, Norway being an hereditary kingdom. They had a son called Magnus.

The people of Sweden must have suffered greatly during these years, not merely from the battles raging in various parts of the country, but also as a result of the extra taxes squeezed out of them by the king and his brothers to pay for the loans they had taken. In addition to this, the climate had deteriorated and the harvest failed more frequently than before.

The king was meditating revenge, but revealed nothing of his designs. In 1317 he amicably invited his brothers to celebrate Christmas with him at the fortress of Nyköpingshus, where he had been held prisoner ten years earlier. They arrived with sizable escorts, which for reasons of alleged lack of space were billeted in the town. One night in December, the brothers were seized and locked in the tower. There they either starved to death or were assassinated. The king had exacted his revenge in what became known as the Banquet of Nyköping. But now the rebellion attained serious proportions. Soon the dukes' men controlled the whole country and in the summer of 1318 Nyköpingshus, too, was reduced.

The corpses of the royal victims were now buried in state. Birger and his consort fled to Denmark, where they died. Their son Magnus was decapitated in Stockholm in 1320, because although innocent, as successor to the throne he posed a threat.

In the eyes of posterity, these brothers appear equally ruthless and greedy for power, but Erik was probably the most gifted and the one who found it easiest to win supporters. A typical contender for power, who united in himself both the good and the bad aspects of the age of chivalry.

In the spring of 1319, Håkan V of Norway had died and the realm had been inherited by his grandson, the three-year-old Magnus Eriksson. In July 1319, at the traditional location for such events – the Mora Stone in the parish of Lagga, south of Uppsala – the Council assembled together with representatives of the nobility, the high clergy, the law-speakers of each province and a number of free peasants from each jurisdiction, and elected the infant Magnus king. As part of the celebrations paying homage to the new king, a Letter of Privilege was drawn up, in which the king was promised loyalty and he in

his turn (in reality of course the regents in his name) gave his pledge

- not to introduce new taxes without the consent of the Councillors of the Realm
- not to appoint foreigners as Councillors of the Realm or royal bailiffs, and
- to govern by law and not to imprison any person without due examination and process of law.

Around 1350, when a unified set of laws known as Magnus Eriksson's national code of laws was promulgated to apply to the whole kingdom, the above provisions were included. It was also laid down that Sweden was an elective monarchy. A new redaction of the code in 1442, which was somewhat more favourable to the nobility,

There are many manuscripts, some of them illustrated, of the national code of laws promulgated by Magnus Eriksson in 1350. The picture shows part of a fifteenth century manuscript, and depicts the division of an inheritance in accordance with the inheritance code. The man says: "Give me the pitcher, you can have the butter-churn", and the woman answers: "The pitcher is better".

Saint Birgitta (1303-73) died in Rome after returning from a pilgrimage to the Holy Land. Nicolò di Tommaso met her shortly before this in Naples and then painted her famous vision of the birth of Christ. The depiction of Birgitta in the right-hand corner is reproduced here. This is the oldest contemporary image we have of the now elderly woman who was soon to be made a saint.

mense sum of 32,000 marks (6,432 kg of silver!). This debt and future expenses were to weigh down the king for the duration of his reign. What is more, Magnus would eventually lose these rich southern provinces, and he was unable to create a Nordic Union. Such a Union, however, would later be achieved by Queen Margrete (see below).

Having completed his *eriksgata*, his progress through the realm, in 1335, Magnus married Blanche of Namur (in present-day Belgium), a relative of the king of France. In the course of his *eriksgata*, the last of the thralls had been liberated, although by now there were probably few such slaves remaining.

The marriage produced two sons, Erik and Håkan. In 1343, the latter became the king of Norway at the tender age of three. Erik was only five years old when Magnus decided it was appropriate to pay homage to the successor to the throne as the "elected king" at Mora Stone in 1344. Soon the deteriorating finances of the realm began to create palpable problems, and the king's desperate taxation policies brought him into conflict with both the nobility and the Church – a powerful enemy. For a time, he was excommunicated. These are probably some of the reasons why the noble Birgitta Birgersdotter, who would become the only Swede ever to be canonized (as Saint Birgitta, or Bridget) by the Pope, condemned Magnus with such vigour in a number of her revelations. Birgitta had eight children with her husband, the Law-Speaker Ulf Gudmarsson, who died in 1344. As a widow she founded a convent in Vadstena which subsequently became the headquarters of the religious order she established. After

also contains these important principles, which have been called Sweden's first Constitution and have been compared to the English Magna Carta of 1215. This national code of laws was to apply, naturally with many changes and additions, until 1734.

Magnus Eriksson had been thoroughly groomed, but his reign was to prove a bed of thorns. Declared to be of age in 1331, he and the Council of the Realm faced a gigantic expense in the very next year. Denmark was in a state of dissolution, and almost the whole realm was in pawn to the neighbouring dukes of Holstein. A delegation led by the archbishop of Lund requested that Magnus should agree to be their overlord. After negotiations, the provinces of Skåne and Blekinge were redeemed for the im-

leaving Sweden in 1349 she mainly resided in Rome until her death in 1373.

The fact that the king had a favourite, Bengt Algotsson, who was elevated by Magnus to become Sweden's only non-royal duke, did not make matters any better in the eyes of the great men of the realm. Unsubstantiated allegations of homosexuality were levelled at the king, a crusade to the east was a failure, and Denmark now had a new king, Valdemar Atterdag, who was not prepared to accept the loss of Skåne. This led to a number of wars between the two kings. In addition to all these problems, the horrifying epidemics associated with the Black Death struck in the mid-fourteenth century. The bubonic plague ravaged the whole of Europe, and in some areas wiped out more than a third of the population. Sweden and Finland together had some 700,000 inhabitants around 1300, but after 1350 they certainly had less than 500,000. Many farms were abandoned, and it was as difficult to find soldiers as it was to get hold of labour. And naturally one result of this was to reduce the revenues to the Crown obtained from taxes. Magnus's problems just grew worse,

A fresco from St Peter's church in Næstved, Denmark, depicting Valdemar Atterdag.

When Valdemar Atterdag conquered Gotland in 1361, there was a great battle outside Visby in which the king defeated the peasants. Since it was summer, the slain were buried immediately. The location has been excavated and the picture shows the skull of a soldier still in his chain-mail.

until they became too great for him to handle.

The most powerful men in the realm used the teenage Erik, the king elect (in effect, crown prince) for their own purposes. Misfortunes dealt Magnus blow upon blow. In 1357, Erik and the magnates rebelled, and the teenager was hailed as king in large parts of the country. However, the young king, his consort and their newborn son all died in 1359 of the "children's plague", most probably chicken pox. Magnus convened a Diet in Kalmar, and for the first time all classes of property owners were assembled together, including the burgesses of the towns. This may be considered the beginnings of the Swedish parliament, the Riksdag. It has not been fully established that the Diet actually took place in Kalmar, however. A reconciliation was also effected with the Church and the magnates.

But then Valdemar Atterdag took up arms once more. In 1360 he recaptured Skåne and Blekinge, and in 1361 he conquered Gotland and defeated the island's once so powerful peasants.

Albrekt of Mecklenburg, who ruled Sweden 1364-89, with his queen Rikardis. Tomb at Doberan monastic church near the Baltic city of Rostock, Germany.

Persuaded to do so by Germans and powerful Swedish magnates, Magnus's son Håkan entered Sweden from Norway and imprisoned his father. They became reconciled, however, and Håkan was only king of Sweden for a brief period. They abandoned their association with the Germans and went to Copenhagen, where Håkan married Valdemar's ten-year-old daughter Margrete in 1363. By now the magnates had lost all patience. They sent a delegation to Mecklenburg, where Magnus's sister was married to the reigning duke. Their son Albrekt was more than ready to be king of Sweden, and so the delegation and Albrekt sailed back from Mecklenburg with a not inconsiderable fleet. Kalmar and Stockholm immediately went over to their side, and in early 1364 Albrekt was hailed as king at Mora Stone. Magnus made an attempt to regain the throne, but was defeated, was held prisoner in harsh conditions in Stockholm for a number of years, was ransomed by his son Håkan and then resided in Norway until he died in 1374.

The reign of Albrekt of Mecklenburg was an

unending series of humiliations for the monarchy. The German knights who escorted the king to Sweden did not help win him any popularity. The most powerful man in Sweden was a native Swede, however, Bo Jonsson Grip. No Swede has ever owned such extensive estates. He became Lord Chief Justice in 1374, and eventually became Lord of the Fief at ten fortresses. He was the true ruler until he died in 1386, but the ten man council that was to administer his estates after his death had no desire to accept his wishes regarding their disposition. Instead they and the other magnates invited Margrete Valdemarsdotter to become queen. At Dalaborg in Dalsland she was paid homage as "Sweden's plenipotentiary Mistress and true Lord". How had it been possible for a woman to attain this station?

THE KALMAR UNION 1397-1521 ❧ We saw above that Margrete was married off as a child. She had a divided upbringing – first in Denmark, then in Norway, under the strict surveillance of one of Saint Birgitta's daughters. Her husband Håkan was born in Sweden. They had a son, Olav. Håkan died in 1380 and Margrete

became the guardian of their son. In 1376, Olav had been elected successor to his maternal grandfather Valdemar Atterdag in Denmark, but he met an early death in 1387 and so never became king of Sweden. The queen to whom homage was shown at Dalaborg was thus a childless widow.

Albrekt and his German army were thoroughly defeated in 1389 and Albrekt himself remained a prisoner for several years while his captors held out for a handsome ransom payment. But no calm ensued. Pirates roamed the Baltic and avaricious Germans controlled Stockholm and Gotland. The agrarian crisis of the late Middle Ages was now taking its political toll throughout Europe. This crisis had been unfolding for at least a hundred years. A smaller population meant that cattle were given preference over grain cultivation. Sweden developed a not inconsiderable export trade in meat and above all butter.

Queen Margrete, the regent of Sweden, now ruled all three Nordic countries – a vast realm facing huge problems, not least in the area of communications. In 1397 the spiritual and temporal nobles of all three countries were sum-

The parchment letter of homage of 1397 with all its seals. Valid documents typically looked like this.

33

moned to a Diet in Kalmar. Here a very young prince from Pomerania was elected, crowned and paid homage to as king of the Nordic countries. His name was now Erik, as his original name, Bogislav, was considered inappropriate. He was Margrete's grand-nephew and thus had a suitable pedigree from the Danish, Norwegian and Swedish royal houses, all of which had expired with the exception of the now childless Margrete. The countries were all to retain their own laws and privileges, however, and the highest offices were not to be given to foreigners. A letter of homage was drawn up on parchment, signed and sealed. The union char-

ter itself, however, was written on paper and is incomplete. This document is currently considered to be a draft which Margrete was unwilling to authorize in this particular form. The powers of the monarchy were not to be unduly weakened.

This association of the countries, known as the Kalmar Union, remained in force for the remainder of the Middle Ages, even though it soon began to function less than smoothly. Sweden broke away several times – for good in 1521 – but Norway would remain united with Denmark until 1814. In Denmark, however, the powers of the nobility had been drastically curtailed and the nobles were in no strong position to oppose the Union monarchs.

Margrete ruled Sweden with an iron hand and reduced (i.e. took back into the possession of the Crown) a large number of noble estates. Nor did the Church escape unscathed. Taxes were raised despite earlier promises and the effects were particularly harsh on the peasantry. Margrete died in 1412. The journal at Vadstena Convent notes that "she was very fortunate in the things of this world", which was a way of saying that she had a lot to answer for in the next, despite her many visits and donations to the convent!

Erik of Pomerania appointed a growing number of foreign bailiffs. He felt he was better able to rely on them and furthermore they would not be tempted to show any consideration to the interests of the peasants, who in Denmark and Germany virtually had the status of serfs. The nobility felt robbed of many of its most lucrative fiefdoms, which passed into the hands of foreigners, mainly Danes and Germans. The king was also constantly waging war on the southern borders of Denmark, and his successors were to emulate him in this – the Union monarchs have been said to be more interested in the small counties and duchies of northern Germany than they were in the whole of their vast Nordic realm. The Hanse was not particularly enamoured of the Union, either. They considered that their trade would benefit most if the Union were kept weak or if it actually disintegrated. So the Hanse initiated a trade blockade that affected the iron and copper producing region of Bergslagen with particular severity.

And it was in this very region that the great rebellion against Erik of Pomerania began. In 1434, Engelbrekt Engelbrektsson, a wealthy mine-owner from the minor nobility, led the peasantry in a revolt against the tyranny of the bailiffs. One bailiff's stronghold after another was burnt down. It is not very helpful to view a revolt of this kind with modern eyes. The peasant armies did not have what we understand by national sentiment. They were not especially hostile to the Union either, as a matter of fact, but were extremely sensitive to the economic oppression they were subjected to and to the brutality of the bailiffs. At a meeting in Vadstena, the great magnates also agreed to back the revolt – although it is uncertain how enthusiastic their support was. After this, Engelbrekt and his forces controlled large parts of the country, including the eastern half of the realm in Finland. But by breaking agreements wholesale, Erik of Pomerania slithered his way out of trouble. At this point a Diet was summoned to be held in Arboga in January 1435. The Diet of Arboga is often considered to be the first Swedish Riksdag or parliament, but this is hardly the case since the peasants were not represented. Engelbrekt was appointed as Captain-General and came to

Margrete, the Union queen. An unfinished alabaster bust from the 1420s, probably intended for her tomb. According to the custom of the time she is depicted as relatively youthful, although she was 60 when she died in 1412. Sankt-Annen Museum, Lübeck.

A fresco from Aspö church in Skåne, depicting the simple, arduous life of a peasant at his plough.

an accommodation with Erik in May 1435. When the agreement was to be ratified that autumn, a Swedish magnate called Karl Knutsson Bonde appeared on the scene and was appointed Earl Marshal. He was well educated and widely travelled, but he was also ambitious and ruthless.

But the king did not honour the agreement, and in early 1436 the revolt erupted in earnest. Karl Knutsson and Engelbrekt took Stockholm and the royal castle was besieged. Engelbrekt was compelled to share the position of Captain-General with Karl Knutsson, and tensions were soon to be observed between these representatives of the rich upper aristocracy on the one hand and the lower nobility at the head of the peasantry on the other. Returning to Stockholm by boat from his fiefdom of Örebro, Eng-

elbrekt was murdered in May 1436 on a small island in Lake Hjälmaren. The deed was perpetrated by his personal enemy Måns Bengtsson Natt och Dag. Historians have searched in vain for a political motive for the assassination. Karl Knutsson took advantage of the absence of his rival, however, and protected the assassin. Engelbrekt was buried in Örebro and the peasants considered him a saint.

The popular rising was resisted by the nobility and two of its leaders were executed. But king Erik's days in power were numbered. Karl Knutsson became Protector of the Realm and in 1439 the Union monarch was deposed for good. A pro-Union party emerged among the nobility, creating a division that would last until 1521. Nor should it be thought that the whole of the peasantry was opposed to the Union.

Women also worked as building labourers. The woman behind the mason in this picture from the Union period is mixing mortar in a trough. Brunnby church in Skåne.

Things did not work out as Karl Knutsson would have liked, however, and in the autumn of 1440 the nephew of Erik of Pomerania, Kristoffer of Bavaria, was elected king, hailed as monarch at Mora Stone and finally crowned in the following year. He was also able to argue blood ties to Saint Erik. Now every country in the Union was to run its own affairs. Karl Knutsson was Lord Chief Justice and had extensive fiefdoms. In reality, the monarchy had lost a great deal of its power. Those who gained most from the new order were the nobility and the Council of the Realm, but the peasants had nonetheless made one or two gains. They now usually had representatives at the national diets and for a long time to come no revolt or civil struggle would have any chance of success without their support.

The Riksdag, a parliament originally based on the representation of the Estates, first appeared in this period, even though its powers had not been regulated, let alone its procedures. As we have seen, however, its deepest roots go back to the fourteenth century.

Kristoffer, called the "Bark King" after a famine in which the peasants were compelled to mix bark with their bread to survive, died unexpectedly in early 1448. That summer Karl Knutsson succeeded in obtaining election as king, homage at Mora Stone and coronation. To be on the safe side, he forged a pedigree for himself to prove his family relationship with "holy king Erik". He even became king of Norway for a brief period. And then the Union collapsed. The Danes elected Christian (I) of Oldenburg, a petty German prince descended from

37

St George and the Dragon, by the German sculptor Bernt Notke. The group was commissioned to commemorate the victory at Brunkeberg in 1471.

Notke's wooden statuette of Karl Knutsson. The work was created after his death, probably for the St George and Dragon group. It is Sweden's earliest verifiable royal portrait and is now at the Swedish National Portrait Collection at Gripsholm Castle.

also came into significance in this period.

The first revolt broke out in 1457. Karl fled to Gdansk, and the archbishop (an Oxenstierna) and Erik Axelsson (Tott) called in Christian I, who was duly shown homage and crowned. He showed his gratitude by such acts as embezzling the crowns of the king and queen of Sweden and "losing" Mora Stone, which has never been recovered. The people soon learned the reason for the king's nickname of "empty and bottomless moneybag". By 1464, they had had enough, and Karl Knutsson was recalled. This time his reign was very brief. At the end of the same year, bishop Kettil Karlsson (Vasa) proclaimed himself Protector of the Realm and Karl was once more driven into exile. The bishop died of the plague during the summer of 1465, and first the archbishop and then Eric Axelsson held the regency. In 1467 Karl was recalled and became king for the third time

With Karl Knutsson's death three years later, the office of Protector of the Realm took on crucial significance. Sten Sture the Elder seized power and was able to manoeuvre so skilfully that no negotiations with the Union monarchs were actually concluded before 1497. Christian I invaded Sweden with a large army, but was defeated at Brunkeberg near Stockholm in 1471. In the 1490s Sten Stu-

all the Nordic royal houses. There is good reason to consider the end of the Middle Ages a rather chaotic and turbulent period.

Karl Knutsson proved to be almost as oppressive an extractor of taxes as his predecessors. The nobility resented his claims to power. The members of the Oxenstierna and Vasa families emerged as his principal enemies. A number of brothers of the noble Danish (Skåne) family, the Totts, known as the Axelssons, were also to play a prominent part in the ensuing struggles. They had a vacillating position with respect to the Union. The Trolle family re had to face serious problems, including war with Russia. His ruthless acquisition of estates was a source of great irritation, and in 1497 his opponents in the Council of the Realm got the upper hand and king Hans of Denmark-Norway now also finally became king of Sweden and was crowned in due order. But his reign did not last long, even though he managed to get his son Christian acknowledged as his successor. Sten Sture the Elder took power again. In the autumn of 1503, he died and his successor was Svante Nilsson of the Natt och Dag family. Svante Nilsson faced grave economic problems, including a large annual payment he had been compelled to make to king Hans for as long as the king was not allowed to return to Sweden. But like his predecessor he had solid support among the peasantry and the mining magnates, especially in Dalarna.

In the late autumn of 1511, Svante was in Västerås for negotiations with the mining magnates of Sala, whose silver mine had proved to be very productive. At the end of the year he died suddenly, however. (His skeleton is in Västerås Cathedral, and an examination of it revealed that Svante was the first Swede we know to have suffered from syphilis, a disease imported from America by the men who sailed with Columbus.) The Council of the Realm now proposed a supporter of the Union, Erik Trolle, as Protector of the Realm, but he had to abandon his claim in the summer. With the support of the peasantry, Sten Sture the Younger, the son of Svante, was appointed. This ruthless power-seeker desired the monarchy, and soon came into conflict with the new king of Denmark-Norway, Christian II. The newly appointed archbishop, Gustav Trolle, did not appreciate the ambitions of Sten Sture, and instead allied himself with Christian II. Sten retaliated with great vigour. Backed by a parliamentary decision, he deposed the archbishop and laid siege to his stronghold at Stäket near Stockholm, capturing and destroying it. Christian II, who marched on Stockholm with an army, was defeated at the battle of Brännkyrka in 1517.

But the Danish king returned in early 1520. The Swedish forces were defeated in a battle on the ice of Lake Åsunden in which Sten Sture the Younger was fatally wounded. He died on his way to Stockholm. Within a few months Chris-

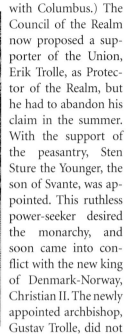

Christian II, the last Union king, as depicted in the "bloodbath paintings" (now only preserved as copies in the form of copperplate engravings), commissioned by Gustav Vasa as propaganda against the "tyrant" and his Swedish exploits, which culminated in the Stockholm Bloodbath and other atrocities.

tian controlled the whole country. The defence of Stockholm was led by Sten Sture's widow, Kristina Gyllenstierna, but eventually she too was forced to capitulate. In November 1520, Christian II was paid homage as hereditary king at Brunkeberg ridge, where his grandfather had suffered a heavy defeat in 1471. He was then crowned in Stockholm Cathedral by Gustav Trolle in the presence of the most prominent members of the nobility and the Council. But immediately after the coronation banquet, the archbishop suddenly uttered grave accusations of heresy. He held up the parliamentary decision of 1517, signed and sealed, in which he was declared deposed. This was naturally nothing more than a well-rehearsed performance to justify what was to follow. More than eighty Swedes were executed in the Great Square in what was to become known as the Stockholm Bloodbath: among them nine Councillors of the

Realm, including two bishops, many members of the high nobility and a large number of burghers who had been loyal to the Stures. When Christian the Tyrant, as he came to be called in Sweden, shortly afterwards undertook his bloodsoaked *eriksgata* through the nation, his path was lined with further executions and he thought his place on the throne was safe. But before long he was deposed from all his kingdoms and went to live in exile. Attempting to regain power with the help of his brother-in-law, the emperor Charles V, he was imprisoned in 1532 and subsequently remained a prisoner in Denmark until his death in 1559.

Kristina Gyllenstierna was the widow of Sten Sture the Younger and led the prolonged resistance to Christian II's siege of Stockholm in 1520. Detail from a triptych at Västerås, on Lake Mälaren.

THE EARLY
MODERN AGE

THE EARLY VASA PERIOD (1521-1611) ❧ It is difficult to get away from the traditional division of history into periods, but such a division seems quite justified at this point in Swedish history. It is impossible to ignore the man who now came to power and, for better or worse, founded modern Sweden. Gustav Eriksson, a member of the Vasa clan, a family with a prominent position in the Council of the Realm, is the epitome of all that is centralized and regulated in Swedish administration.

Few people have dominated their age so completely and left such a legacy after them as this Gustav Eriksson. (Oddly enough, for more than a hundred years he has been consistently misnamed in all the literature as Gustav Vasa, although this was never his name.) He was born in Uppland, most probably in 1496. His schooling was neglected, although he learnt German and possibly a little Latin. It was a matter of course for him to understand Danish, as did the whole of the ruling class of the age. In his teens, he came to the court of Sten Sture the Younger and received instruction in the military arts and other useful noble accomplishments. He was imprisoned by Christian II as a hostage in 1517, but in 1519 he fled to Lübeck. The following year he returned to Sweden. King Christian II was at the zenith of his power, he had succeeded in restoring the Union for a brief period, and a few months later thought he had clipped the wings of the opposition with the Stockholm Bloodbath in the late autumn of 1520. In fact he had made things easier for Gustav, for the executioner's sword had removed many potential competitors. Gustav himself had wisely refrained from coming to Stockholm for Christian's coronation. Now he learned that his father had been decapitated and that his mother and sisters had been seized and taken to Denmark.

Gustav was a man of action and rode north to Dalarna to instigate a revolt. Having failed to persuade the leading men of the province to

A man on snowshoes leading a horse in a wintry landscape. Gustav Vasa's flight in Dalarna in the winter of 1520-21 probably resembled this illustration from Olaus Magnus' *Historia de gentibus septentrionalibus*, 1555.

Gustav was a thrifty king, and had his accounts bound between the durable parchment leaves of confiscated church records. Modern researchers have been able to partially reconstruct mediaeval church libraries with the help of such binders. Here a page from a *graduale* from ca 1500.

take part in his rebellion, he headed for Norway through the dark, snow-heavy December forests, where if you had no guide you had to follow a trail of marks blazed in the trees, aided at night only by the light of the moon. But the men of Dalarna thought better of their refusal and sent a number of skiers after him. They caught up with him near Sälen – this long chase constitutes the historical background of the famous annual ski marathon, the Vasa Race, although Gustav himself was unable to ski and used snowshoes instead. He was escorted back to Mora, where he was elected Captain-General of Dalarna in January 1521. This was followed by one success after another. He became Protector of the Realm early in the summer of 1521, and with the financial backing of the Hanse, which was opposed in principle to the idea of the whole of the Nordic area being under a single ruler, he was elected king on 6 June 1523 (a day to be chosen much later as Sweden's national day). He was not crowned until 1528, however. Despite many rebellions and other vexations, he reigned until his death in

Stockholm in 1560. In Sweden's case, what historians were later to call the Modern Age most definitely started during Gustav's reign.

With an iron fist, Gustav organized a centralized administration, suppressed all opposition, confiscated the greater part of the Church's estates and treasures, pushed through (with rather more caution) the Reformation, instituted a system of hereditary monarchy and made the Riksdag, the Swedish parliament, which at the time consisted of the four Estates, a part of all future Swedish forms of government. From what was known as his Chamber he governed his officials and bailiffs, supervising everything himself. Perhaps paradoxically, Gustav's very personally coloured mode of governance laid the foundations for Sweden's state bureaucracy, which Gustav's grandson Gustav II Adolf would reshape, extend and modernize after 1611 together with his Chancellor Axel Oxenstierna.

Monetary policy was of central importance for Gustav. He was undoubtedly the most distinguished economist to have occupied the throne of Sweden, and had a natural talent for the field. Although no pioneer in many respects, there is a great deal of the monetarist in him, four hundred years before Milton Friedman. For many years Gustav

had great problems with what would nowadays be called his budget. The heaviest burden was the vast debt the country owed to Lübeck. The way he was able to transform this state of affairs and end his reign as one of the few monarchs in Europe free of crippling debts is a remarkable story.

THE DIET OF VÄSTERÅS ∾ In the summer of 1527 Parliament was summoned to meet in Västerås. The significant decision that initiated the Reformation in Sweden was taken here – although not without ructions – and the king was able to bend the law in his own favour to justify the confiscation of Church estates and monastic property and also to take into his possession "superfluous" objects of gold and silver kept in the churches. The nobility was also allowed to join in the feeding frenzy.

From this period onwards, the lands owned by the Crown become very extensive. It should be pointed out that Gustav also saw to it that his private inheritance was extended to the utmost. All monasteries with the exception of Vadstena were eventually transformed into the property of the Crown or claimed to be Gustav's just in-

An historical painting by C. G. Hellquist from 1883 showing Gustav Vasa at the Diet of Västerås in 1527. The king is allowing Olaus Petri, the principal protagonist of the Reformation in Sweden, to defend his Lutheran faith. The king is on the right, surrounded by his closest associates.

heritance. And the only distinctions made between these two categories of property were of a formal, bookkeeping nature.

OUT OF DEBT! ❧ In the autumn of 1531, Christian II invaded Norway. During his exile in the Netherlands he had eventually managed to gather together a fleet of 25 ships. A shared fear of Christian "the Tyrant" united Denmark, Sweden and Lübeck against him as their common enemy. Christian was lured aboard the Danish fleet, and once ashore in Copenhagen, he was seized and imprisoned for the remainder of his life, as recounted above.

New problems were already accumulating, however. The death of Frederik I of Denmark-Norway in 1533 was followed by chaos and rebellion. The supporters of the imprisoned Christian II among the merchants, burghers and peasants turned against the nobility, and Lübeck changed tack and wished to force the Danes to forbid trade with the Netherlands and also wanted to be rid of Gustav in Sweden, who was balking at paying the final instalments of the debt. A war broke out in 1534, that has become known as the Count's Feud. Gustav had no choice but to support Christian III, who had been shown homage as king in Jutland earlier in the year. He had to crush the supporters of Christian "the Tyrant" and put an end to Lübeck's constant interference in Nordic affairs. He also seized the opportunity of getting

out of paying the rest of his debt. The other Hanse cities only gave half-hearted support to Lübeck in this conflict.

The decisive battle took place in Denmark. Gustav and Christian III emerged as the victors. Lübeck lost its power and Sweden was able to write off its national debt.

FARMS, ESTATES AND CASTLES ❧ The rest of Gustav's reign also had its share of problems, including the Dacke Feud of 1542-43 in which the peasants of Småland rose under Nils Dacke in a powerful rebellion that it required the ruthless mobilization of national forces to put down. In the 1550s, Gustav was forced to make war on Russia on his Finnish borders. On the whole, however, the last twenty years of his reign went well for him, and both he himself and the Crown became very wealthy. Even the emperor of Germany tried to borrow money from the king of distant Sweden, but he was refused.

It is well-known that Gustav was an exceptionally pragmatic gentleman. When it suited him he would cite "the old laws of Sweden", but when it didn't, he could just as easily call these very same laws "a heap of old letters and privileges we consider not worth a bilberry". Tax revenues were accumulated at the royal castle in Stockholm and at the castle of Gripsholm on Lake Mälaren, but the Crown also prospered. Above all it was the large-scale confiscations of

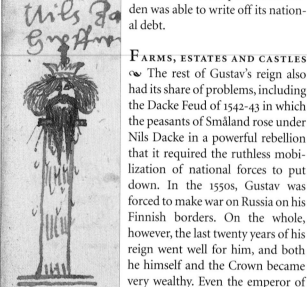

In 1542, Nils Dacke's head was displayed, wearing a copper crown, on a spike in Kalmar, as a warning to anyone with rebellious designs. From Joen Klint's chronicle of Gustav Vasa.

Church property, culminating in the 1540s, that brought much of the property into the possession of the Crown. It is noteworthy that the estates of the Crown increased during Gustav's reign from just under 6 per cent to 28.5 per cent. The nobility had a slightly larger share than they had had in 1527 (just over 21 per cent), and the share of the peasantry was practically unchanged. The Church's property had been conjured away, transformed into Crown estates or the king's private land. The attitude of the king towards forests and other land that could not be immediately associated with any existing piece of property clearly emerges in his well-known comment: "Such land belongs to God, Ourselves and the Crown".

In a number of ways Gustav had a rather old-fashioned view of the realm. When he felt his end drawing near, he made Parliament grant his sons generous dukedoms. Erik was to be king, but Johan had much of Finland, Magnus Östergötland and Karl, the youngest, was to rule Södermanland, Närke and Värmland. It would prove difficult for them to abide by expectations that they should subordinate themselves to the monarch.

THE SONS OF THE VASA DYNASTY ✆ With Gustav Vasa's sons, the European Renaissance finally came to Sweden, more than a century after it had conquered continental Europe. They had none of the caution that had distinguished their father's policies, and had their eyes fixed on the countries around them and were not at all reluctant to consider expanding Swedish territory.

Erik XIV reigned 1560-1568 and was the only

Gustav Vasa in the 1550s, wearing puffed breeches. A contemporary portrait ascribed to Willem Boy of Flanders.

son by Gustav Vasa's first marriage to Katarina of Sachsen-Lauenburg. He was given a very solid education in the fashion of the day – in addition to matters of state, languages, art, music and astrology were also studied – and became one of Europe's best educated and linguistical-

ly gifted monarchs. At the early age of seventeen, he was already working for his father in the administration of the realm. Eventually he obtained a residence of his own in Kalmar, where he lived with a small-scale Renaissance court with artists and musicians in his employ. He had men on his staff who would accompany him when he ascended the throne, including Göran Persson, the son of a priest, whom Gustav had cast out of his own chancellery. He had large-scale plans for foreign policy and commerce, and this was something that Gustav regarded with suspicion. Among these plans were those he has become best known for, his repeated wooing of Queen Elizabeth of England – and also her mortal enemy, Mary Queen of Scots. As early as 1559, his stepbrother Johan

had sailed to England to deliver Erik's second proposal to the queen. Everyone at the English court thought Johan a most cultivated young man and an excellent Latinist, but where marriage was concerned Elizabeth, as always, expressed herself in very vague terms.

Following Gustav Vasa's last parliament, at which his sons received their titles and lands, Erik decided to sail to England himself to ask for Elizabeth's hand, but he had to abandon his enterprise at Älvsborg (present-day Gothenburg), because his father had died.

The new king – Sweden's first hereditary monarch – had no wish to share his power with his brothers. He promulgated the Articles of Arboga in the spring of 1561, which quite drastically restricted their autonomy. Most an-

Dancing peasants depicted in the Gripsholm tapestry, commissioned by Gustav Vasa in the 1540s. It is based on German copper engravings and probably gives a good idea of contemporary festivities. The costumes of the peasants are more old-fashioned than those of the minstrels. Note the bagpipes, which were still in general use at the time.

gered by this was probably Duke Johan, who felt himself to be fairly independent in Finland. At the end of June, Erik celebrated his coronation in Uppsala with unusual pomp and splendour – the regalia were newly made and very expensive. After his coronation, the new king elevated some members of the high nobility to the rank of counts and barons. This meant Sweden now had a titled nobility. Even though counties were distributed, the high nobles had their subordination to the monarch duly prescribed to them. More exacting requirements of wartime military service and supplies to the Crown were imposed. At the same time as he needed its services, Erik was very suspicious of the high nobility (and not wholly without reason).

Erik XIV selected commoners lacking titles and distinguished ancestors to be his closest advisers and collaborators, and in this he resembled his father. Among these advisers was the above-mentioned Göran Persson, the highly-educated son of a priest who has rather unfairly come to be regarded by posterity as Erik's evil genius. A new court, the Royal Commission, was instituted, with Göran Persson as prosecutor. The Commission gradually gained notoriety as an arbitrary tool of royal policy.

Before long the brothers were in conflict. Erik was irritated by Johan's independent policies in Finland, particularly with respect to the collapse of the former territories of the Teutonic Order on the Baltic. Erik's sovereignty was acknowledged in 1561 by the city of Reval

(Tallinn) and by the Estonian-German nobility, largely due to the fear they felt in relation to Russia and its ruler, Ivan the Terrible. Estonia was long to remain part of the Swedish realm. These steps mark the beginning of Sweden's period as a great Baltic power. In 1562, Duke Johan married the daughter of the king of Poland, Katarina Jagellonica, and simultaneously obtained a number of fortresses in Livonia, whose territories lay adjacent to Estonia. Erik did not want this marriage – neither did tsar Ivan, who had had his eye on the same princess – and saw his brother as an obstacle to his grand design for dominating east-west trade. Åbo castle was captured after a brief siege and Johan and Katarina were taken as prisoners to the castle of Gripsholm, where they were kept in custody until 1567 and where their son Sigis-

mund was born. Their closest friends and servants were tortured and executed.

After 1559, a young and power-hungry king, Frederik II, had also been on the throne in Denmark-Norway. He viewed Erik XIV's plans with suspicion and what is more also wished to restore the Kalmar Union. In 1563, the Nordic Seven Years War began. It is remarkable for its cruelty and bloodshed. Sweden was also ranged against Poland and Lübeck. At the time it was impossible to know that this marked the start of a prolonged period of warfare that would last until 1721 and only be broken by the occasional brief armistice or peace agreement. Erik, who was better as an administrator than a field marshal, took part in large-scale marauding in Blekinge, but soon handed over the blood-soaked business to others, who could then be given the blame for setbacks. Älvsborg, Sweden's only port to the west, was lost, and could only be partly compensated for by the capture of Varberg. The Swedish fleet, created by Gustav Vasa, fared better.

Erik regarded the high nobility with deeper and deeper suspicion, and a number of fiefdoms were confiscated and once more became Crown property. Nils Sture was one of those who incurred royal disfavour and was forced to endure public humiliation in Stockholm. In the spring of 1567, several representatives of the high nobility, among them some members of the Sture clan, were accused of conspiring against the king, and one or two of them were sentenced to death by the Royal Commission. The Estates were assembled in Uppsala to confirm the sentences, and at the end of May the king himself read out the charges. The following day, Göran Persson continued the prosecution. The main features of what followed are clear, even though they were recorded by Erik's enemies. For some time the king had been restless and nervous. He began to behave in a confused way, going to the prison to ask for the friendship of the imprisoned Svante Sture. Shortly afterwards, he returned in an utterly different mood, stabbed a knife into Nils Sture's arm and had him murdered. Then he ran from the prison and ordered everyone to be killed "except lord Sten", which saved the lives of both Sten Leijonhuvud and Sten Banér. The king's guards then took the lives of Svante and Erik Sture and some of the other leading nobles. The king was now obviously utterly confused, and after having his old tutor killed when he had tried to calm him, he ran off into the forest.

A latent mental disorder had broken out. The incident is referred to as the Sture murders.

It took several days to find the king. He was roaming the countryside and clearly of unsound mind. He thought he had been deposed and was obsessed by a number of compulsive ideas. The Council took over the reins of government, Johan and Katarina were released from prison as autumn advanced and the king immediately reconciled himself with them. A large fine in silver was paid to the survivors of the Sture murders. Göran Persson was seized and sentenced to death.

While he was waiting for his official propo-

This drawing is believed to depict Karin Månsdotter, the consort of Erik XIV. It was discovered in the margin of a book used by the king during his captivity, and is ascribed to the king himself.

Johan III, the step-brother and successor of Erik XIV. Copy of an original by J. B. van Uther.

secret. It became public knowledge in December, and in early 1568 they had a son, Gustav. While this was happening, the war continued and the Danes ravaged Östergötland, but they had to withdraw. Erik's mental health improved and he was able to take part in the winter campaign, and after new raids on Danish territory he returned in triumph to Stockholm. Göran Persson was set free and reinstated in his former office.

Many of the country's leaders felt concern. What was decisive, however, was Erik's official betrothal to Karin Månsdotter and her coronation as queen in the summer of 1568. His brothers Johan and Karl were invited to the coronation, but did not come. Instead they launched a rebellion, partially financed by the money that had been paid in fines for the Sture murders. After a few minor victories, Erik saw the enthusiasm of his supporters wane. Eventually, he only controlled Stockholm. Göran Persson was handed over, broken on the wheel and executed. The gates of the city were thrown open, and on 29 September 1568 Erik left his castle and surrendered. He was thrown into prison with his family. He had been king for exactly eight years to the day. From now on, Erik was to be held in different prisons in Sweden and Finland, and towards the end he was separated from his family. In 1577, after a brief illness, he died, probably of poison. Karin Månsdotter was allowed to settle in Finland.

WAR, EXPENSES, INFLATION ∽ Erik's brother, Johan, assumed the throne without delay – he was proclaimed king the day after Erik was put in prison. He was the oldest son by

sals of marriage to be accepted, Erik had kept a number of mistresses. One of them, Karin Månsdotter, won his heart. She was the daughter of a soldier and thus of very humble origins. The Council and the Estates had conceded Erik the right to marry a Swedish woman, but no one had even contemplated the possibility that the king might wish to marry a commoner. In the summer of 1567, however, they married in

Gustav Vasa's second marriage, to Margareta Leijonhuvud, who died young but nonetheless bore him ten children. Johan had inherited his father's quick temper, but otherwise there was little similarity between them. He had no financial sense, and the value of money, which had already deteriorated grievously under Erik, sank once or twice to unprecedented depths. Towards the end of his reign Sweden had a rate of inflation of 800 per cent over just two years. This problem, with its ten-fold price increases, was above all caused by a huge deterioration in the coinage. Admittedly, the virtually permanent wars were also a contributory factor. The two Books of State from 1573 and 1582 constitute a kind of budget, presenting the regular revenues and expenses of the state during one year. The books must have made gloomy reading for the king and his Council. Expenses outran revenues quite dramatically. In the first year mentioned, 1573, state revenues came to some 410,000 *riksdaler*, and expenses amounted to some 590,000 *riksdaler* (not including the costs of war).

As soon as Johan became king, of course, the war with Poland ceased. Sweden negotiated an expensive peace with Denmark in 1570 – it had to pay a heavy ransom to regain Älvsborg and a special tax was levied for the purpose, for which everyone was assessed and compelled to pay. The surviving taxation records gladden the hearts of historians, but the people of Sweden were able to suppress their mirth. And now war with Russia became a burning issue. The correspondence between Johan III and tsar Ivan the Terrible is probably unique in the annals of diplomacy for the scarifying invective and ac-

cusations hurled at each other by their majesties. A gain for Sweden was the conquest of Narva (on the eastern border of present-day Estonia) in 1581, but Russia transferred the bulk of its trade to the northern port of Archangelsk, so the benefit to Sweden was not as great as had been hoped. With only brief interludes of peace, this war continued throughout Johan's reign. Peace was not concluded until 1595, and by then both the antagonists were dead. But Sweden had further extended its Baltic dominions.

Johan's consuming passion was building castles – "building is Our greatest delight". His father had also built a great deal, but his focus was on castle fortresses built for defence, for storage and for administrative purposes. Johan continued this work of his father's, but transformed the fortresses into castles or built new ones – Stockholm, Åbo (Turku), Vadstena, Kalmar (commenced by Erik XIV), and Gävle, to name but a few. Now the aesthetic aspects became predominant and art historians speak of Johan III's Renaissance. He was also the first monarch to concern himself with the care of Sweden's historical monuments, primarily the churches. Today Johan would be regarded as "high church" in theological terms, and he made certain approaches to the Roman Catholic Church, which still had many sympathizers in the country. A papal legate stayed for a time at Johan's court, and the school on Riddarholmen was run by a Catholic. But nothing came of the reconciliation, the only monument of which is Johan's liturgy, known as the "red book" because of the colour of the binding.

The relations between Johan III and his

younger brother Karl soon worsened after their common rebellion. Karl was a zealous Protestant, almost a Calvinist, and throughout his large duchy it would have been a foolish worshipper indeed who flaunted the "red book". Karl was quick to intervene in the business of the realm, but tolerated no interference in his own domains. A reconciliation took place in Vadstena in 1587, in the autumn of which year Johan's son Sigismund was elected king of Poland-Lithuania. Like his mother, Sigismund was a Catholic, a fact that was to bode ill for the future.

Johan missed his son. At a meeting in Reval in 1589, he stated his wish that Sigismund should return to Sweden. The Swedish Councillors who were present were adamant in their opposition to this, and Sigismund remained in Poland. This caused the embittered king to break with the high nobility and to dismiss many of its members from their positions in his administration. Their influence was now a thing of the past. Duke Karl, who had never enjoyed good relations with the Council nobility, gained in influence at their expense. By now most of the mediaeval fiefdoms had disappeared and been replaced by allocations from Crown revenues or confiscated Church property. Johan's abysmal finances compelled him to make over certain tax revenues from the farms of freeholding peasants. Most administration was managed by bailiffs, who were formally responsible to provincial governors. The king often corresponded directly with the bailiffs, however, who were controlled as well as circumstances permitted.

In 1592, Johan died and was succeeded by his son Sigismund, which united Poland and Sweden in a personal union.

THE STRUGGLE FOR POWER 1592-99 ∾
On the death of his brother, duke Karl assumed the reins of government. His nephew was still in Poland. Right from the start it seems that the blunt and short-tempered regent had decided that the Catholic king would never gain any real influence on affairs. In 1593, he and the Council jointly summoned the whole of the clergy to the Synod of Uppsala, at which it was reaffirmed that Sweden was to be a Protestant-Lutheran kingdom. The Confession of Augsburg was adopted and Johan III's liturgy fell into disuse, but (against Karl's wishes) the reformed doctrine (Calvinism) was also condemned.

Shortly after this, Sigismund and his queen came to Sweden. A coronation parliament was summoned at Uppsala in 1594, and the king was forced to make a number of concessions. He conceded more than he wished, and less than the duke's party demanded, so all sides were dissatisfied. The decisions of the Synod of Uppsala were accepted by Sigismund, which meant that no one confessing an alien faith (except himself) might be appointed to state office. Thus it was that the king and queen Anna were compelled to submit to a Protestant coronation ceremony.

The remainder of the 1590s was a struggle between the duke and his nephew the king, which the latter was to lose. Karl summoned a number of parliaments in quick succession, which gave him their support – the nobility with reluctance, but the commoners gladly. Sigismund had forbidden the summoning of Parliament, and had decided that the Council should rule (with his uncle as a member, nonetheless) in his absence. But the king's intentions were not realized. Most members of the Council had their doubts about breaking with the king, even if they were not papists. Finland was controlled by Klas Fleming, a supporter of the king who was at least as brutal as the duke. The harsh rule of Fleming and the Finnish nobility provoked a peasant revolt known as the war of the clubs, which was conducted with great cruelty by both sides. The duke naturally supported the peasants against Fleming – his propaganda portraying him as their one true friend. The Arboga parliament of 1597 once more decided to support Karl's policies, and shortly afterwards he left for Finland, which he subdued and brought under his dominion. Fleming had died shortly before, but the duke's other opponents felt the full force of his retribution and had their heads cut off. This was the final straw for the Councillors, some of whom retired to their estates, while others fled to the king in Poland.

In the summer of 1598, Sigismund came to Sweden with a fleet and an army. He took Kalmar and open war broke out. Negotiations were of no avail. At Stångebro in Östergötland Karl defeated the troops of the king. Sigismund was humiliated in Linköping – the Councillors of the Realm who had fled to Poland and accompanied the king to Sweden were handed over and the king had to send home his army. He was also commanded to come to Stockholm and appear before Parliament, but he fled back to Poland instead and tried to mount a commercial blockade.

Soon the whole of Sweden was in Karl's power. Since Sigismund had not sent his eldest son to Sweden to be raised as a Protestant, as the Estates had demanded, he was deposed in 1599 and duke Karl was appointed Protector of the Realm.

KARL IX – A NATIONAL MONARCHY 1599-1611 ∽

The meetings of the Estates were frequent. The next parliament took place in

Karl IX as Protector of the Realm ca 1600. The Protector used harsh methods and executed several of his opponents. His most notorious action was the executions of 1600 known as the Linköping Bloodbath. Unknown artist.

Linköping in 1600. The duke offered to govern as the guardian of either duke Johan of Östergötland, Sigismund's younger half-brother, or of his own son Gustav Adolf, born in 1594. Parliament, however, wished to proclaim Karl as king, but he refused – for the time being. At the same parliament a special court was set up with the duke as prosecutor. On trial were the Councillors of the Realm who had been handed over by Sigismund. Four of them, from the clans of Bielke, Sparre and Banér, were condemned to death and decapitated in what became known as the Linköping Bloodbath. These were by no means the only executions to take place, and more were to come.

It was not until 1604 that Karl was ready to accept the title of king with the consent of a parliament held in Norrköping, which also decided that his relatives would inherit the crown after him. In 1607 he was crowned with great pomp and ceremony, and two years later he made his progress through the nation, his *eriksgata*. He was to be the last king to perform this ritual according to the old traditions. It was naturally a matter of some importance for someone who had deposed the legal monarch to observe the formalities. In his restless and complex personality, Karl combined ambition and brutality with a constant desire to have the law and Parliament behind him – hence his eagerness to have all the formalities enacted so he could be seen to observe them. He was very attached to his family, and they were to him. The children received a very thorough education, and Gustav (II) Adolf was to become one of the best-read monarchs Sweden had ever had, with rare linguistic gifts and a training in oratory that would stand him in good stead in the Council and before Parliament.

During his brief reign, however, there were many who hated and loathed king Karl. A great number of contemporary pamphlets illustrate this. Some of the high nobility, however, including Axel Oxenstierna, chose to cooperate with Karl. This they did from conviction, but with little enthusiasm.

Karl, the youngest son of Gustav Vasa, was the one who most resembled him. He was a stickler for thrift, and kept his bailiffs under a surveillance that was characterized by a good deal of suspicion. He was very interested in matters of industry and commerce, founded the city of Gothenburg, improved communications, and encouraged the setting up of mines and mills, which he frequently inspected. Copper and iron became more and more significant export commodities and their quality improved. Foreign, especially Dutch, merchants were permitted to settle, and they dominated the new city of Gothenburg. Finnish immigration from the eastern part of the Swedish realm gave rise to regions in a number of provinces that became known as Finnish lands, or *finn-marker*. Karl did not ignore the vast northern regions of his kingdom, and laid claim to land up to the Arctic Ocean. He was the only Swedish king to adopt the title of "King of the Lapps in the North Country", which utterly enraged Christian IV of Denmark-Norway. He reorganized the collection of taxes among the Sami and was the first to seriously set about converting them to Christianity.

Looking abroad, we may note that Sweden immediately found itself at war with Poland following the deposition of Sigismund. Karl IX was no great general and suffered not a few setbacks during his campaigns in Estonia and Livonia. As did the Polish king, he interfered in the struggles over the succession to the throne in Russia during the "Great Confusion" as the period is known. Towards the end of Karl's reign, his general Jakob De la Gardie had a number of successes in the field and eventually took Moscow in 1610 (although he was unable to hold it for long) and Novgorod in 1611. For a while, Karl's youngest son Karl Filip was being considered for tsar.

The young Danish king Christian IV attacked Sweden in 1611 and took Kalmar (thus initiating the so-called War of Kalmar). During the fighting there, the still hot-tempered Karl became so enraged that he challenged Christian to single combat. An extremely impertinent answer from the Dane only served to enrage him further. Shortly afterwards, and perhaps as a consequence of the incident, he suffered a stroke and died in October 1611. He left behind him a kingdom with great inner tensions, war on all fronts and a son who was still a minor.

COMMERCE AND SOCIETY ∾ During the whole of this period, that is to say, from Gustav Vasa's accession to the throne, agriculture remained the principal occupation of the country and its people, as it had been in the Middle Ages. Salt had now joined the few indispensable imported products, otherwise domestic produce satisfied the country's needs. The amount of grain needed had increased, but many of the basic foodstuffs were still based on dairy products, meat and not least fish. Even if the Lenten fast disappeared with the Reformation, fish was still eaten perhaps 150 days a year, in most cases in dried, salted or fermented form. After the harsh conditions resulting from the deterioration in the climate and the Black Death in the fourteenth century, the population was once more increasing slowly but steadily and with it domestic production. In the sixteenth century Sweden still had a not inconsiderable export trade in such goods as furs, butter and dried fish, most of which had been supplied in payment of taxes.

Some peasants lived in communal villages, tilling the land and managing the forest in

"On the hunting expeditions of the Lapps". Olaus Magnus, 1555.

common, and some lived in self-contained, individual farms – although the latter were to be found in the forests or in newly cultivated lands in sparsely populated areas of Sweden. Towards the end of the sixteenth century foreign visitors reported that conditions were very simple, to be sure – whole families and some of their animals could share a single room – but that the peasants had food for the day and often a small collection of silver spoons. The need for money was so minimal that if a peasant ever did earn some money, the silver was melted down and a local goldsmith would transform it into this kind of "reserve capital". Should a famine occur it would always be possible to sell the spoons or exchange them for grain.

Sweden was almost unique in Europe with respect to the ownership of the land. Taking the whole realm (including Finland) into account, more than 60 per cent of the land was owned by peasants (the figure was slightly less than 50 per cent for Sweden proper). At the end of the sixteenth century, the nobility owned some 25 per cent of the land (much less in Finland) and the Crown 30 per cent. This meant that the peasantry had an independence and a degree of self-confidence that astonished those foreign visitors who found their way to Sweden. The peasantry was also represented in Parliament as the fourth Estate, and at times it was unruly and difficult to govern. On the other hand, the king always found a reliable ally in the peasantry if he was having trouble with the nobility.

Generally speaking, the towns had little significance and were mainly inhabited by craftsmen. Stockholm, the newly-founded Gothenburg and Kalmar, however, were cities with a genuine burgher class and merchants, who were often of German, Dutch or sometimes Scottish descent.

SWEDEN AS A GREAT POWER 1611-1718

In 1612, the situation was as follows: Sweden was at war with Denmark, as we have seen, and the Danes, despite some minor Swedish successes and some cruel Swedish ravages in Skåne, had the upper hand. There was no peace in the East, either, even though there was no open fighting. King Gustav II Adolf was young and untried,

and had only recently been declared of age. In the spring of this year, the newly appointed Chancellor, Axel Oxenstierna, wrote the following letter to the wilful dowager Queen Kristina, the king's German-born mother from Holstein-Gottorp:

"First of all, it is general knowledge that all our neighbours are our enemies, the Poles, the Russians and the Danes, so no place in Sweden, Finland or Livonia may say that it is safe from the enemy. Second, we have absolutely no friends at all whose hearts are affected by our discomfiture. Third, there are none of our enemies who are not, or at the least do not consider themselves to be, more powerful and

stronger than us. Fourth, the long-enduring feud of fifty-two years, with no respite, in which we have been engaged with several enemies by land and by sea, has so scraped bare and impoverished the commerce and the subjects of this realm that there is nothing left to which we may have recourse. The best of our warriors are no longer with us but are fallen to the sword, so that no man will soon be of age before he has passed on. No store of cannon, powder or other munitions of war. No victuals in store, either for campaigns on land or for the fleet. No money in store, nor any clothing, nor any such necessities."

Axel Oxenstierna belonged to the old nobility and his family had played a significant role in Swedish history as early as the fifteenth century. He had received a thorough education at German universities and formed part of the group we mentioned above – the nobility choosing to work with Karl IX from a sense of duty but with little enthusiasm. He had an unusually

Axel Oxenstierna (1583-1654). Drawing executed by Daniel Dumoistier while the Chancellor of the Realm was in Paris in 1635.

other, the king on his travels or in the field and the Chancellor "at his office" – although he too would soon be spending a good deal of time away from Stockholm. By 1614, the king had created him a baron, while the title of count was bestowed on him by Queen Kristina in 1645.

As we have seen, Gustav Adolf had been given a thorough education. He had two mother tongues (Swedish and German) and a fluent command of four additional languages. He was the most gifted and also the most harmonious of the monarchs of the Vasa line. The less desirable traits he had inherited included only the quick temper and impatience, which, however, with time, he taught himself to control to a certain extent. In addition, he found it easy to persuade others of his views (with the help of his knowledge of oratory!) and to charm people. He won the confidence and trust of those around him, something neither his father nor his grandfather had been able to do very often.

With the help of a growing group of able officials, gifted generals and skilled businessmen – many of them immigrants – the king and his leading adviser now proceeded to construct a new Sweden. Before dealing with the wars and foreign entanglements this involved, however, we must devote some attention to the national administration.

long career and was Chancellor of the Realm (a position roughly equivalent to prime minister) longer than anyone else. In fact he held the position until his death in 1654. Not without justification, he has been called the greatest statesman Sweden ever produced. But in 1612 he saw nothing but gloom and doom – paradoxically enough just a few years before the whole situation would be reversed and Sweden would embark on its explosive but short-lived career as a Great Power.

The new king had rapidly been declared of age, sworn his royal oath and embarked on a steadily improving course of cooperation with Oxenstierna. They became more and more indispensable to each other, even if they resided for lengthy periods at great distances from each

REFORMS ∾ During the reign of Gustav Adolf, there were eleven meetings of Parliament. At the Diet of Örebro in 1617 a parliamentary ordinance was adopted which at last regulated the way in which the four Estates were to work and the type of decisions they were to make in conjunction with the king. At the same time, Sweden obtained commercial legislation – referred to at the time as a trade ordinance – and laws regulating the onerous carrying obligations that fell upon the peasantry. The Ordinance of the House of Nobility of 1626 contained stipulations regarding the organization of the highest Estate. All the noble clans were to be introduced and to receive a number, in order to make the nobility more accountable and to prevent the intrusion of false nobles. The nobility was divided into three classes: lords (counts and barons) comprising 12 families, knights (relatives of members of the Council of the Realm) comprising 23 families, and squires (those remaining) comprising 92 families, that is to say a total of 127 families in all. The head of each clan had place, voice and vote, while other (male) members of the clans were encouraged to attend to "listen in silence". Proceedings in the chamber were presided over by the President of the House of Nobility who was appointed by the king. By Gustav II Adolf's death the number of families was already approaching 300.

Legislation was also passed governing court procedures, and the Svea Court of Appeal became a permanent high court, followed by the Åbo (Turku) Court of Appeal in 1623 and the Göta Court of Appeal (in Jönköping) in 1634. It was, however, possible to appeal to the king and the Council, a function they had until 1789, when the Supreme Court was instituted. The religious statutes adopted in Örebro in 1617 became an instrument of the state in this century of intolerance, and constituted a response of sorts to the Catholic Counter-Reformation. All Catholics had to leave the country within three months, and any person converting to Catholicism lost all rights "as if deceased". Any contact with Sigismund and his dynasty was strictly forbidden.

In a significant cultural development, Upp-

The Swedish Land Survey Office dates from 1628. It has played an extremely significant role in Swedish agriculture. It has also accumulated a collection of maps that ranks with the finest in Europe. Here three surveyors are shown at a drawing board wearing broad-brimmed hats, elegant coats and swords of office. Detail from a Survey Office map from the end of the seventeenth century.

sala university found itself on a stable economic foundation when the king granted it the Gustavian hereditary estates as a gift. The office of the Keeper of National Antiquities was instituted in 1630 and the first person to be appointed to the post was Gustav II Adolf's old tutor Johannes Bureus. This marked the beginnings of Swedish research in ancient history and of a growing interest in and desire to preserve the cultural monuments of the nation. A university was also founded in Estonia (Dorpat, now Tartu).

New towns were founded and important settlements were granted urban privileges. Gothenburg, which had been destroyed during the War of Kalmar, was rebuilt and its trade and commerce were promoted in every conceivable way. The Swedish state bureaucracy – for many years the envy of other nations – began to develop. The taxation system was reviewed and revamped and grew more and more burdensome – we shall frequently be reminded of this as our story unfolds.

PEACE AND THE SECOND ÄLVSBORG RANSOM ∾ As we have seen, the War of Kalmar was conducted mainly within the borders of Sweden as they were at the time. It was the last war to be fought with no real battles. It was extremely brutal, nevertheless, and for most of the time, the Danes had the upper hand. But Christian IV and his supporters were unable to capitalize on their successes and in 1613 peace was concluded at Knäred in the province of Halland, which was then Danish territory. Conquests were restituted, but Denmark kept the fortress of Älvsborg, Sweden's only port to the West, until Sweden paid a new ransom of no less than 1 million *riksdaler*, corresponding to more than 25,000 kg of silver, to be paid in six years.

The sum of this second ransom greatly exceeded the national Swedish budget of the time, and the country's resources had to be scraped together to meet it, a task which would have been completely impossible without the copper from the mine in Falun, where production during the decade in question rose to 1,500 tons a year and during the 1640s to over 2,000 tons. The world market price was high, and Sweden had the best production figures in the world during at least the first half of the seventeenth century. The copper was sold – most of it in Amsterdam – and the payment, in ringing Dutch *rijksdaalder*, was freighted back to Sweden only to pass straight to Denmark in part payment of the ransom.

In addition an extraordinary tax was levied on the whole population – no one was exempt. It was the first genuinely progressive tax to have been levied in Sweden (although taxation based on wealth had been exacted previously). The king had to give 20 per cent of his civil list, a bishop 50 *riksdaler*, a peasant 2 or 3, a farmhand 1 and a maid half a *riksdaler*. But there were too few *riksdaler* in the country, and the Danish king insisted on being paid in this currency and no other – it was the euro of the age. As a result, Swedes paid their taxes as best they could, with other coins or with goods, and the government had to convert it all to silver. Much of the money was used for other purposes as well. If we assume that Sweden (including Finland) at the time had some 1,200,000 inhabitants, then the tax would have yielded more

than 1 million *riksdaler*. And in fact it did, bringing in four times the sum required. And Denmark received its money on time. But as is apparent from Oxenstierna's letter to the dowager queen (see above), cash was in short supply. Much of the tax went to armaments and to the war with Poland, which soon broke out again.

WAR, PEACE, ARMISTICE ∽ Other wars, too, were drawing to a close. The long struggle with Russia was led by Jakob De la Gardie, and Gustav II Adolf took part in the fighting in 1614 and 1615. Once Russia had attained stability under a new tsar from the Romanov clan, which was to reign until 1917, all thoughts of putting the king's brother on the throne in Moscow were abandoned and the Peace of Stolbova was concluded in the winter of 1617. This peace considerably extended the territory of the Finnish part of the realm, and in addition Sweden obtained Ingria and handsome reparations. In his turn, the tsar obtained Novgorod. Now Sweden ruled the whole of the Gulf of Finland and Russia no longer had any ports on the Baltic. But the Swedes did not win as much as they had hoped for in terms of commerce, as the Russians had the port of Archangelsk on the White Sea, which they increasingly turned to instead.

The Vasa, a Swedish man-o'-war, capsized and sank in Stockholm harbour during her maiden voyage in 1628, to the great embarrassment of the fledgling Great Power. The ship was located in 1956 and its subsequent raising and restoration resulted not only in one of Sweden's most popular museums but also in valuable research findings.

The war with Poland dragged on for many years. Once Sweden had made peace with Russia, new troops were equipped and the king prepared a new strategy. Then he took part for years on end in the war being conducted on the far shores of the Baltic, first in Livonia, where Riga became Swedish in 1621 and Dorpat in 1625, and then in Lithuania and in Poland itself. Livonia, which to a great extent occupied the same territory as present-day Latvia, was to remain Swedish for ninety years. It was allowed to keep its system of governance, but the king appointed a Swedish Governor-General, who had great powers of decision. High-ranking Swedes were granted fiefs in the new province.

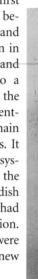

Gustav II Adolf. Red chalk drawing by L. Strauch, 1632.

From 1626 onwards, the war spread into West Prussia. At the time, Prussia was divided, with the Elector of Brandenburg ruling one part and the king of Poland another, including Danzig, Elbing and Thorn. Here Sweden enjoyed great success under the leadership of the young king, who proved to be an outstanding general and strategist. Elbing was captured and administered by Sweden – and from the city, at Oxenstierna's suggestion, debased coins were distributed which wreaked havoc in the Polish economy. By this time the thought of a Swedish Baltic Empire had become more than a distant aspiration. The majority of the Council agreed with the king that sooner or later Sweden would be drawn into what was to become the Thirty Years War, which had been blazing in Germany since 1618. On one side were ranged the German-Roman Emperor and the Catholic German states, and on the other the Protestant states, principally based in northern Germany. Christian IV had already tried to intervene, but had been defeated by the imperial army under the skilled generalship of field marshal Tilly.

First, however, it was necessary to bring the Polish war to an end. This happened with the armistice of Altmark of 1629, which was to hold for six years. Sweden gained not only some territories but also economic advantages, including the right to levy customs duties on the rivers Vistula and Neman. A large part of the grain export trade of eastern Europe passed along these rivers, and quite considerable sums of money accumulated in the coffers of the Swedish representatives. Indeed it was almost the equivalent of Sweden's annual tax revenues.

THE THIRTY YEARS WAR ∾ This long-drawn-out, brutal and devastating war constitutes a most complex skein of events, with on the one side the Habsburgs – that is to say, the Holy Roman Emperor, his relative the Spanish king and a number of minor German states that practised Catholicism – and on the other all the German princely houses who wished to increase their own power at the expense of the emperor. All the dissensions were exacerbated by religious fanaticism – but then again, Catholic France, led by Cardinal Richelieu, was in the camp of the enemies of the Habsburgs for reasons of Great Power realpolitik. When Sweden made its accommodation with Poland, the fortunes of war were favouring the imperial camp, and a large part of northern Germany was occupied by Catholic troops.

Sweden and its king had enjoyed good relations with the emperor's opponents, and now considered that it was time to take a more active part in the fighting. And if this participation also happened to promote the creation of the projected Baltic Empire, so much the better! Naturally there were other factors involved such as the political situation of the country, the threat to the economy if the export trade were to end, the threat to Protestantism, etc. The king deployed his most eloquent rhetoric and won the support of the Council and Parliament, and the Church made its contribution by fanning the agitation that portrayed the war as a battle against the hydra of Catholicism. In the summer of 1630, the greatly expanded fleet conveyed the Swedish army across the Baltic and set it ashore in Pomerania. Even at this early stage the Swedish army contained a fair number of mercenaries, and these were to play an increasingly significant role as the war progressed. There were quite simply not enough Swedes for the purpose. There was a not inconsiderable influx of foreign officers into the Swedish army – principally Scots and a few Englishmen, but also nobles or nobles-to-be from the Baltic territories, Germany and France – who were to settle in Sweden after the war and whose descendants still live here.

The duke of Pomerania now entered into an alliance with Sweden. He became completely dependent on the Swedes and remained so until his death in 1638. In 1640, the duchy was transformed into a Swedish possession. At the same time, the Catholic League had succeeded in persuading the emperor to dismiss his principal general, Wallenstein, and replace him with Tilly, who was soon to confront the Swedes. Initially, Gustav II Adolf had few allies. Brandenburg acceded under compulsion, Hessen-Kassel and Magdeburg rather less reluctantly. Funding was a great problem for the remainder of the year 1630, and bills of exchange and loans increased the debt burden. By the Treaty of Bärwalde of early 1631, Sweden received large subsidies from France, whose political leader Cardinal Richelieu did not hesitate to support the leaders of the Protestants in order to weaken the power of the Habsburgs. Intensive propaganda boosting the "Lion of the North" was conducted in all the anti-Catholic regions of Germany. The Swedish campaign soon went more on the offensive, and the famous battle of Breitenfeld took place on 7 September 1631, at which the Swedes led by Gustav Adolf defeated the imperial army under Tilly. In the initial stages of the battle, Gustav's ally the Elector of Brandenburg and his troops fled the field "and did not stop until they got to Eulenburg", as the king himself expressed it in his description of the battle. It was becoming clearer and clearer that the Swedish king was a general of genius.

The Swedish army with its growing complement of Germans and mercenary foreigners was now able to continue its victorious march to southern Germany. New territories had to contribute to the war effort (that is to say, were forced to hand over money and provisions), although the discipline of the soldiery is said to have been considerably better in the Protestant army than in the imperial one – at least as long as Gustav Adolf remained alive. After his death the Swedes and their mercenaries gained an evil reputation for the same brutal behaviour as all the other armies in the ever more grievously ravaged and plundered German Empire, whose civilian population suffered more in this than in any previous war.

Negotiations with the German states and cities were conducted by Axel Oxenstierna. He also dealt with the French, who were not yet openly involved in the war. Historians have discussed Gustav Adolf's real plans at this stage of the war at great length without being able to reach a consensus. Was he merely hoping to become the leader of an evangelical alliance, or did he aspire to a Protestant imperial crown? What is clear, is that he knew his own strength and was able to confront his allies with force and ruthlessness. He showed tolerance towards the Catholics of southern Germany – in contrast to his behaviour in Sweden – but he made them contribute enormous resources to the maintenance of his army. Swedish and foreign officers were granted fiefs in Germany.

The emperor now attempted to save the situation by recalling Wallenstein, who joined the Bavarian army and met the Swedes at Nuremberg, but the battles ensuing there were indecisive. Gustav Adolf attempted to storm the imperial camp, and failed, but Wallenstein did not dare engage in an open battle. Finally the area became so devastated that both armies had to leave it. During the autumn Wallenstein marched on Saxony, whose Elector called for Swedish help. Gustav Adolf marched rapidly to assist him, and met Wallenstein at Lützen, some dozen miles southwest of Leipzig, on 6 November 1632. In the ensuing battle the king, who had been riding at the head of the Småland brigade but had evidently lost touch with them in the heavy mist, was slain. The Swedish army won a narrow victory, and Wallenstein retired to Bohemia. Gustav Adolf's plundered corpse was not found until the following day. The war was now to enter a new phase.

THE REGENCY AND THE CONTINUATION OF THE WAR ∾ The death of Gustav II Adolf put an end to any wide-ranging plans for foreign dominion, even though it proved impossible to disengage Sweden from the German war. The immediate problem was a domestic one: how was Sweden to be ruled during the minority of Gustav Adolf's daughter, the six-year-old Kristina? The decisive role in handling this question was played by Chancellor Oxenstierna. He proposed a constitutional framework that was finally adopted in 1634. The Councillors of the Realm were placed in charge of the administrative offices organized on a collegiate basis, and the composition of Parliament and the meetings of the parliamentary committees were regulated. The regency government would be constituted by the five highest officers of the realm: the Chancellor, the Lord Chief Justice, the Earl Marshal, the Admiral of the Fleet and the Lord Treasurer. In this government the Chancellor, Oxenstierna himself, had the greatest influence. These "lords of the realm" should not be imagined as the equivalent of today's civil servants, however. It was not their custom to appear at the office every day and several of them spent long periods on their estates. At times the Council was a bearpit of contention and in Parliament the unprivileged Estates were constantly grumbling at the nobility.

In the years immediately following the death of Gustav II Adolf, the conduct of the war in Germany was in the hands of the Chancellor, who resided there until 1636. Wallenstein was no longer a factor in the war, as he had been assassinated by his own officers in 1634 while oc-

Gustav II Adolf is killed during the battle of Lützen on 6 November 1632. Historical painting by Carl Wahlbom, 1855.

cupying himself with obscure intrigues against the emperor. In this same year, however, the Swedish-evangelical army suffered a heavy defeat at Nördlingen. Axel Oxenstierna, who merely wished to obtain Swedish possessions in Germany in order to sustain the Baltic Empire, had no desire to give up the struggle, but was ready to envisage a separate peace in order to be able to march on Poland instead. Nothing came of this plan, however, as the regency government in Stockholm prolonged the armistice in 1635 and returned the Prussian ports to Poland against the will of the Chancellor, a measure which drastically reduced Swedish revenues. It now became even more important to carry the war effort in Germany to its intended conclusion. The Chancellor travelled to Paris and met Cardinal Richelieu at Compiègne. In 1638 Sweden entered into a formal alliance with Catholic France, which actively joined the struggle against the emperor and increased its subsidies to Sweden. The Swedish generals Johan Banér and Lennart Torstensson enjoyed notable successes, and the young prince Karl Gustav, the queen's cousin, who had not yet been recog-

nized as the successor to the throne, took part in the campaigns. Long drawn-out peace negotiations were initiated in 1643, but the war continued as before, as bloody and destructive as ever.

WAR WITH DENMARK ∾

While Swedish military operations were at their height, open hostilities broke out with Denmark, which had been given cause for concern by the Swedish successes in Germany as well as around the Baltic. The principal issue for Christian IV was to defend Denmark's commercial position and the right to levy customs duties in the Sound. He engaged in energetic diplomatic activities. The inspections to which the Danes subjected Swedish shipping became more and more intrusive. The Dutch, who were most heavily affected by the customs duties, drew closer to Sweden and concluded a treaty with the Swedes in 1640. Oxenstierna was able to win both the Council and the Estates to his view that the growing number of disputes with Denmark could only be resolved by force of arms. At the end of 1643, Lennart Torstensson broke into Holstein and Jutland with his army. Christian mobilized his land and sea defences, however, and Torstensson was unable to cross

Queen Kristina comes of age in 1644. To the left of the young queen, holding the regalia, the five highest officers of the realm may be seen, while on the right are the spokesmen of the four Estates. Silver medal by Sebastian Dattler.

the Little Belt. In 1644, in the naval battle of Femern near Kiel, Christian was wounded. The Swedish fleet was able to escape to Stockholm, and the Dutch fleet entered the Baltic in support of the Swedes. In a new naval battle in the autumn of 1644 the Danes lost twelve ships.

With French mediation, peace was concluded in Brömsebro on the border between Småland and Blekinge in 1645. Sweden obtained the provinces of Jämtland and Härjedalen, the islands of Gotland and Ösel, and Halland for 30 years. Sweden's traditional freedom from customs duties in the Sound was reaffirmed, and the Dutch were granted more favourable rates. After these events it was often said that the keys to the Sound were to be found in the Amsterdam stock exchange.

THE PEACE OF WESTPHALIA, 1648 ∾ In 1648, the Peace of Westphalia was concluded. It was signed in the cities of Münster and Osnabrück, and finally put an end to the ravages of the Thirty Years War. Sweden obtained Western Pomerania including Stralsund, Stettin and the mouth of the Oder, the city of Wismar, the bishopric of Bremen-Verden (which did not include the city of Bremen itself) and a number of smaller territories, including the county of Wildeshausen (see the map on p. 74). For the first time in fifty years, Sweden was now at peace.

As the possessor of fiefdoms within the German Empire, the Swedish monarch now had the right to a seat on the princes' bench at the German Reichstag, with the titles of the duke of Bremen-Verden and Pomerania, the prince of Rügen and the lord of Wismar.

THE SUCCESSION ∾ In December 1644, the young queen came of age. She had received a thorough education specifically designed for her rank. She was instructed in theology by the tolerant scholar Johannes Matthiae, which eventually made the orthodox Protestantism of her native country distasteful to her. She was very interested in philosophy and she was well acquainted with the literature and art of her day, although her knowledge was not always profound in every subject. Axel Oxenstierna characterized her as having "an extraordinarily

Queen Kristina in 1650, the year in which she was crowned. Portrait by David Beck.

Iron dealing by the
great iron scales
near Järntorget
("Iron Square") in
Stockholm at the
end of the seven-
teenth century. The
iron porters sur-
vived until the nine-
teenth century.
From *Suecia Antiqua*
by Erik Dahlberg.

splendid mind" and as being "not at all like a woman". He himself instructed her in matters of state.

The regency always viewed it as a matter of urgency that the queen should marry and produce heirs. Her suitors included the Elector of Brandenburg and above all her cousin, the Count Palatine Karl Gustav, with whom she became secretly engaged. However, Kristina was unwilling to marry, and in the years immediately following her coming of age her principal interests were politics and the business of government. She wished to assert the powers of the monarchy as against the nobility, and wanted to resolve the question of the succession without marriage. The influence of the Council of the Realm and of the Chancellor waned, and at the parliament of 1649 she was able to obtain her objective of having Karl Gustav become her successor if she should die without heirs. The following year this decision was confirmed by a new parliament, and thus Karl Gustav and his male heirs, should he have any, became the hereditary princes of Sweden. Kristina was able to push this decision through by skilfully playing off the unprivileged Estates against the nobility, as the former were crying out more and more insistently for a Reduction of the noble estates and the curtailment of noble privileges. Once she had got her way, Kristina shifted her support to the nobility and was able to have the projected Reduction postponed.

IMMIGRANTS, TRADE AND COMMERCE, COLONIES AND FINANCE ∾ Swedish trade and commerce had been expanding greatly, without however affecting the majority of the population. Foreign merchants, traders and engineers came to Sweden to live. Among the engineers were many Walloons (from what is now Belgium), who improved the forging of iron and helped Sweden obtain better prices for its products. The most prominent of the merchants, Louis De Geer, from the Netherlands, was responsible for setting up metalworking plants in places like Finspång (blast furnaces, bar iron manufacture, cannon forges, etc.) and Norrköping (a rifle factory and a brass works), owned other metalworks throughout the country, lent money to the Crown and equipped a fleet of his own. As we noted above, Sweden was producing copper on a very large scale. This had a bizarre impact on the minting of copper coinage, as the government introduced a series of huge solid copper "coins" in 1644. The largest of these weighed almost 20 kg! It was to prove difficult to get the public to accept this as a means of payment, although smaller denominations were gradually taken into use. Those having to use this currency were compelled to cart around "coins" weighing many kilos until 1776, when they were finally withdrawn from circulation.

In 1649, De Geer was able to persuade the government to establish a trading company for Africa, and a Swedish colony was set up on the Gold Coast at Cabo Corso, where the fortress of Karlsborg was built. Sweden was unable to retain this colony, however, and by 1663 it had been lost for ever.

The colony of New Sweden (1638-55) was of greater significance. It was established in Delaware in North America on the initiative of Axel Oxenstierna, and its trade was handled by the West Indian (or American) Company. A number of plantations were established, and many Swedes emigrated. The colony was conquered by the Dutch, however, and later fell to the English.

Despite the string of victories and the growing export trade, the long drawn-out wars had undermined the country's finances and they were in a state of near-dissolution. The Crown had sold or donated a large part of its estates to the nobility in return for support in the wars, and the growing revenues from customs fees and other charges were unable to completely compensate for the wealth generated by the Crown's estates. There was also a threat to the

The world's largest coin was struck at Avesta mint in 1644-45. It had a value of 10 *daler* and consisted of 19.7 kg of pure copper from the famous copper mine at Falun. These coins were struck partly because Sweden needed money and had more copper than silver, and partly because they could be exported as pure copper in years when the metal fetched a good price in the world market.

liberty of the Swedish peasant, or the perception of a threat, due to tax revenues having been pawned off for cash or made over as gifts. Eventually in one way or another the nobility came to own 50 per cent of the land which had generated revenues for the Crown before 1611. The unprivileged Estates were being weighed down more and more by the burden of taxation. Given this state of affairs, the demands for a Reduction of noble property raised at the parliament of 1650 are quite comprehensible. Kristina continued to give away Crown property, however. The upper nobility in particular obtained additional large estates in the new territories, and in consequence now had the financial resources to initiate the many palatial building projects that were undertaken in the seventeenth century preceding the Reduction of Karl XI. These developments lost the Council of the Realm much of its influence over Kristina, and the nobility was expanded by the immoderate creation of new peerages – from less than 300 clans in 1632 when she became queen to a total of 767 clans in 1654, the year of her abdication.

THE ABDICATION ∾ By 1650, the queen had made up her mind to abdicate. The French philosopher René Descartes, who had resided in Stockholm in 1649-50 and died there, had brought Kristina closer to Catholicism in their long morning conversations. To her, it appeared to be a more tolerant and more cultivated doctrine than Lutheranism. In 1651, she got in touch with the General of the Jesuit order, and two Jesuits were secretly dispatched to Sweden to instruct her. The Council of the Realm

was long opposed to Kristina's desire to abdicate, but she continued with her preparations for leaving Sweden. In February 1654, she reiterated her unshakable decision to the Council, and on 6 June the same year she put off her crown before the Estates in the Hall of State at Uppsala Castle, at the age of 27.

The queen, who had been assured maintenance by towns and territories in Sweden and its possessions, immediately left the country and headed for the Spanish Netherlands. On her journey to Rome she publicly converted to Catholicism in November 1655 and made her solemn entry into the Holy City just before Christmas. In her early years of exile, she took part in the political intrigues of Europe, and visited Paris, for instance, in order to obtain Naples. But as time went on she devoted less and less time to such projects. She made one or two brief visits to Sweden, principally to resolve problems relating to non-payment of her maintenance. Her principal place of residence was Rome, where she lived at the Palazzo Riario, pursuing literary and philosophical studies but also taking part in disputes concerning her sovereign status. She began writing her memoirs and noted down her thoughts ("Maxims") on various subjects.

THE CONQUEROR TAKES POWER ∾ Karl X Gustav was 32 when he ascended the throne. His mother was the daughter of Karl IX, his father a petty German prince who had settled in Sweden. With him, the Palatine dynasty had succeeded the Vasa dynasty.

The new king had to ensure the continuation of his dynasty, and in the autumn of 1654 he married Hedvig Eleonora of Holstein-Gottorp. Their only child, Karl XI, was to become king at a very early age.

One of the problems requiring resolution was the ever more insistent demand for a Reduction of the noble estates. The parliament of 1655 decided on a relatively moderate measure of this kind, known as the Quarter Confiscation. It was partially implemented, but ground to a halt due to the wars that Sweden almost immediately became involved in.

In 1653, Russia had attacked Poland, which proved to be very weak. Karl X Gustav saw an opportunity to further Swedish expansion at the expense of the latter country. A formal cause was found in the Polish Vasa dynasty's old claims on the Swedish crown and Livonia. With the consent of Parliament, the attack was launched from Pomerania in the summer of 1655. The campaigns were initially successful, culminating in the three-day battle of Warsaw. The whole of western Prussia (except Danzig) was occupied, and the Elector of Brandenburg briefly acknowledged Swedish sovereignty over East Prussia.

The successes did not last, however, as the Swedish army was too small to control the whole of Poland. The population rose against

The old Stockholm royal castle, much later known as "Three Crowns" from the national coat of arms on the great tower, and part of the surrounding city. Coloured copper engraving from the mid-seventeenth century.

Karl X Gustav. Part of a painting by A. Wuchters.

the invaders, and Russia attacked Sweden in June 1656. In the following year, first Austria and then Brandenburg concluded treaties of alliance with Poland. In addition to which war was declared on Sweden by Frederik III of Denmark-Norway.

Karl X Gustav decided to postpone his Polish plans for the time being, and instead marched on Denmark as rapidly as he could through northern Germany, as he considered it necessary to defeat Denmark if he was to avoid a war on two fronts. Jutland was taken and negotiations were conducted with Cromwell, the English dictator, to assist with landing Swedish troops on Zealand. The severity of the winter solved this particular problem in a spectacularly unexpected fashion, however. In January 1658, the Swedes were able to make their way across the ice to the island of Funen, where the Danish army was defeated, and on 6 February the renowned march across the Great Belt began (via Langeland-Lolland) – the whole army had completed the crossing by the twelfth of the month. With mediation by the French and the English, the Peace of Roskilde was concluded on 26 February, and Denmark was compelled to hand over Skåne, Halland, Blekinge, Bohuslän, Bornholm and the county of Trondheim to Sweden. Hostile fleets were not to be allowed to enter the Baltic. With this peace, Sweden had attained its objective of freeing the Sound, which was no longer under the sole dominion of Denmark. The ultimate objective of Karl Gustav, however, was that his defeated neighbour would "in time combine with Sweden".

During the summer of 1658 it was to emerge that Sweden was rather isolated, however. Negotiations with England and France led nowhere, the Netherlands were reluctant to see any further strengthening of Swedish control in the Baltic, while Brandenburg, Austria and Poland were still engaged in active hostilities. An accommodation was reached with Russia alone, in that an armistice was signed. Denmark was an unpredictable factor in this sensitive situation, and for this reason Karl Gustav decided to conquer the whole country. The war began immediately, in August 1658, but it did not turn out as well as the Swedes had anticipated. Denmark was supported by the Netherlands, Bornholm and the county of Trondheim were lost and the siege of Copenhagen dragged on longer than expected. In December 1659, a large-scale assault came to nothing.

Karl Gustav now left for Gothenburg, where he had summoned the parliamentary Estates to obtain their support. Once there, however, he contracted a sudden illness, and died in February 1660, leaving Sweden facing a war on several fronts, but also having made significant territorial gains, the most important of which were to remain with Sweden permanently.

Count Magnus Gabriel De la Gardie and his wife, Princess Maria Eufrosyne of the Palatinate. De la Gardie long enjoyed high office, and his wife was Karl X Gustav's sister. The picture indicates her higher rank by having her husband stand one step below her. The small dog is a symbol of fidelity and the bean pod in Maria's hand indicates that she is pregnant. De la Gardie was greatly interested in culture and was an enthusiastic builder of palaces, but he was ineffective as a head of government and died a ruined man as a result of the ransacking of the regency and Karl XI's Reduction. Painting by H. Münnichhoven, 1653.

THE REGENCY ∽ For the third time in fifty years, Sweden faced the problems of a regency government. The new king, Karl XI, was four years old when he assumed the throne, and a long regency was in prospect. The regency government was made up of the upper nobility and the dowager queen, and its most promi-

nent figure was count Magnus Gabriel De la Gardie, a politically weak individual with strong cultural interests. He was long the favourite of Queen Kristina, until he incurred her displeasure in 1652. Karl X Gustav used him for many commissions, and he became Chancellor and a member of the regency govern-

NORWAY
Danish
until 1814

FINLAND
Swedish
until 1809

LADOGA

SWEDEN

INGRIA

ESTO-
NIA

DEN-
MARK

LIVO-
NIA

The Baltic
provinces
ceded to
Russia in 1721

THE BALTIC

POMERANIA
Swedish until 1720
Swedish until 1815
WISMAR Swedish until 1803
BREMEN-VERDEN Swedish until 1719
WILDESHAUSEN Swedish until 1679

den to possess Livonia and Johan Kasimir (Vasa) renounced his claims on the Swedish crown. Sweden had previously had to give up its control of the Prussian ports. By the settlement with Denmark in May the same year, Sweden handed back Trondheim county and Bornholm, but retained Skåne, Blekinge and Halland, in addition to Gotland, Bohuslän and Jämtland.

In the autumn of 1660, Parliament managed to force through certain changes in the government and to add a clause to the Constitution of 1634 which increased the powers of the Estates and the Council. The regency government was never able to remedy the shortcomings in the finances of the nation. In 1661, the Stockholm Banco, founded under Karl X Gustav and run by Johan Palmstruch of Riga, had made Europe's first ever issue of bank notes. The government's imprudence meant that this new means of payment, which was initially welcomed, was greatly abused, and the bank foundered. Palmstruch was sentenced to death (but was pardoned) and the Bank of the Estates of the Realm was established in 1668, the first national bank in the world, which both initially and subsequently was under parliamentary management (even during the period of absolutism). But it did not obtain authorization to issue banknotes until 1701.

The conflicts between the upper nobility and the Council of the Realm on the one hand and the lower nobility and the three unprivileged Estates on the other became more strongly marked during subsequent sessions of Parliament. There was also dissension in the sphere of foreign policy, but here De la Gardie was able

ment in accordance with the king's will. His influence was great, but by no means uncontested. He was no statesman, but played a significant role in the development of Swedish culture thanks to his interest in Uppsala University and his antiquarian studies. He made important donations and encouraged many young scientists. Sweden's first law on cultural monuments was passed in 1666 on his initiative, and probably constitutes the oldest legislation of this kind in the world.

The first task facing the regency was to make peace with the nation's enemies. In April 1660, at the Oliva monastery near Danzig, peace was concluded with Poland, Brandenburg and the emperor. Poland recognized the right of Sweto negotiate a treaty with Louis XIV which would relieve some of the country's financial distress. This treaty tied Sweden into the French system of alliances.

THE KING COMES OF AGE AND WAR BREAKS OUT ∾

In 1672, shortly after the treaty with France had been concluded, the 17-year-old Karl XI was declared to be of age. He was shy and inexperienced and had received a poor education, in addition to which he suffered from dyslexia. His diaries reveal that he constantly misplaced letters in words. Throughout his life he found reading difficult, and was dependent on oral reports.

Initially the young king let himself be guided by the opinions of his mother and the Council. The Chancellor had great influence over him. The gaps in his knowledge made it easy to sway him, but he nonetheless kept a firm grip on certain fundamental ideas such as the sovereignty of the monarch and the true evangelical faith.

As a consequence of its alliance with the French, Sweden was drawn into the European war in 1675. Friedrich Wilhelm of Brandenburg, "the great Elector", defeated the Swedes at

The battle of Lund in December 1676 was the bloodiest in all wars between Denmark and Sweden. Karl XI defeated the Danes but half of those fighting, some 9,000 men, never left the battlefield. After this Karl XI fought no more wars but ensured that Sweden was well-armed. Oil painting by J. P. Lemke, 1696.

Karl XI was an industrious and conscientious man of simple habits. His only pleasures were hunting and military manoeuvres. He is simply clad in this painting from 1685 by David Klöcker Ehrenstrahl, the royal family's favourite painter.

Fehrbellin. This in itself insignificant setback gave the Netherlands, the emperor and Denmark the courage to declare war on Sweden forthwith, which immediately exposed the inadequate level of military preparedness and the poor financial management of the regency. At the request of Parliament, a commission was set up to investigate the administration of the high officials of the realm, a measure known as "ransacking the regency".

Karl now assumed the main responsibility for both administration and the conduct of war, and his anger fell heavily on the negligent officials. De la Gardie retired from public life and the king reigned alone. In the ensuing war with Denmark, fought mainly in Halland and Skåne, Karl was an inspiration to his troops thanks to his indomitable, warlike spirit and his

unwillingness to give up. In the summer of 1676 he briefly appeared to lose heart. With Dutch help, the Danes had won an important naval battle off the southern point of Öland, during which the magnificent flagship *Kronan* (The Crown) had exploded and sunk. (The wreck has since been located and marine archaeologists have made valuable discoveries, including a large treasure of gold coins, now on exhibit at the county museum in nearby Kalmar.) What is more, the enemy had occupied large areas of Skåne, and in the Göinge district the *Snapphane* guerrillas raised veritable mass levies against the Swedish cavalry. The king received valuable assistance from Councillor of the Realm Johan Gyllenstierna, who was soon summoned to the army and proved to be an excellent adviser. A minor victory at Halmstad was followed in December 1676 by the gory battle of Lund, in which Karl's aggressive spirit carried the day and the Danes were finally obliged to withdraw. The Swedes remained in Skåne. They suffered yet another naval defeat in the battle of Köge Bay in 1677, but not even this was able to bring the Danes any nearer victory. The subsequent battles were of no great significance, and in 1679, following the intervention of Louis XIV several peace treaties were concluded whose only substantial content involved the cession of some insignificant territories to Brandenburg.

The remainder of Karl's reign was peaceful. He broke with France, concluded an alliance with Denmark and lost no time marrying Ulrika Eleonora (the Elder), the princess of Denmark, in 1680. He had already been betrothed to her before the war. The proclamation of pardon to the rebellious Scanians was adhered to, but an intensive programme of Swedish "harmonization" was launched. The Swedish fleet was relocated to Blekinge, where the naval port of Karlskrona was established.

ABSOLUTISM AND REDUCTION ∾ Johan Gyllenstierna, a brutal advocate of the primacy of *raison d'état* above all personal considerations, died in 1680. But those who were hoping that the king would moderate his policies to any great extent were in for a disappointment. Other advisers and assistants took over and proved to have the same view of what needed to be done. The parliament of the autumn of 1680, the first after the war, marked a great change. A declaration by the Estates made the king virtually an absolute monarch – he no longer needed to reign with "the advice of the Council" and was not bound by the Constitution. But before this declaration was passed at the request of the king, the Estates had adopted a number of other important proposals. The ransacking of the regency officials was intensified, and they were to be brought before a court which would include representatives of the Estates. Of even greater importance was the decision concerning the Reduction, that is the return to the Crown of all recent fiefdoms granted to the nobility. It should be noted that there was never any question of this measure affecting the traditional estates of the nobility, but only lands given in fief or as pledges by the Crown.

Even the counties and baronies were abolished and these marks of rank were from now on merely titles. Subsequent parliaments approved even stricter execution of the measures. Certain noble clans, particularly the more recent ones, were ruined. De la Gardie, who had been severely affected by both the ransacking of the regency and the Reduction, was allowed to keep just one of his many palaces, and this only until his death. It should not, however, be passed over in silence that a number of newly ennobled individuals in the king's circle made themselves new fortunes with suspicious rapidity.

An important consequence of the Reduction was that it permitted the state to extend to the whole nation a system of maintaining the officers and men of the army that had been previ-

Taverns began to appear on a large scale in the seventeenth century, and the abuse of akvavit culminated in the eighteenth and early nineteenth centuries. Painting of a seventeenth century tavern by G. Camphuysen.

ously practised partially and locally. Known as the *indelningsverket* (the Distributive System, subdividing the country into maintenance districts), it involved officers being provided with houses, and soldiers with crofts, for the equipping and maintenance of which a number of tax-paying peasants were responsible. The towns, too, were brought into the system, and were obliged to maintain sailors. The system was not new, but its implementation by Karl XI was – he imposed it with ruthless severity and made strict demands on all classes of society.

Also active in revamping Swedish military capabilities was the renowned builder of fortresses Erik Dahlberg. Without the Reduction, this military revitalization and the Distributive System for maintaining officers and men would not have been feasible. In this way the "distributed" army and navy became the core of the Swedish military organization, that would not be finally dismantled until 1901. The new system relieved the peasants of the burdensome levy of soldiers, at least in peacetime. There are many soldiers' crofts and officers' houses preserved today that serve as monuments of the Distributive System. Constant musters and journeys of inspection, often undertaken by the king himself and involving scrutiny down to the minutest detail, contributed to keeping national defence readiness at a high level. Arms were rationalized to a few types only, and the simple Carolingian uniform was introduced.

The Reduction was also implemented in the Baltic provinces. It aroused a great deal of opposition among the nobility there, which had a repressive relationship to the peasantry, and provoked these nobles into conspiring against the Swedish Crown. The best known of these conspirators is Johan Reinhold Patkul, who eventually had to flee and was sentenced to death *in absentia*. He subsequently manoeuvred clandestinely to coordinate the Great Northern War, which broke out in 1700. Karl XI was enraged at the system of serfdom prevalent in these provinces, and opposed it, but was unable to abolish it. At this time, Sweden was a multilingual nation with no nationalism in the modern sense. Languages spoken within its borders included Swedish, Danish, Finnish, Sami, German, Ingrian, Latvian and Estonian. But Swedish historians were concerned to boost the remarkable history of the nation and had no qualms about claiming that it was the original home of all the world's peoples. This was the doctrine taught by professor Olof Rudbeck at Uppsala University, for instance.

The Reduction improved state revenues by some two million silver *daler* annually, in addition to what was obtained from the ransacking of the regency administration. Injustices indubitably occurred, with many people being affected with unnecessary severity by unfair demands. But the absolutist regime seldom committed serious violations outside the financial sphere, as the king regarded himself as being subject to the law rather than standing above it. The Reduction prevented Sweden from developing into a feudal state with a regime in the hands of the nobility, as happened in Poland, for instance, and the freedom of the peasantry was preserved, but the upper nobility usually managed to keep its older lands, and became transformed into a class of great landowners rather than feudal lords. But its political power

"The Castle Fire", an historical painting by J. F. Höckert, 1864. Karl XII (un-historically dressed in uniform) and his elder sister help the dowager queen Hedvig Eleonora down the steps. In the background the corpse of Karl XI is being rescued from the fire. The youngest sister, Ulrika Eleonora, is seen leading the way.

was finished, and its role would gradually be taken over by officials from the lower nobility.

THE DEATH OF THE KING ❧ In 1697, not yet 42 years old, Karl XI died of cancer of the stomach, for which the medicine of the time had no remedy. At the same time the whole country had been struck by a series of bad harvests and a famine lasting many years, which decimated the population and severely depleted state coffers. Shortly after the king died, the royal castle in Stockholm went up in flames.

The Reduction and the Distributive System have been condemned by later critics, who charge that they bound Sweden to the archaic relations of a subsistence economy and an obsolete system of taxation. To some extent this may be correct. The "distributive" army was in no sense nimble, and proved inadequate in prolonged conditions of war. In peacetime, however, the system worked well, and it is legitimate to ask what other system of taxation a "financial housekeeper" like Karl XI might have been able to introduce in the conditions of seventeenth century Sweden.

A TEENAGE KING ❧ On his accession to the throne in 1697, the new king had not yet reached the age of 15. He was the oldest of Karl XI's sons, and the only one of them to reach adulthood. In contrast to his father he found it easy to learn things and received a solid education. He enthusiastically participated in his father's outdoor activities, which mainly consisted of hunting and military exercises. Karl XII learnt at a very early age that the monarchy was held by "the grace of God", and that he was an "absolute, all-commanding sovereign". From the 1680s onwards, "His Majesty's Council" and "His Majesty's Estates", as they were now called, were the obedient or at least powerless tools of the monarchy. Religious instruction contributed to fixing these ideas of absolutism in his mind; Karl became a convinced Lutheran. Like his father, he was extremely law-abiding, but his stronger sense of logic and his lack of a capacity for compromise at times led him to make decisions that would have dangerous consequences.

Ever since Voltaire's hero-worshipping biography in the eighteenth century, everything written about Karl XII has been so coloured by the times and the values of the authors that there are few if any objective accounts available. This is amplified by the king's own great reticence, which made it difficult to uncover his plans at the time and still does today. The regency administration that had been appointed wished to be rid of the task as soon as possible. In the late autumn of 1697 it resigned, and the king assumed the full powers of government at the age of 15.

THE GREAT NORTHERN WAR AND THE END OF SWEDEN AS A GREAT POWER ∾ The rapprochement with Denmark (see p. 76) had soon changed into the usual distrust. Sweden had close contacts with Holstein-Gottorp, Denmark's enemy, whose duke, Frederik IV, had become Karl's brother-in-law in 1698. In 1698-99, there were busy rounds of negotiation between Russia (Peter the Great), Poland (August the Strong of Saxony) and Denmark (Christian V and later Frederik IV); these negotiations were energetically encouraged by the exiled Baltic nobleman Patkul mentioned above. An hostile alliance was eventually concluded and in 1700 all three allies launched their attacks on Sweden; the Great Northern War had begun.

Karl XII and his generals launched an almost instantaneous counter-offensive and landed in Zealand, which had inadequate defences. Denmark was compelled to seek peace and to abandon its claims to Holstein-Gottorp. This was Karl XII's first taste of the war that was to be the main preoccupation of the remainder of his reign. While the brief Danish campaign was being concluded, August the Strong had used his Saxon troops for a failed attack on Riga. Tsar Peter of Russia crossed the border into Ingria in September 1700 and began to besiege Narva. It was intolerable for the energetic Russian leader to be excluded from the Baltic, and his objectives were clear: the conquest of Ingria, the division of the Baltic provinces with Poland and if possible a favourable adjustment of the border with Finland.

In October 1700, the Swedish army left Karlshamn in the province of Blekinge and sailed to Pernau (now Pärnu). After landing, it hurried to relieve Narva. On 20 November the superior Russian siege forces were attacked, thoroughly defeated and driven to flight or slaughtered. In describing the division of responsibility it is usually said that the quarter-master-general, Carl Stuart, drew up the plan of attack, and the king made the crucial decision to carry it out. Stuart also had the technical responsibility in the campaigns of 1701, in which the Saxons were repulsed, but in 1702 Karl assumed leadership in every respect. There is no doubt that he had great gifts of military generalship, both in relation to planning and preparation as well as during the actual fighting on the battlefield.

The peace terms offered by the defeated enemy were rejected by the king – against the views of many of his advisers – and the goal of the continued campaign became to strip August of the Polish crown. This was finally accomplished, despite the skilled generalship of the Polish king, and in 1704 the aristocratic Polish republic elected Stanislaus Leczynski as king and concluded an alliance with Sweden. In 1706, to put a definitive end to August's ambitions, Karl marched into the defeated king's hereditary realm of Saxony by way of Silesia. The treaty of Altranstädt forced August to abdicate the Polish throne, recognize Stanislaus and break off the alliance with Russia. His adviser, the Baltic noble Patkul was handed over to the Swedes and the pending death sentence was executed in all its brutality. In addition the Electorate of Saxony had to pay for the maintenance of the Swedish army for the whole of the winter, an amount that was probably in excess of 15 million *taler*; the sum was raised by means of a tax on all groups of society, not by pillage. During his sojourn in Altranstädt, Karl compelled the German emperor to guarantee the right of the Silesian Protestants to exercise their religion. The victorious English general John Churchill, the duke of Marlborough, paid a visit to the young warrior king, whose plans were the object of widespread speculation as the War of the Spanish Succession was going on at the same time, and observers wondered if Karl intended to change his plans and back one or the other of the parties involved in that great trial of strength.

Karl's goal was clear, however. He wished to defeat Russia, which had moved into Sweden's Baltic provinces and succeeded in conquering Narva and Dorpat. An additional irritant was the founding by the tsar of St Petersburg in 1703 on what had been Swedish territory. Karl's well-equipped troops made their move in 1707. His

Karl XII in Altranstädt in 1706. The king realized the propaganda value of a realistic depiction in a simple uniform, with no wig or royal attributes. Painting by D. von Krafft after an original by J. D. Schwarz.

The *kalabalik* of Bender, 1713 – as depicted in an early nineteenth century hand-coloured print by P. A. Huldberg.

intention was to occupy Moscow and compel Peter to sue for a peace that would restore Sweden's possessions. It is unlikely that he had any plans for expansion at Russia's expense, as he had not given any indication of such desires in Poland. After successes in 1707 and 1708 he suffered a harsh blow – in the late summer of 1708 he was unable to establish contact with general Lewenhaupt, who was to have reinforced him with supplies and troops.

THE DEFEAT AT POLTAVA ∾ Karl now moved to the Ukraine, where he was counting on a Cossack revolt against the tsar. Lewen-

haupt and the remains of his army joined the king, but they had lost all their supplies. The harsh Russian winter of 1708-09 had decimated the Swedish forces, and neither Swedish nor Polish reinforcements arrived in time to help prevent the great defeat at Poltava on 28 June 1709, in which field marshal Rehnskiöld was in command, as Karl had been wounded in the foot and was in the grip of fever. After tsar Peter's victory the king and what remained of his army withdrew towards the Turkish border. At Perevolochna, where the river Vorskla empties into the Dnieper, there eventually gathered 16,000 men, many of them wounded. The king, still ill, thought his army would follow him and had himself ferried across the river with a few hundred men. Shortly afterwards, however, Lewenhaupt capitulated to prince Menshikov, the Russian commander, and the rest of Karl's army was led away into captivity.

THE KALABALIK OF BENDER ∾ Karl remained in Turkey until 1714, residing for most of that time in the small town of Bender in present-day Moldavia. His five-year sojourn so far from Sweden appeared most peculiar to his contemporaries, but it may be partially explained by his desire to press Turkey into declaring war on Russia. This in fact happened a number of times, but with no tangible results, at least as far as Sweden was concerned. Eventually the Sultan and his advisers tired of their troublesome guest and had him forcibly taken into custody in February 1713, in the incident known as the *kalabalik* (tumult) of Bender (thus introducing into Swedish one of a number of Turkish words borrowed during this period). Tired, depressed and shaken, the king was taken from Bender and held as a prisoner partly in Demotika and partly in Timurtash.

THE KING'S RETURN AND HIS DEATH ∾ In the meantime Sweden's dominion as a Great Power was crumbling. The Baltic possessions were rapidly captured by the Russians, including Finland (1713-14). Saxony re-entered the war and August regained his Polish throne. The invasion of Skåne by the Danes was beaten off by Magnus Stenbock at Helsingborg in 1710, to be sure, and this same general won a victory in Mecklenburg over a Danish-Saxon army, but

the following year he was forced to capitulate and was taken off into lifelong captivity. In the autumn Stettin (now Sczeczin) in Pomerania capitulated.

Conditions naturally grew more and more problematic in Sweden the longer the king remained in Turkey. He insisted on resolving important issues himself, and this entailed great inconvenience given the slowness of postal deliveries. Between 1710 and 1712 there was a plague epidemic, large-scale levies for a new army provoked discontent, and the state coffers were at times so empty that officials were only able to receive part of their salary.

The Council, most of whose powers had been removed by the king, started making its presence felt once more, and took over some aspects of government. At last, in 1713, a parliament was summoned, at which it was planned to proclaim the king's sister, Ulrika Eleonora the Younger, as regent. Secret discussions were held about abolishing the absolute monarchy. As soon as Karl XII got news of the parliament, however, he ordered it to disperse, and it did so immediately.

Karl finally realized that he would not be able to achieve anything in Turkey, and left Demotika in the autumn of 1714. He accomplished the final stages of his journey at breakneck speed and in November 1714 arrived at Stralsund with just a single companion. He stayed in Pomerania's last remaining Swedish city for a year. From the summer of 1715 it was heavily besieged by a Danish-Prussian army, once Brandenburg-Prussia and Hanover had decided to join forces with Sweden's enemies. Karl led the defence of the city with new-found energy, but was finally compelled to acknowledge that the situation was hopeless. He sailed by night from Stralsund with a number of officers, having granted the city permission to capitulate, and arrived back in Sweden in December 1715 after an absence of more than fifteen years. His headquarters were initially set up in Ystad, and then in Lund. He never visited Stockholm.

Baron Georg Heinrich von Görtz, from Holstein, soon emerged as the king's principal adviser in matters of both domestic and foreign policy. Comprehensive measures were undertaken to get the country back on to its feet again. The Council was pushed aside completely, the government of the nation was vigorously centralized, strict new taxes were imposed on all subjects and new soldiers were enlisted. A reconstruction of the tax system was overdue, and had already been prepared by the king and his advisers. A kind of personal tax return was introduced. Supplementary taxes were levied on every kind of commodity, including wigs (as is well-known, the king himself did not use a wig). Credit coins were issued in great numbers in order to make money available. These were known as emergency coins and functioned as a kind of paper money in the form of copper. The idea behind this has been attributed to Görtz, but erroneously. Görtz fully understood the potential of this new device for obtaining money, however, and the whole responsibility for the scheme was laid on his shoulders after the death of the king.

The newly instituted Office of Contributions, whose task was to oversee the supplementary taxes, eventually issued what became known as coin-notes, and old coins of copper

sheet were withdrawn from circulation to be restamped at higher nominal values. All in all some 42 million emergency coins were issued during a period of three years, and despite various decrees they gave rise to an inflation of some 30-50 per cent or more and eventually led to the partial bankruptcy of the state.

Karl had succeeded in mobilizing a new army, but also devoted time and energy to diplomatic negotiations with both England-Hanover and Russia and Prussia. Towards the end of his reign he focused his efforts more and more on Russia, with Görtz conducting negotiations for him in the Åland islands. He gave the tsar to understand that his nephew Karl Fredrik of Holstein-Gottorp would inherit the Swedish throne and marry the tsar's daughter. The other claimant to the throne was the king's sister Ulrika Eleonora the Younger, who had married landgrave Friedrich of Hesse in 1715.

In the autumn of 1718, Karl marched on Norway with an army of almost 40,000 men. He never disclosed the reason for the campaign. It is possible that he wished to replace the territories he had lost in the east or to compel the Danes to accept peace terms and separate them from their allies, but more wide-ranging plans have been attributed to him. Perhaps he just wanted to secure his rear in preparation for the reconquest of Finland and the Baltic provinces. A number of indicators point to this possibility, including the gathering of a considerable number of transport vessels in Stockholm and other ports.

The campaign came to an abrupt end, however. On 30 November 1718, during the siege of the fortress of Fredriksten (Fredrikshald), the

36-year-old king, who was standing in a trench, was hit by a bullet in his left temple and died immediately. It has never been ascertained whether the bullet came from the fortress or from the gun of an assassin.

After Karl's death, the whole campaign was immediately called off. Friedrich of Hesse took the initiative with an energy he was rarely to show later, distributing the campaign coffers among the officers and arresting Görtz when he arrived to report on the progress of negotiations with Russia. Ulrika Eleonora let the Council pay her homage as hereditary queen in December 1718. Karl Fredrik of Holstein-Gottorp had been outmanoeuvred.

The witch-hunts of the late seventeenth century form a tragic aspect of Swedish history. This German copper engraving from 1670 illustrates the priest E. Skragge's narrative of the trials in Mora by showing witches being burnt at the stake.

THE SEVENTEENTH CENTURY – GLORY AND POVERTY

∽ Becoming and remaining a Great Power of the Baltic was nothing that the majority of Sweden's population had ever desired. During the sixteenth century conditions in Sweden had been relatively good, as contemporary accounts by the few foreign visitors to the country corroborate. There were few failed harvests to torment the country, most of whose inhabitants were and would long remain peasant farmers. A certain level of exports of foodstuffs and mining products provided the revenues needed to pay for necessary imports such as salt. But after 1611, things changed. Many taxes were introduced (the first being to pay off the Älvsborg ransom 1613-20) that weighed heavily on all subjects. War services were and long remained a crippling burden that could in places empty whole villages of their male population, at least of the able-bodied. It was not at all uncommon for these poor peasants to succumb to some campaign disease before they even got to confront the enemy. In the latter stages of the Thirty Years War, Sweden mainly fought using mercenaries, since its own population was insufficient – as were its own revenues, despite the subsidies mentioned above.

It became more and more difficult to pay the officers. The Crown began to give its lands in fief to nobles who were serving as officers or who were to be compensated for other reasons; eventually 50 per cent of the land which had previously generated revenues to the Crown had passed into the hands of the nobility. Many mines, mills and forges were also being pawned to the big capitalists (often Dutch), whose principal representative was Louis De Geer. These men had settled in Sweden and were able to run their enterprises, sell the products, bring skilled specialists (such as the Walloon smiths) to Sweden and lend large sums of money to the Crown. The peasantry was concerned for its freedom, since it was almost unique in seventeenth century Europe in possessing both liberty and parliamentary representation. The year 1650 was a particularly restless one in Sweden, even in Stockholm, and a number of minor rebellions were brutally suppressed. The peasant Estate complained to Queen Kristina, but she rode out the storm and the reforms were put off for a few more decades.

By the 1650s the Crown's revenues were already considerably reduced as a result of the fiefdoms granted to the nobility, but it was not until after the wars of the 1670s that Karl XI began to tackle the ills this had given rise to. The problems facing the peasants were resolved in two ways, the first being the Distributive System and the second the Reduction. With the assent of Parliament, the king assumed absolute powers. The great landowning magnates lost both land and influence, and there remained a nobility of high officials and officers, many recently ennobled, who came to form the king's intimate circle. The highly orthodox Lutheran clergy also retained its influence, but then, the priests were all loyal to the king. The state coffers were in good shape once more, and between 1679 and 1700, peace reigned.

At this time it was impossible to protect yourself against such perils as bad harvests or the plague. Both of these evils afflicted the peasants first and worst. It is not as if the authorities did not care for the well-being of the population, but they found it very difficult indeed to do anything effective about it. Transportation problems meant that grain did not reach areas in the grip of famine, and there was no way of combating disease. The king and the government were able to remove themselves from an outbreak of the plague, but ordinary people had no such option. The bad harvests of - 1695-97 were therefore catastrophic in their effect. More people died of starvation than were killed in all the wars fought by Karl XII. The plague of 1710-12 was another heavy blow for Sweden, coming hard on the heels of the defeat at Poltava.

THE AGE OF FREEDOM 1719-72

A QUEEN ON A LEASH – THE FALL OF ABSOLUTISM ∾ The death of Karl XII marked the abrupt end of both absolutism and Sweden's status as a Great Power. The inevitability of this seems to have been obvious to all – the country was practically bankrupt, at war with all its neighbours, partially occupied, had lost all its possessions and was being squeezed by high taxes and inflation. To this must be added the great squandering of life in the previous 18 years of warfare, amounting to 200,000 or more perhaps in terms of those killed, wounded and taken prisoner, and the even greater numbers who died of starvation or during the plague epidemic of 1710-12.

The parliament that was summoned in January 1719 refused to recognize the homage to Ulrika Eleonora as hereditary queen which the Council had been persuaded to give immediately after the death of Karl XII. Instead she was forced to once again receive the crown from the Estates and compelled to accept the new Constitution in advance. She had already given up her "sovereignty", that is to say her absolute powers, in her summons to the parliament.

Ulrika Eleonora and her consort Friedrich of Hesse had no choice but to approve what was laid before them, as there was still a serious rival for the throne, the above-mentioned nephew of Karl XII, duke Karl Fredrik of Holstein-Gottorp. The proposal for the Constitution of 1719 was prepared by a committee in which the peasantry was not represented. The lower nobility and the commoners were able to ensure that the new Constitution was not unduly favourable to the upper nobility.

The crucial importance of the new Constitution, however, resided in the radical departure it represented from the state of affairs before 1680, a return to which had been declared as its purpose. With a number of modifications added by the parliament of 1720, the new Constitution meant that real power passed into the hands of the Council and the Estates. The

87

monarch was bound to follow the decisions of the Council in all important matters, and the Council in its turn was bound to follow the Estates, since these appointed new Councillors of the Realm – three candidates were nominated and one of them had to be appointed. The monarch had two votes in the Council. This was an unfortunate rule, as it meant that the head of state did not remain aloof from the incessant party strife that was to break out later. The Council was obliged to report to Parliament, and after 1723 its members could be removed by a decision of the Estates. Parliament had to be convened every three years, and its approval was required for such matters as declarations of war, changes in the composition of the coinage and the monarch's journeys abroad. A form of words was included in the royal oath which bound the monarch to the decisions of the Estates, thus laying the foundations of Swedish parliamentarism. The ensuing period of Swedish history, which would last until 1772, is known as the Age of Freedom.

The new form of government did not represent a social revolution. The nobility was still the most influential Estate, with the lower nobility retaining the preponderance it had obtained as a result of the Reduction. The importance of the non-privileged Estates grew slowly throughout the Age of Freedom and serious conflicts between them and the aristocracy occurred as early as 1719. Initially, the noble Councillors of the Realm, who were formally advisers, also headed the most important government agencies or had positions in the administrative colleges. They led the whole bureaucracy, with its permanent and irremovable administrative officials, quite in keeping with the traditions of the seventeenth century. In collaboration with the Estates, these magnates swept away both the bad and the good centralizing reforms of Karl XII. His government by privy council disappeared along with other newly created bodies, and the emergency coinage was recalled, redeemed and abolished.

On his own initiative, Friedrich of Hesse had had Görtz arrested immediately after the death of Karl XII. The trial of the king's hated minister was little else than a parody of justice, and in February 1719 he was beheaded.

THE PEACE TREATIES OF 1719-21 ❧ Once the Estates and the Council had regulated the national debt by way of a limited national bankruptcy in conjunction with other measures, there remained the task of ending the wars. This proved arduous. The first agreement was reached in the autumn of 1719 with England-Hanover (a personal union united these states between 1714 and 1837). Sweden made over Bremen-Verden to Hanover for a sum of 1 million *riksdaler*, and concluded a defensive alliance which proved to be of little benefit. An armistice was concluded with Saxony, but full peace had to wait until 1732. In a peace agreement reached in 1720, Brandenburg-Prussia obtained a large part of Pomerania (including Stettin) in return for 2 million *riksdaler*. Denmark, which had launched one last offensive in the summer of 1719, also made peace in 1720. Sweden abandoned its alliance with duke Karl Fredrik of Holstein-Gottorp, and paid a large sum of money to regain occupied territories in what remained of Swedish Pomerania and Wis-

mar. Sweden also renounced its duty-free status in the Sound.

The most difficult task was making peace with Russia, which had occupied all Sweden's Baltic possessions and Finland. From 1719 the Russian fleet had raided the Baltic coast of Sweden during the summer months. The most dangerous of these attacks took place in July 1719, when Stockholm itself came under threat. All the coastal towns of Uppland and Södermanland provinces were burnt as well as a large number of mills, manorial estates and farms. In the summer of 1721, when peace negotiations had reached a decisive juncture, coastal towns in Norrland were put to the torch. The peace treaty was signed in Nystad in August 1721. Sweden surrendered all its Baltic possessions (Livonia, Estonia and Ingria) as well as part of Karelia and the county of Viborg. The rest of Finland was returned, and the tsar conceded the right of duty-free grain exports from Livonia to Sweden. Russia also agreed not to interfere in Sweden's internal affairs or its royal succession – an important clause, as duke Karl Fredrik of Holstein-Gottorp had drawn close to the tsar and hoped for his support in backing his claims to be recognized as the successor to the Swedish throne. In 1725 he married the tsar's daughter, Anna, and became the progenitor of the later Russian imperial dynasty. He never became the

Ulrika Eleonora the Younger and her consort Fredrik I of Hesse, 1733. Part of a painting by G. E. Schröder.

Illustration from P. Strandberg's dissertation "On the improvement of agriculture", 1749, demonstrating how to plough and harrow, and showing proposed kinds of sowing machinery. The greatest problem facing every attempt at rationalizing agriculture was the number of narrow plots under separate ownership in each field and meadow. An ordinance in 1757 on a large-scale redistribution of landholdings made it more feasible to introduce measures of rationalization. Copper engraving by Jean Erik Rehn.

king of Sweden, however, although a party was working in Sweden on his behalf.

THE ABDICATION OF ULRIKA ELEONORA
Ulrika Eleonora was uncomfortable with her role as reigning queen. She had many good qualities, but these did not include patience or a grasp of state affairs. She accepted the new Constitution, to be sure, since she had sworn to do so, but frequently bypassed the Council out of sheer thoughtlessness, and was mostly content to follow the lead of her notoriously unfaithful husband. At the parliament of 1719 she already found herself at loggerheads with the Council of the Realm and the Lord President of the Council, Arvid Horn, Sweden's most prominent statesman at the time.

The queen found her position more and more distasteful, and wanted to have her consort elevated to the rank of monarch. The Council and the bureaucracy were soon per-suaded of the necessity of a change, since what royal power remained was in actual fact being exercised by Friedrich of Hesse by way of the queen, and it would be just as well for him to have this position officially. The queen's appointments and her elevation of a large number of people to the nobility without consulting the Council had also aroused anger. At the parliament of 1720, accordingly, Ulrika Eleonora abdicated her crown in favour of her consort – she had not been permitted to share power with him – and Friedrich of Hesse was elected king as Fredrik I. The marriage was childless, and the Palatine dynasty in Sweden expired in 1741 with the death of the queen.

RULE BY PARLIAMENT AND COUNCIL. THE AGE OF ARVID HORN
Upon his accession to the Swedish throne, Fredrik I had been compelled to accept further restrictions to the powers of the monarch and to approve a re-

vised Constitution whose main provisions were to remain in force for the rest of the Age of Freedom. The Councillors of the Realm, whose number was set at 16, were now separated from their posts as the heads of the administrative colleges. Only the Lord President of the Council and his deputy retained their positions in both the Chancellery and the Council. In modern terms, the former became the head of government and the Councillors formed a Cabinet, in which the king presided. Minor matters were decided by the king in the presence of two Councillors of the Realm. If the king's view diverged from the proposals presented by the college in question, the matter had to be discussed in council. Parliamentary business was disturbed by a renewed spate of serious disputes over the privileges of the nobility, which the non-privileged Estates wished to curtail.

From now until late 1738, the wise and prudent Lord President of the Council, Arvid Horn, would be guiding Swedish policy. The king made one serious attempt at extending his powers, with the support of the peasants, at the parliament of 1723, but it was a complete failure and he had to make a public apology and resign himself to further curtailments of his prerogatives instead. After this humiliation, Fredrik had no more influence on policy and played the part of a constitutional monarch until his death in 1751. The sloth for which he was criticized was in fact more of an asset for the Council, which had no cause to feel uneasy about royal diligence or curiosity disturbing them in their work of government. Fredrik's private life and base morals gave rise to much repugnance, however, not least among the clergy.

At the meeting of the Estates in 1723, a set of parliamentary procedures were ratified which were based on earlier praxis and decisions. This code of procedure was subsequently regarded as one of the basic constitutional laws of the Age of Freedom, and contained stipulations concerning the forms parliamentary activities should take. The Secret Commission of Parliament was given wide-ranging powers, but the peasantry was not represented on it. The Commission dealt mainly with matters of foreign policy, defence and financial policy. The Secret Deputation, in which all the Estates were represented, scrutinized the minutes of Council meetings. The Great Secret Deputation was appointed for matters of extraordinary importance and included 25 peasants. Additional deputations were subsequently created and corresponded to what are today called parliamentary committees. It should perhaps be mentioned that between them three of the four Estates – the nobility, the clergy and the burghers – represented 4-5 per cent of the nation's (male) population. But it was still almost unique in Europe that the peasantry had any say in national policy at all.

Arvid Horn devoted his best energies to preserving the peace and allowing the country to recuperate. In this he undoubtedly enjoyed the support of the whole people. In foreign policy, Horn primarily sought assistance from England, and in 1727 Sweden joined the so-called Hanoverian alliance between England and France. When this broke down in the 1730s, Horn began having problems.

The exhausted country and its exhausted people – Finland in particular had been very hard hit – recovered with surprising rapidity. In 1730 it was at last possible to abolish the supplementary contributional tax, which had been levied to pay off the national debt. Agriculture made progress and the number of peasants owning their own land increased thanks to what were known as tax purchases, that is to say, those who lived on Crown property bought what is known as birthright, which meant that they and their children obtained the real right of ownership, although they continued to pay interest to the state. Throughout the eighteenth century population growth was strong, however, which meant that the number of propertyless people on the land grew even faster than did the free peasantry or the urban proletariat. This led to the emergence of the *statare* towards the end of the Age of Freedom – these were married agricultural labourers who were employed on short-term contracts and paid mainly in kind. This was a notorious and humiliating form of employment which was to survive until after the Second World War. Wages fell as the supply of labour power rose.

The East Indian service with a Linnea floral pattern ordered by Carl von Linné from Canton.

COMMERCE AND INDUSTRY ∾ The commercial policies pursued by Horn and his successors have been characterized as cautious mercantilism. This term refers to the economic system that had been in force in Europe since the sixteenth century and which entailed an attempt to create economically unified states, to ease the system of internal customs duties and tolls and to favour domestic industry so that production would rise and as little as possible would need to be imported. Protective tariffs and import prohibitions – in themselves no novelty – were imposed. The Produce Proclamation of 1724 forbade foreign vessels to carry other goods to Sweden than those manufactured in their home country or its colonies. All other freight to Sweden was to be carried in Swedish vessels. Hopefully, the surplus in the balance of trade would lead to the introduction of hard coinage in the form of gold and silver. Everyone had a superstitious belief in the power of noble metals. A typical case is that of the Ädelfors gold mine in the province of Småland, which was discovered in 1738 and worked until the end of the century. A study has shown that the value of the total amount of gold produced (1 kg a year!) was far lower than the costs of production incurred.

In 1731, the East India Company was founded. After some difficulties in the early years, it carried on a profitable trade with China in particular, and noted an initial average profit of over 40 per cent per voyage, rising considerably as the century progressed. The Company was a very significant factor in the flourishing growth of Gothenburg, and there was a not inconsider-

able trade in the re-export of luxuries such as the tea, silk, porcelain and spices that were sold by auction when a ship reached Sweden.

A typical feature of the Age of Freedom is the flourishing growth of the manufacture system, principally in the textile industry. Initially the machinery used was of the simplest kind. The great enthusiast and promoter of manufacture in Sweden was Jonas Alströmer, who had studied the industrialization that was beginning its triumphal march in England and believed that Sweden would be able to increase its prosperity in the same way. In 1724 he was granted the privilege of starting a manufacturing mill in his home town of Alingsås, and many prominent people put money into his "society". Sweden's first shares were printed. It should be pointed out that Alströmer's enterprises, which covered such activities as tobacco cultivation and sugar refining, were far from solid, and that the foundations for establishing manufacturing mills

had been laid earlier. His importance, however, lay in his enthusiasm and his desire to use domestic raw materials. Today Alströmer is principally remembered as the man who introduced the potato to Sweden, but this characteristically Swedish tuber, which was to play such an important part in feeding the nation, was in fact little appreciated until long after his death.

Among the most important domestic events of the first period of the Age of Freedom was the enactment of the new Code of Law by the Estates in 1734. It is still in force, although of course there have been innumerable amendments and additions made to it. Many of the penalties stipulated in it strike us as extremely severe, but by international comparison, Swedish punishments were not particularly harsh. Everything is relative, but it should be noted that torture, for instance, has never been used as widely in Sweden as in the rest of Europe.

Trading emporia in Canton, where commercial transactions with the Chinese were settled in cash. The East India Company made big profits during the Age of Freedom. The Company primarily exported metal and timber goods which were sold in Cadiz for the silver so coveted by the Chinese.

The policies of the Hats favoured trade and business. The first laudatory medals were struck in this period to encourage enterprises of the most varied kinds, such as the peasant-farmer ploughing up virgin land or "the woman who spins with such skill and diligence" –

THE FALL OF ARVID HORN AND THE HATS IN POWER 1738–65 ∾ Initially, opposition to Horn was limited to the nobility and primarily concerned foreign policy. But the gradual alienation of England and France from each other during the 1730s gave fresh fuel to suspicions regarding the alliance policies of the Lord President of the Council. His desire for peace was attacked as weakness and he was charged – with a certain degree of justice – with neglecting the defence of the country. Among Horn's opponents were Councillor of the Realm Carl Gyllenborg, the culturally eminent Carl Gustaf Tessin, Anders Johan von Höpken and others. Horn was already having problems at the parliament of 1734, and two political parties may now be considered to have come into existence in Sweden. Horn's supporters were called the Caps ("nightcaps" in the view of some – echoing the disparaging words of Fredrik I to the Council of the Realm: "You are all nightcaps!"), and his opponents were known as the Hats.

The storm erupted at the parliament of 1738-39. The Hats turned on Horn, who was accused of representing a senile upper nobility and of neglecting the country's need for new laws better able to promote trade and industry. Above all the Hats were working for an alliance with France and were dreaming of a war with the arch-enemy Russia which would regain Sweden's forfeited possessions. The opposition controlled the nobility and the burghers and the Secret Commission. The new alliance with France was pushed through in October and its terms were mainly drafted by Tessin. Horn accepted the consequences of his political defeat and resigned in December 1738. His supporters among the Councillors were removed by a process called "licensing", which meant that they retained their title of Councillor of the Realm but lost the confidence of the Estates and were no longer entitled to exercise their office. It was a kind of retirement. The alliance between the lower nobility and the burghers had led to the victory of parliamentarism.

In many respects it was Parliament that reigned. During the Age of Freedom, the Council of the Realm was in some ways more subject to parliamentary constraint in its actions than are the governments of today.

THE WAR WITH RUSSIA 1741-43 ∞ Carl Gyllenborg succeeded Horn as Lord President of the Council, and set about his new tasks by changing course and steering the country towards a war with Russia. Broadsheets had already been used in pre-parliamentary agitation, and when major Malcolm Sinclair, at once a spy and a courier, was murdered by specially dispatched Russian agents while returning to Sweden from Turkey in 1739, a huge wave of indignation blew up. Feelings were deliberately inflamed and everyone was singing the Sinclair Ballad, which tells how the dead officer meets Karl XII and hears him urge vengeance on the arch-enemy. Parliament gave its fullest backing to the war policy. Sweden appeared to have a useful ally in the Russian princess Elizabeth, who herself wished to assume the crown after the death of empress Anna in 1740, but was obliged instead to see the one-year-old Ivan proclaimed tsar. The government offered her its help, and the declaration of war was approved by the Council with the king's casting vote. In July 1741, the war had got under way.

The Swedish fleet was superior to the Russians, but the army was poorly prepared and incompetently led. When general Charles Emil Lewenhaupt finally launched an offensive against Viborg and Karelia in the late autumn, it was already too late. A few days later Elizabeth carried out a *coup d'état*, deposed the tsar and his weak regency government and had herself proclaimed empress. Lewenhaupt allowed himself to be persuaded to agree to a truce and the opportunity of obliging Russia to cede territories had evaporated. Elizabeth could not recall having made any binding promises, and in any case she was now firmly in power and no longer needed any Swedish help. During the winter the Swedish army was decimated by disease and the officers busied themselves with political discussions, in which some of them agitated for making Prince Karl Peter Ulrik of Holstein-Gottorp, who was to become Peter III, the successor to the Swedish throne. When the Russian army violated the truce, the result was close to panic. The

or building a house of stone in the countryside, or growing mulberry trees so Sweden could breed its own silkworms and would no longer need to pay for expensive imports. Silver medals from the Royal Coin Cabinet.

The Forsmark works in Uppland. Swedish mill towns were whole societies in miniature; in this picture we see the manor house and the church at their respective ends of the typical mill town main street.

poorly conducted war led to one minor defeat after the other, and finally to capitulation in Helsinki in August 1742. Soon the Russians had occupied the whole of Finland as far as the border with the province of Västerbotten, just as they had done during the Great Northern War.

THE PEACE OF ÅBO. THE REBELLION IN DALARNA AND THE ELECTION OF THE SUCCESSOR TO THE THRONE ❧ At the parliament of 1742-43, discontent with the Hats

was rife, particularly among the peasantry, who mistrusted the aristocrats in the ruling bureaucracy and the Council even more than they did the monarchy. The Hats were able to stay in power thanks to some deft manoeuvring, including the timely manipulation of the question of the succession to the throne. At first the Estates elected Karl Peter Ulrik of Holstein-Gottorp and sent a delegation to Elizabeth to inform her of this step and at the same time to obtain peace on the same terms as in the Peace of Nystad of 1721. The ambassadors discovered on their arrival that the young prince had been appointed successor to the Russian throne and had converted to the Russian-Orthodox faith. The empress demanded the whole of Finland and war reparations and also required Sweden to elect Adolf Fredrik of Holstein-Gottorp, the prince-bishop of Lübeck and the uncle of the new successor to the Russian throne, in place of Karl Peter Ulrik.

After a couple of other candidates to the throne had been proposed and the peasant Estate had even elected the Danish crown prince – there was no chauvinistic hatred of the Danes to be found among the ordinary people of Sweden – the matter was postponed to await the outcome of the peace negotiations in Åbo (Turku), which were now definitely coupled with the question of who was to succeed Fredrik I. While these were in progress, the last great peasant revolt in Sweden broke out in 1743. It is known as the Great Dance of Dalarna, and a great number of peasants from towns and villages in this province marched towards Stockholm. They got as far as what is now Gustav Adolf's square in the centre of Stockholm and panic broke out in the capital. The peasants demanded the recognition of the Danish crown prince and refused to believe reports that peace had been concluded in Åbo. Finally the troops were sent in and the peasants were easily defeated, leaving hundreds dead or wounded. Six of the peasants were later sentenced to death, while others were sent to prison.

Peace with Russia meant that the greater part of Finland was returned to Sweden. Russia kept certain eastern areas. The arrangement had already been approved by Parliament in the midst of the peasant rebellion, and the day after the rebellion was crushed, Adolf Fredrik was elected as successor to the throne. Sweden was now subject to powerful Russian influence, and Russia even had 12,000 troops stationed in the country for a period – at the government's own request!

The Hats had managed to retain power, but they desperately needed scapegoats for the military debacle. Accordingly, the two highest commanders in Finland, generals Lewenhaupt and Buddenbrock, were sentenced to death and executed, as a repugnant sacrificial sop to the discontented nation. Parliament dissolved in September 1743, and a few weeks later Adolf

A tiled stove in a manor house setting. The tiled stove had been used for heating since mediaeval times. In eighteenth century Sweden its design was improved and it became more efficient, and Swedish dwellings were reputed to be the best heated in the whole of Europe.

Adolf Fredrik helping an infirm old man at the side of the road. Painting by Pehr Hilleström (1732–1816). Adolf Fredrik is here presented as a model enlightened monarch caring for his subjects.

Fredrik came to the capital. He was immediately given a place in the Council and the right to use the king's double vote during his absence. The amiable and placid hereditary prince seemed the right person to occupy the largely representative post of monarch. Initially he adopted a docile attitude towards Russia and empress Elizabeth, since he had them to thank for his exaltation to the monarchy. In the summer of 1744 he married Princess Lovisa Ulrika of Prussia, the sister of Frederick the Great.

The years immediately following the peace were ones of humiliation for the government, but it was able to ward off a war with Denmark in the spring of 1744, and in the summer of that year the last Russian troops finally left Sweden.

The country was treated more or less as a Russian vassal state, and in June 1745 it was compelled to conclude a defence alliance with its powerful neighbour. The Hats had sufficient audacity to draw closer to France, however, whose relations with Russia had deteriorated during 1744. Despite the reverses France had suffered in the War of the Austrian Succession Louis XV was still able to pay subsidies to Sweden. The Swedish crown prince, under the influence of his gifted and power-hungry consort, had begun to manifest a greater degree of independence, and the most prominent of the Hats, Carl Gustaf Tessin, who became Lord President of the Council in 1747, was a very influential personality at his court. Adolf Fredrik broke with the Russian court, which led the Russians to seek a new ally, which it found in Denmark. Russia and Denmark then agreed to jointly ensure that the Swedish Constitution was preserved. At the parliament of 1746-47, following the custom of the time, very generous bribes were distributed to the Caps, mainly through the Russian ambassador. The Hats, for their part, drew closer to France and exploited the indignation aroused by Russian complaints about the successor to the throne. The Hats still controlled Parliament, and in 1747 they concluded an alliance with France and Prussia. For a time, Sweden was faced with a serious Russian threat, as both Russia and Denmark were planning to attack her. Thanks to pressure applied by Sweden's allies and England, however, and to an energetic Swedish programme of rearmament, an agreement was reached with Denmark in 1749, and the threatening rumblings from Russia ceased. A treaty was concluded in 1751, arranging a future marriage between the crown prince's eldest son Gustav (III) and the Danish princess Sofia Magdalena, and the regulation of Sweden's borders with Norway helped to further reduce old tensions and possible causes of conflict.

A NORTH GERMAN DYNASTY ❧ Adolf Fredrik, who succeeded Fredrik I in 1751, had family ties with both Sweden and a number of other royal houses. One of his sisters was the mother of Peter III's consort, soon to become Catharine the Great, who was thus a cousin of Adolf Fredrik's children. The ducal dynasty of Holstein-Gottorp formed a branch of the Danish house of Oldenburg. The blood ties with the

house of Oldenburg in Denmark were soon forgotten, however, and deep hostility reigned between the dukes of Gottorp and their more powerful Danish neighbour. Adolf Fredrik had also been the guardian of his young relative Karl Peter Ulrik, whose aunt Elizabeth, as we have seen, assumed power in Russia and had herself proclaimed empress. In this way the young prince became the successor to the Russian throne.

It was natural for the Russian empress to wish to favour her relative, and in this way he became her candidate for the Swedish throne in 1743. Since Sweden had been defeated, she got her way. Adolf Fredrik was not very gifted, and with his weak interest in politics and his simple pleasures (he enjoyed shaping wood on a lathe, for instance), in combination with a dignified presence, he was cut out to be the ideal head of state in a parliamentary monarchy. As mentioned above, he fell very much under the influence of his consort, Lovisa Ulrika of Prussia, however, and later under that of his eldest son, Crown Prince Gustav. Relations between the parties in power and the monarchy were to deteriorate considerably during his twenty-year reign. Gradually, the friendly relations between the successors to the throne and the Hats cooled off. The Hats had no intention at all of resigning any of their political power. At the parliament of 1751-52, a new grouping, known as the court party, worked to promote the interests of the royal couple, but it remained without influence. It was the view of both Carl Gustaf Tessin and Parliament that the task of the king was merely to execute the decisions of the Estates and to represent the nation.

Carl von Linné, the great Swedish botanist (1707-78). Portrait after an oil painting by Alexander Roslin, executed when Linné had been ennobled and received the Order of the Northern Star.

Title page and illustration from Linné's 1751 account of his travels in Skåne.

Parliament had to tackle the country's poor financial situation and the continued deficits, which had increased the national debt from the already considerable dimensions it had attained as a result of the war with Russia 1741-43. Carl Gustaf Tessin, who had long been a welcome visitor at court and shared the queen's cultural interests, now fell out of grace and found his position so uncomfortable that he resigned as Lord President of the Council. He was replaced by Anders Johan von Höpken. Tessin remained as tutor of the crown prince until 1754, when he had a row with the royal couple whose upshot was that he resigned from all his posts.

The disputes between the king and the Council, especially in connection with appointments, became more and more serious, and the royal couple did their best to humiliate the leading Hats. The dissensions became known to the public by way of publications like the journal *En ärlig svensk* (An honest Swede),

published by one of the Hats.

From this period there is clear evidence for the influence of the press on politics. New and talented Hats emerged alongside von Höpken, particularly Axel von Fersen the Elder, who became President of the House of Nobility, and the scheming Carl Fredrik Pechlin. The king suffered a number of defeats in Parliament, on issues such as his right of appointment. Against the will of the monarch and his consort, the Estates appointed Carl Fredrik Scheffer as tutor to the crown prince, and chose new teachers for him. Their instructions were to instil in Gustav an understanding that power originated with the people. These newcomers were initially disliked by the court, a circumstance which did not fail to make an impression on the crown prince. He learned the art of dissimulation by listening to the diametrically opposed views propounded by his parents on the one hand and his teachers on the other, and by concealing his own views.

The inventor Christopher Polhammar (1661-1751), dubbed Polhem when ennobled, came from very simple origins and had an illustrious career. This contemporary portrait is reproduced from a modern Swedish banknote in which his lock Slussen in Stockholm, joining Lake Mälaren and the Baltic inlet of Saltsjön, is also depicted.

A FAILED COUP. THE SEVEN YEARS WAR

∾ The Estates further decided to make a name stamp, to be used if the king refused to sign a parliamentary decision into law. This reduced the significance of the monarch to practically nothing. The royal couple became desperate, and the queen pawned her jewels in order to be able to fund a revolution, but this merely led to her further humiliation when one of the Estates demanded an inventory. At the last moment she was able to have returned to her from Berlin certain jewels that the parliamentary commission considered to be public property and wished to see, but which she had regarded as her own private property. At the same time the court party's attempted revolution was to have taken place, but it was betrayed and heaped more humiliation on the head of the royal couple. They were now compelled to sit through the reading of a document prepared by the Estates which was full of recriminations. Eight of the conspirators were executed, among them Marshal of the Court Horn and count Erik Brahe, the most prominent noble of the country.

Relations between the Council and the now completely powerless royal couple long remained poor and the nation's financial situation deteriorated. The Ordinance concerning superfluous goods ("luxuries") of 1756 and other measures were ineffective and the expenses of the state rose, principally because the Hats decided for the second time to involve Sweden in a war (1757). On this occasion they had hopes of winning some easy victories over Prussia, which under its king Frederick was facing a crushing array of enemies including France, Russia and Austria, in what was to become known as the Seven Years War. For Sweden's part, the war was conducted from Swedish Pomerania, and it revealed once more that Sweden was no longer a military power. There were no victories and the generalship was abysmal. All the resources available in Sweden were used up. In 1762, a separate peace had to be concluded with no territorial gains having been made. It was humiliating for the Council to have to ask the queen to mediate the first approach to the Prussian king, her brother. The conclusion of peace was so much the more necessary because empress Elizabeth of Russia had died and the new tsar, Peter III, who was a fanatical admirer of Frederick, had at once ended the war and entered into an alliance with his former adversary. Later the same year, however, he was deposed by his German-born consort, Catharine, and murdered. During her long reign, which would last until 1796, the new empress was to cause much distress to Sweden.

As we have seen, the finances of the nation had deteriorated continuously under the Hats. Neither increased taxation nor more borrowing helped in the face of the wantonly spendthrift habits of the government. Money was poured into subsidies for trade and manufacturing, party kickbacks, pensions and other such payoffs, and to this was added the Pomeranian war, whose debt of 11 million silver *riksdaler* had for the most part been run up illegally, without due decision-making process. After the peace of 1762, Sweden had the same national debt as it had at the end of Karl XII's wars. The value of banknotes fell throughout the period, and by 1745 they had ceased to be redeemable against copper coin or silver, and Sweden was on a paper standard.

THE BANKRUPTCY OF COMMERCIAL POLICY ❧ Parliament was summoned in 1760 and continued until 1761. Once again, the Hats managed to cling to power, but they found it increasingly difficult. The Caps were now rejuvenated and stronger. Negotiations became more and more difficult for the government and a number of Councillors decided it was expedient to resign, including the Lord President of the Council.

As a gesture of reconciliation some Caps were elected to the Council, but they still found themselves in a minority. A number of legislative constraints on trade and industry were eased, with certain import prohibitions being lifted. The distillation of spirits for household use, which had been prohibited, was once again permitted. Some factory subsidies were reduced. In general, however, the policies which were ruining the finances of the nation were continued regardless.

THE CAPS TAKE POWER ❧ The following years were catastrophic for the Swedish economy. The actual rate of exchange for banknotes was only one third of the nominal value, and all coins disappeared from circulation. A great and generalized European commercial crisis, which erupted in 1763-64 after the end of the Seven Years War, meant that it was no longer possible to obtain credit, and bills of exchange were called in. One commercial and business enterprise after another went bankrupt and the government had no means of bailing them out. Factories closed down and skilled workers moved abroad. On top of all this, the country was afflicted by a severe epidemic of cattle plague and had to purchase expensive imports of grain. The whole optimistic edifice of Swedish commercial and industrial policy collapsed.

In January 1765, the Estates met for a parliament which was to last for more than a year. The Caps now had a majority in the non-privileged Estates, but not in the House of Nobility, where the alliance with the court party had ended. From this parliament on, it is possible to note that the "younger Caps" had begun to represent primarily the interests of the burghers and the peasants, while the Hats had their main body of support among the nobility. The tensions between the nobility and the commoners were increased by an imprudent decision of the House of Nobility during the preceding parliament not to introduce newly ennobled families until further notice. This gave the House of Nobility the character of a closed Estate during the latter years of the Age of Freedom. This caused problems because it had long been praxis for commoners who had ascended the social ladder (for instance, the sons of bishops, high officials and officers) to be more or less automatically ennobled, which had maintained a degree of social circulation.

During this parliament, Russia and Denmark renewed their treaty, in one section of which they had pledged themselves to ensure that the

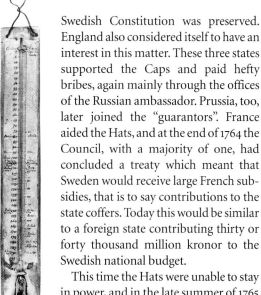

Swedish Constitution was preserved. England also considered itself to have an interest in this matter. These three states supported the Caps and paid hefty bribes, again mainly through the offices of the Russian ambassador. Prussia, too, later joined the "guarantors". France aided the Hats, and at the end of 1764 the Council, with a majority of one, had concluded a treaty which meant that Sweden would receive large French subsidies, that is to say contributions to the state coffers. Today this would be similar to a foreign state contributing thirty or forty thousand million kronor to the Swedish national budget.

This time the Hats were unable to stay in power, and in the late summer of 1765 all the leading Councillors of the Realm resigned or were removed from office. Responsibility was exacted for the abuses that had occurred. Besides a great ransacking in relation to the mismanagement of the offices of exchange and other government agencies, Parliament passed a number of laws reducing the elements of compulsion in relation to industry and trade. Some towns in Norrland and Finland were granted the right to sail to foreign countries with their products rather than being forced as they had been previously to sell them in domestic markets or carry them to Stockholm. The most important of the proposals to be adopted, however, was the Ordinance on the Freedom of the Press 1766. This law removed all censorship for all publications except those relating to theology. It was now permitted to write on any subject, with the sole proviso that

The Age of Freedom was a great period for Swedish scientific research. Anders Celsius (1701-44), a professor of astronomy, was one of the many researchers and inventors who won worldwide renown and earned Sweden a splendid reputation. He invented the hundred degree thermometer shown here. Initially, however, the boiling point was set at 0 and the freezing point at 100 degrees.

A view of Stockholm by J. Sevenbom, 1768.

neither the evangelical doctrine nor the constitutional laws were to be opposed, nor was it permitted to slander the royal family or private persons. Public documents that had not been declared secret could be published freely. Procedures in trials concerning the freedom of the press were closely regulated. The Ordinance was to be considered to be "an unshakeable constitutional law".

The government and fall of the caps ∾

The Caps now broke with France and drew closer to Russia, Denmark and England, which had funded them in the parliamentary elections and during the meetings of the Estates. The Hats, under pressure, began to collaborate to a certain extent with the royal couple, who had won nothing from the shift in power. From now on, some of the leaders of the Hats, including count Axel von Fersen the Elder, gradually changed their views on the Constitution and were able to countenance a certain increase in the power of the monarch.

It soon transpired that the Caps and their policies of thrift were no better than the Hats and their spendthrift ways had been. Trade stagnated, money was short and there was great unemployment. Relations between the Council and the government agencies were bad, since most officials were Hats, and the tension even led to the arraignment of the Board for Public Lands and Funds for lese-majesty. The situation was skilfully exploited by the royal family, where Crown Prince Gustav had now to a great extent assumed his mother's role as the driving force behind the weak king. The court also consulted with the Hats and with the French ambassador. The objective of the manoeuvring was to compel the Council to summon the Estates, something the Council wished to avoid at all costs. In December 1768, the king attended the Council, accompanied by Crown Prince Gustav, and lodged a protest at the arraignment of the Board for Public Lands and Funds. The Council refused to change its views. At this, the officials at all the offices in the Council chambers were called in and the crown prince read a statement in which the king demanded that the Estates be summoned, or else he would boycott his duties. The Council refused the king's demand and Adolf Fredrik carried out his threat.

The Council's attempt to rule with the help of the name stamp failed, as the administrative colleges refused to perform their duties. Faced with this revolt of the officials, Parliament had to be summoned.

The extraordinary session of the Estates commenced business in Norrköping in April 1769. The Hats and the court party who had prepared a proposal for a new Constitution obtained a majority in all the Estates and in the committees. However, it was not possible to achieve a solution to the constitutional question, as a faction of the Hats were opposed to any extension of royal power. Carl Fredrik Pechlin undertook secret negotiations with the Russian minister Osterman and received money from him. Once the parliament moved to Stockholm in the summer, he announced publicly that he had joined the Caps and took a number of supporters with him.

THE FINAL GOVERNMENT OF THE HATS. THE DEATH OF THE KING ∽ Parliament was not dissolved until January 1770, but it had not been able to achieve a great deal. The same may be said of the short-lived Hat government, which once again increased the national debt. It did some work with respect to issues of defence policy, and the connection with France was renewed. But the great number of anti-aristocratic pamphlets published by the Caps and their supporters boded ill for the future work of Parliament.

Adolf Fredrik was not to live to see the end of these party disputes, however. In early 1771, Crown Prince Gustav left on an educational trip to France. He also had the intention of negotiating French support for a change of regime. On 1 March, when he was at the Paris Opera, he was reached by the news that Adolf Fredrik had suddenly died.

THE AGE OF FREEDOM – A SUMMARY ∾
The favourable developments in culture and science during the Age of Freedom are indisputable. This partly coincides with what is known as the Age of Enlightenment in Europe, which had its origins in England and above all in France and sought to elaborate a view of the world which would eradicate superstition, prejudice and social injustice. The Enlightenment gradually assumed an overtly political character and turned against existing society, and much of its philosophy underpinned the ideologies embraced by those who led the revolution of 1789 in France. The roots of liberalism, which was to become the ideology of the new middle class in the following century, can also be found in the Enlightenment. But it also provided the foundations for enlightened despotism as practised by such monarchs as Frederick II of Prussia, Catharine the Great of Russia and Gustav III of Sweden. A middle class was created, and all the news of Europe quickly reached the leaders of Swedish society. New books by Rousseau or Voltaire very soon found their way to Stockholm. But the majority of the people were left untouched, and studies show that what we call the lower middle class and even more so the peasantry absorbed little of this "enlightenment".

THE GUSTAVIAN AGE 1772-1809

THE END OF THE AGE OF FREE-DOM AND THE OVERTURN OF THE CONSTITUTION ∿ Once he was king, Gustav was able to pursue his negotiations with a completely different authority. Louis XV and his ministers immediately author-ized the payment of old subsidies and promised new ones from 1772. The old king also urged his young colleague not to be over-hasty, but to work cautiously for a reconcilia-tion between the parties and in this way strengthen his own position.

The new parliament met in June 1771, and its first act was to listen to Gustav III eloquently ad-monishing it to reconciliation. For the first time in over a hundred years a native-born Swedish king was speaking to Parliament – and one with a good command of the language to boot. The speech was a success, and was subsequently published. However, the king was unable to dampen party passions, which now even more took on social contours, with the younger Caps in the three non-privileged Estates launching powerful attacks on the nobility and its privileges. The Hats had to withdraw, and the Caps were once more in government. When, as a result, the Council had recom-posed, many of the Hat leaders left the parliament, which was now completely dominated by their op-ponents.

With the help of royalists among the military and senior state offi-cials, Gustav began to prepare a *coup d'état*. He obtained the money he needed from the French. Russia was conveniently occupied with a war on Turkey. Risings were to be launched by the troops in Kristianstad, Skåne, and in Borgå, Fin-land. Both risings were successful. However, the Governor of Stockholm, who happened to be passing Kristianstad on the day of the coup and learned of the rising in progress, went straight to Stockholm and delivered an emergency report to the Council of the Realm and the Secret Com-mission. The king now had to act quickly to avoid being imprisoned and deposed. On the

Part of Carl Gustaf Pilo's unfinished painting of the coronation of Gustav III in 1772. To the right the Danish-born queen, Sofia Magdalena.

morning of 19 August, the king made a speech to the officers of the guard at the royal palace, declared his desire to put an end to the "mob rule of the aristocrats" and restore the old Swedish freedoms of the days before 1680.

All the officers with the exception of one single captain enthusiastically sided with the king and swore an oath that they would risk their lives and their blood for the salvation of Sweden. Next it was the turn of the palace guards to join the royal cause, which they did in a state of euphoria, according to eye-witnesses. The Council was arrested and the king rode out into the city to be greeted by jubilant crowds. On the following day, the public authorities joined the king. The overturn had been accomplished, and no blood had been shed.

On 21 August, the Estates had to listen to a royal dressing-down, full of recriminations for their party dissension and for allegedly visiting lawlessness and confusion upon the nation. This was followed by the king's proposal for a new Constitution, which was approved unanimously.

THE CONSTITUTION OF 1772 ❧ The new Constitution did not grant the king unfettered powers, but was consciously designed to embody the principle of the distribution of powers. The king appointed the members of the Council – seventeen in number – and they were responsible to him alone. Only in certain cases was he compelled to consult the Councillors of the Realm – when it was a matter of concluding a peace, a truce or an alliance, of undertaking trips abroad, or of dealing with senior appointments, dismissals and questions of law. If the Council was unanimous in the matter of a peace or an alliance, the monarch had to follow its declared opinion. The Estates and the king were jointly responsible for making laws, and they had a reciprocal right of veto. The right to authorize taxation remained with Parliament, whose consent was required in wars of aggression, modifications of privilege and declarations of war.

The Council's parliamentary responsibility before the Estates had now ceased, inadequate control was exercised over the administration, and since all regulations enacted after 1680 had been rescinded, working procedures became unclear – it was, for instance, no longer officially stipulated how often Parliament should be summoned. And many provisions of the Constitution had probably been left vague by the king and his secret advisers as a matter of policy.

OPINIONS OF THE AGE OF FREEDOM ❧ The Age of Freedom had a bad reputation among Swedish historians during the whole of the nineteenth century. It was regarded as a period of internal and external weakness, economic decay and dependency on foreign powers, who bribed Swedish politicians. In this view, Sweden ran the risk of sharing Poland's fate, and it was only thanks to the intervention of Gustav III that Sweden avoided being partitioned by its neighbours. But for over six decades now, there has been another and different view of this epoch. It is seen as an age of promising developments under governments appointed by Parliament, that was destroyed by a power-hungry and reckless king, who in addition suffocated the newly established freedom of the press and finally dragged the country into an unnecessary war with Russia, which he himself had started, thereby violating the Constitution. Whichever interpretation the observer chooses, however, it is imperative to avoid seeing the eighteenth century with the eyes of our own age, and to refrain from choosing sides according to a modern set of political convictions. Parliament was definitely not based on the democratic principles we observe today – the three "higher" Estates comprised a mere 4-5 per cent of the population, and the peasantry the rest, but few of the broad masses had the right to elect members of Parliament – at first only Crown peasants and peasants with enough property to be on the tax-rolls, then eventually mine-owners. And these electors had a varying number of votes depending on the size of their property. Peasants owing obedience to the nobility and those with no prop-

There were many beggars in Sweden in olden times, even if those in charge of parish poor relief tried to reduce their number by organizing forced labour or driving them into neighbouring parishes. Drawing by Elias Martin (1739-1818) from Stockholm: "The decrepit old woman offers her spectacles for sale to obtain bread".

erty had no vote. The number of peasants with the franchise did not increase until the nineteenth century. In 1750, the population of Sweden was somewhat less than 1.8 million, not including Finland, and most of them made their living from the land – but there were only some 190,000 peasants who owned their own land. The agricultural population increased mainly through the growing numbers of crofters, cottars and landless labourers.

In spite of everything, the Swedish parliament had long been forced to listen to the peasants, who in most other parts of Europe had no influence whatsoever. They were also more loyal to the monarchy than the other Estates, and it was eventually an alliance between the monarch and the commoners that would break down the old society and its feudal privileges.

The systematic use of bribery has also been castigated, but it was perhaps even more widespread in the famous English Parliament, although the providers of the money there were not foreign ambassadors. But the bribes seem rarely to have made a decisive difference in relation to the most important decisions.

We may at least note that it is an open question whether or not the Constitution of the Age of Freedom threatened Sweden's national independence. The treaty of 1773 between Russia and Denmark still contained a secret agreement, to be sure, that they would restore the Constitution of 1720 in Sweden at some appropriate juncture, and these states, governed as they were by absolute monarchs, had no sympathy whatever for parliamentary developments in Sweden, but the fact remains that they never intervened for this purpose. It is a different matter altogether that the situation in 1772 indubitably included disarray in the administration, state finances on the verge of bankruptcy and the whole country suffering from the effects of a bad harvest, which the government neglected. The first two problems were resolved by a number of excellent reforms during the 1770s, whereas bad harvests were to recur throughout Gustav III's reign. The king was an enthusiastic and energetic reformer, but he also bore the responsibility for the new financial problems that arose during the 1780s.

THE PERSONALITY AND FAMILY LIFE OF GUSTAV III ∾ The following period of Swedish history bears the stamp of Gustav III to such an extent that we need to consider his person at this point. His complex personality both fascinated and repelled his contemporaries – and still has the same effect today. Assessments of him are continually changing, and he still inspires polemically animated exchanges. He generates an interest that no other Swedish king is able to rival, with the possible exception of Gustav Vasa.

Gustav received a thorough and, for its time, modern education (it included very little Latin, for instance). He had a perfect command of French, and was very well read in contemporary literature and philosophy as well as in history, mathematics and constitutional law. His childhood and youth were full of tension, as he was exposed both to the influences of his cul-turally interested but domineering mother and those of his teachers, who had been appointed by the detested Estates since 1756. The intellectual-aesthetic atmosphere in which he grew up gave him his lasting interests: literature and art, history and the theatre. The theatrical enthusiasm for which his contemporaries so often criticized him should not be allowed to hide the fact that he had a burning interest in politics that was fuelled by both a romantic desire for glory and a greed for power. His need to be permanently occupied was practically an obsession, and thanks to his great capacity for work he was able to accomplish more (for good or ill) than most other Swedish monarchs. Gustav was a very contradictory individual. Although

The poet and troubadour Carl Michael Bellman (1740-95), singing and playing his zither. Bellman, a dominant figure in the tradition of Swedish minstrelsy, has been translated into a number of other languages and new interpretations and translations are still being produced. A contemporary watercolour by Pehr Hilleström.

A more tolerant social climate arose during the Age of Freedom. Gustav III was a child of his time and persuaded Parliament to mitigate the harshly repressive religious laws. After 1781 those confessing foreign faiths were allowed to settle in Sweden. On the other hand it was still impossible for Swedes to convert to an alien faith – on pain of exile! In this picture Pehr Hörberg (1746-1816) depicts two Jewish rabbis from Poland visiting Finspång in Östergötland.

Judiska Präster ifrån Pålen som för almos besökte Finspång den 25 Juli 1793 och ... å blefwo aftecknade

he often dressed in a slovenly manner and was poorly groomed, he liked to be surrounded by splendour and elegance. Although he was full of the ideas of the new epoch, he introduced an antiquated system of court etiquette using the France of Louis XIV as his model, and he devoted much of his time to questions of precedence and the various orders he had in his gift. He was seduced by the resounding names of the old noble families and fond of surrounding himself with courtiers from the upper nobility, but in the end it was he himself who put an end to most of the privileges of the nobility, in collaboration with the commoners of the non-privileged Estates. Although he was domineering and vain, he was magnanimous towards his enemies and showed a surprising degree of tolerance towards those who dared to contradict or upbraid him.

In 1766, Gustav married Sofia Magdalena of Denmark for political reasons. The marriage was unhappy, as the partners were far too different. The marriage produced two sons, one of whom died young. The intimate intercourse that led to the offspring had to be managed in detail by the king's master of the horse, A.F. Munck, which led to rumour claiming him as the father of the king's son, Gustav Adolf, who was born in 1778. It is probably not possible to gain complete proof one way or the other in this matter, but Munck's written report, which is brutally frank, indicates what seems to be an astonishing degree of sexual inexperience on the part of the royal couple.

The rumours surrounding the birth of the king's first son led to a complete rupture between Gustav and his mother, Lovisa Ulrika. Not until 1782, when his mother was on her deathbed, did a formal reconciliation take place. In other words, Gustav's family life was far from happy, and he sought recreation and relaxation in the life of the court instead, in the company of favourites and cultural luminaries, and not least in the theatre. He founded both the Opera and the Royal Dramatic Theatre in Stockholm, and himself wrote and directed plays and even performed on the stage from time to time. The great collections of paintings and sculptures that he donated to the state and which were made accessible to the public in the Royal Museum after his death, form the basis of the collections in the National Art Gallery.

THE GUSTAVIAN REFORMS ❧ The series of reforms now undertaken in the spirit of the Enlightenment were primarily the work of Gustav III, but he was aided by important collaborators such as Lord President of the Council Ulrik Scheffer and the "finance minister" Johan Liljencrantz.

The reform programme comprised the best ideas of both the Hats and the Caps, which they had been unable to put into practice, plus a great deal of legislation in the spirit of the Enlightenment. The government agencies were given new instructions, and a thorough ransacking of the civil service was undertaken. The regulation of remuneration in 1778 reduced the inclination of public officials to seek bribes. In the legal sphere, slow cases were speeded up,

torture was abolished and the death penalty was restricted on the personal initiative of Gustav III himself. The Freedom of the Press Act, which should by rights have been abolished according to the Constitution of 1772, was replaced in 1774 by an Act prepared by the king himself. It was more limited in scope, and in the 1780s it ceased to have any significance in practice.

Gustav III was a warm supporter of the principle of religious freedom. He pushed a proposal through the parliament of 1778-79, in the teeth of clerical opposition, which granted freedom of religion to all immigrants, and two years later the first legislation permitting freedom of religion in Sweden was passed. One year after this, Jewish immigration to the three cities of Stockholm, Gothenburg and Norrköping was permitted. There is no doubt that Gustav was also aware of the economic advantages of attracting businessmen, craftsmen and other skilled foreigners to Sweden. It has been pointed out that Gustav's interest in the ideas of the Enlightenment did not extend to the point where it might affect his own position, and in this he greatly resembled his royal colleagues in Russia, Prussia and Austria.

The appalling state finances were investigated by a secret commission, but the views that won out were the more optimistic ones held by Johan Liljencrantz. His financial plan of 1774 covered both central government activities and private businesses, and was implemented over the years that followed. In late 1776, the remarkable coinage sale was held, in which the notes circulating during the Age of Freedom were redeemed at half their nominal value, the silver standard was revived and the mediaeval coinage system was abolished. The unit of currency became the venerable *riksdaler*, divided into 48 shillings.

Other experiments in the sphere of financial and taxation policy were less successful. The idea of monopolizing the distillation of akvavit was indubitably a sound one from a financial point of view, but it was implemented in the wrong way. The big government distilleries cost too much to run, and the peasants hated the prohibition, which they opposed in Parliament and diligently violated with clandestine distilling operations. Sweden was a den of drunkenness in the eighteenth century, and the average height of the population fell – at the end of the century the average male height was not more than 163 cm (5 ft 5 ins), whereas today it is 180 cm (6 ft) – Swedes had "shrunk" by a decimetre (4 ins) since Viking times! By 1789 the government had no option but to abolish its monopoly and introduce a system of leasing charges in its place. The monopoly policy had no element of popular sobriety or temperance in it, as was to be the case in later years.

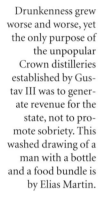

Drunkenness grew worse and worse, yet the only purpose of the unpopular Crown distilleries established by Gustav III was to generate revenue for the state, not to promote sobriety. This washed drawing of a man with a bottle and a food bundle is by Elias Martin.

THE PARLIAMENT OF 1778-79 ∾ Keeping the promise he made during the coup, Gustav summoned a parliament within six years, in the autumn of 1778. Doing so, he restored the antiquated parliamentary procedures from the time of Gustav II Adolf, even including the class divisions in the House of Nobility. The Banco Committee and the Committee of State were appointed to scrutinize the administration of the previous years. Even if the assembly was fairly docile on the whole, and approved the measures proposed by the government and the king, it none the less left an impression of incipient opposition on the part of the nobility. What is more, the Estates felt the lack of an exhaustive and honest account of the financial circumstances of the realm and they were dissatisfied with the system of promotions, the question of the akvavit monopoly and the "pastorate trade" – an abusive institution involving the payment of large sums of money by priests in return for their appointment to a living, in other words, a kind of legalized bribery.

FOREIGN POLICY BEFORE 1785 ∾ The relationship with France remained a cornerstone of Gustav III's foreign policy, which he managed in a very self-willed fashion. He was a true Cabinet politician in the style of the age, carried on a secret correspondence with his own emissaries and exerted himself to the utmost to conceal his intentions, including romantic aspirations to restore Sweden's old Great Power status. Initially, he was cautious in his actions, particularly while Ulrik Scheffer remained Lord President of the Council. A visit to Catharine the Great in St Petersburg in 1777 failed to yield any notable results, but generated a sufficient degree of mutual trust for Sweden, Russia and Denmark to conclude a treaty of armed neutrality in 1780. This treaty protected trade during the war between England and France during the American colonies' war of liberation, and had great significance in international law. At the time of Scheffer's resignation in 1783, a war broke out between Russia and Turkey. The king had long been working to strengthen Sweden's defence forces and now saw an opportunity to attack Denmark, with the objective of conquering Norway. A plan of campaign was prepared, but in a meeting at Fredrikshamn in Finland Catharine refused to abandon her alliance with Denmark, and the offensive had to be postponed. When Gustav returned from his great Italian journey in 1783-84, Turkey had concluded peace with Russia and a scornful letter from Catharine had put an end to official friendly relations. A minor consolation for the king was that he was able to spend time with Louis XVI and Marie Antoinette in Versailles in France on his way home. He had then managed to purchase the small island of St. Barthélemy in the West Indies as a Swedish colony, and had concluded a secret treaty with France obtaining financial subsidies for Sweden to strengthen its defences. The planned offensive against Denmark had to be cancelled, however, but Gustav by no means abandoned his dreams of conquest and military glory.

Domestic policy before 1788 and the parliament of 1786

❧ The setbacks of 1778-79 – the rupture with his mother, the rumours about his son's birth and the nascent opposition – appear to have influenced the king and changed him for the worse. He became anxious, was nervously overactive, and his moods oscillated between depression and euphoria. He occasionally neglected his government duties for the theatre, the secret activities of the orders and other pastimes – but he also founded the Swedish Academy and revived the Royal Academy that his mother had founded. Most of his old advisers left the stage during the 1780s. The vacuum was filled partly

Things looked different in the upper classes. Gustav III and Catharine the Great met in Fredrikshamn in 1783. Politically speaking, the meeting was a failure for Gustav, who wanted support for a war with Denmark. Miniature by C. Høijer.

by favourites, like the Finnish-born Gustaf Mauritz Armfelt, but the king was also sensible enough to make use of able commoners. The order introduced into the nation's finances by the coinage sale of 1776 was short-lived, however, and to a great extent the responsibility for this lay with the king himself, who lacked real financial talent despite occasional thrift in petty matters. The nation suffered from poor harvests and a deficit in its foreign trade. Parliament was summoned in May 1786 and proved to be a great setback for the king. There was now a serious opposition, in which the nobility was the most active element, whose main thrust was against Gustav personally. Its most prominent leader was Axel von Fersen the Elder. Almost all the royal proposals were rejected, the national debt was subjected to a close scrutiny and restrictions in the freedom of the press were attacked. The issue of the akvavit monopoly was also raised and came under strong attack, not least by the peasants. Taxation was approved for no more than four years.

The preceding years had seen a number of improvements in the question of church appointments, and the government also refrained from imposing a tobacco monopoly. This calmed the clergy and the burghers. The peasants were placated by steps to phase out the hated Crown distilleries. What is more, home distillation was permitted on payment of a fee, which further encouraged drunkenness.

THE ATTACK ON RUSSIA AND THE WAR OF 1788-90 ∾ Gustav attempted to restore his former popularity and silence the opposition by engaging in a very active foreign policy.

Sweden was isolated, however, and no help could be expected from France. In the autumn of 1787, Turkey declared war on Russia and the king and his advisers saw in this an opportunity that they had to exploit. The objective was a war against Russia that would force her to restore the territories lost in 1743 and end the support given by Catharine the Great to the Swedish opposition. During a visit to Copenhagen in the autumn of 1787, Gustav tried to persuade the crown prince and his minister Bernstorff (who were governing in the name of the insane Christian VII) to conclude a family treaty with Sweden, but he failed. Nothing came of negotiations with Prussia and England, either. Despite these setbacks, which were concealed, in March 1788 the king decided to start war on Russia – without informing the Councillors of the Realm.

According to the Constitution, Parliament had to give its consent to a war of aggression, and the Russian empress, occupied with the Turkish conflict, was careful to avoid causing the slightest irritation which might provide Gustav with a pretext for attacking her. A "theatrical" monarch is never at a loss when it comes to helping the plot along, however, and in June 1788 he dressed Swedish soldiers in Russian uniforms and attacked a Finnish outpost at Puumala in Savolax. The war was now irrevocable and Gustav was full of enthusiasm. His fleet was superior, and his army was capable of mounting a blitzkrieg, but not more, as its supplies were inadequate. A large squadron sailed from Karlskrona under the command of duke Karl. However, the naval battle off Hogland in the Gulf of Finland in July was indecisive, and this wrecked the planned campaign, which was based on a landing near St Petersburg with the support of the navy. The shortcomings in equipment and supplies and the inadequacy of the king's military understanding became more and more evident, and the campaign of 1788 was a failure. The Swedish officers, many of whom belonged to the noble opposition, began negotiations of their own with the Russian empress. A number of Finnish officers also had secret plans for a union of Finland with their eastern neighbour. The dejected king was sent a letter signed by 112 officers (the Anjala league) in which they pointed out the illegality of the war and the necessity of making peace. In the view of the conspirators, a parliament should be summoned to change the Constitution.

Gustav awoke from his despair – it has been said that a serious crisis always electrified him – and once Denmark had declared war according to its treaty obligations with Russia, he was able to take action. "Je suis sauvé!" (I'm saved!), he is said to have shouted. And now his talents in the fields of diplomacy and demagogy were shown to be in a class of their own. Negotiations were immediately set in motion with England and Prussia, while the king, like a latter-day Gustav Vasa, travelled to Dalarna and levied the peasants. The common people followed him enthusiastically, angered as they were by the traitors in the nobility, who were denigrated mercilessly, and by the attack of the nation's arch-enemy Denmark. The king then rode without delay to Gothenburg, which was under threat from a Danish army marching on it from Norway. Its defences were strengthened

Women in the Nordmark mines in Värmland in 1786, sorting ore from the ore bins. Women working in the mines were a common sight until late in the nineteenth century. Aquatint engraving by J. F. Martin after F. A. von Numers. (Left)

and with the help of the English envoy in Denmark the Danish general was persuaded to break off his offensive. Shortly afterwards a truce was signed with Denmark and the immediate danger was averted.

THE PARLIAMENT OF 1789. THE FALL OF THE NOBILITY ∾

The Estates were summoned early in 1789. The king immediately saw to it that a secret commission was appointed with representatives from all four Estates. The protests of the nobility led to the whole of parliament being summoned to the royal palace, where the first Estate of the realm was given a thorough dressing-down and then shown the door. The three non-privileged Estates remained and when admonished to do so by the king they chose representatives to confer with him about the privileges of the nobility and to enter into a "association for the good of the realm". The draft proposal for an Act of Union and Security presented by the king meant among other things that the powers of the monarch would be strengthened. After nineteen nobles, including von Fersen, had been arrested, the king pushed through the desired changes in the Constitution with the support of the three non-privileged Estates. The main provisions of the new law gave the king complete power over the administration of the nation, allowed him to decide the number of Councillors of the Realm, gave him the right of initiating a war without the consent of the Estates and removed from the Estates the right of taking up other questions of legislation than those laid before it by the king. Taxation, however, was still to be decided in consultation with Parliament. The king now had virtually absolute powers. In exchange, the non-privileged Estates had got the privileges of the nobility diminished – it was now open to members of all Estates to possess and own any type of property except that involving what was known as exceptional privilege – manorial farms with special exemption from taxation – the ownership of which was reserved to the nobility until 1810. Several other benefits were also granted to the non-privileged Estates. This enactment of Sweden's most important equalization of privileges was the result of a just popular demand coinciding with the constrained situation in which Gustav III found himself. It probably spared Sweden a revolution, and from a social point of view it meant a great deal for the expanding peasant class.

The next problem was the national finances. For the first time, the Estates obtained complete access to the accounts and were able to see the actual dimensions of the national debt. To manage the national debt, the National Debt Office was instituted, and it was also given the right to issue notes of exchange. New taxes were authorized and were to be controlled every three years by a committee of authorization to see if there were any need of adjustment.

A subsequent result of these parliamentary decisions was that the king determined the number of Councillors of the Realm to be – zero! By this measure of the king, this institution, which had existed since the thirteenth century, disappeared. Its function as a legal instance was replaced by the Supreme Court, which was set up for the purpose, half of whose members were to be commoners.

THE PEACE OF 1790. GUSTAV III'S FINAL YEARS ∾ The war was resumed in 1789. The Swedes won a number of minor victories on land but the decisive battles took place at sea in the following year. After a success at Fredrikshamn in mid-May 1790, the whole Swedish fleet, numbering 175 vessels, was trapped in the Gulf of Viborg and eventually had to run for it, sustaining heavy losses (the incident is known as the "Viborg gauntlet"). This setback, however, was compensated for by the great victory of the archipelago fleet at Svensksund, not far from Fredrikshamn. Gustav III deserves much of the credit for this victory, since he was the one who insisted on engaging the battle. In August 1790,

Sweden concluded peace with Russia at Värälä. The empress was reluctant to continue a war on two fronts and was also being threatened by Prussia and England. The borders were restored to the status quo, but the Russian guarantee with respect to the Constitution of 1720 was excised from the treaty, removing Catharine's formal basis for intervening in Sweden's internal affairs.

During the autumn and in the following year, Gustav and his advisers struggled to control a growing national debt. The issue of notes, mainly by the National Debt Office, rose far above what had been intended and gave rise to rampant inflation.

New and fantastic opportunities were being

The battle of Svensksund, 1790, in which Gustav III took part, was to be Sweden's greatest naval victory. The Russians lost 60 vessels, the Swedes only 6. Oil painting by J. T. Schoultz, who was present at the battle.

Gustav III was shot and fatally wounded at a masquerade at the opera on 16 March 1792 by captain Jacob Johan Anckarström, who formed part of an extensive conspiracy. The king died of his wounds 13 days later. By A. W. Küftner of Nürnberg.

envisaged by Gustav now, that were far more seductive to his mind than the tedious reality of Swedish affairs, where he suffered greatly from the way the nobility had abandoned him and his court after the parliament of 1789. The king planned to crush the French Revolution of 1789 by putting himself at the head of a coalition of European princes, but his timing was premature. Catharine the Great made encouraging noises, but did nothing except conclude a treaty in 1791 promising subsidies to Sweden. Sweden was now accepting money from its old enemy Russia instead of its traditional ally France, whose payments had naturally stopped dead in 1789. In the summer of 1791, Gustav even travelled to Aachen near the French border in order to prepare his "crusade". He also hoped to be

able to receive the French royal couple, who intended to flee Paris with the aid of Axel von Fersen the Younger, their friend for many years and possibly the queen's lover. The attempted flight failed. The fugitives were discovered near the border and Gustav soon returned to Sweden, without, however, abandoning his plans.

A new parliament was summoned in January 1792 to prolong current levels of taxation. The National Debt Office took over responsibility for the increased national debt, which now amounted to almost 30 million *riksdaler*. On this occasion, too, the king was completely frank in relation to the finances of the realm. Parliament was calm on the surface, and Gustav did not stage any new coup, although the possibility had been whispered about.

THE ASSASSINATION OF THE KING, 1792

∾ A section of the nobility in opposition now planned rebellion and regicide. The most disparate interests were united in this endeavour. The circle around the old intriguer Pechlin mixed those who were bitter over the loss of their privileges with those who were fired by the libertarian ideals of the French Revolution, the great upheaval in France which had put an end to privileges of precisely this kind. Captain Jacob Johan Anckarström, a steely fanatic who nourished a personal hatred of the king, took upon himself the mission of killing Gustav. For several months no opportunity of carrying out the plan presented itself. A masquerade ball at the opera on 16 March 1792 was finally seen to present an appropriate opportunity, however. Once the king had been shot, the conspirators intended to restore the old Constitution by means of a *coup d'état*. The king had been warned, but didn't take the threat seriously. His costume made it easy to recognize him, and Anckarström managed to hit him with a shot in the back above his left hip. The king was heard

The regicide Anckarström was publicly flogged in three locations in Stockholm – one of them here in front of the House of Nobility – and then executed, after which his body was displayed on the breaking wheel, with his head and his right hand cut off.

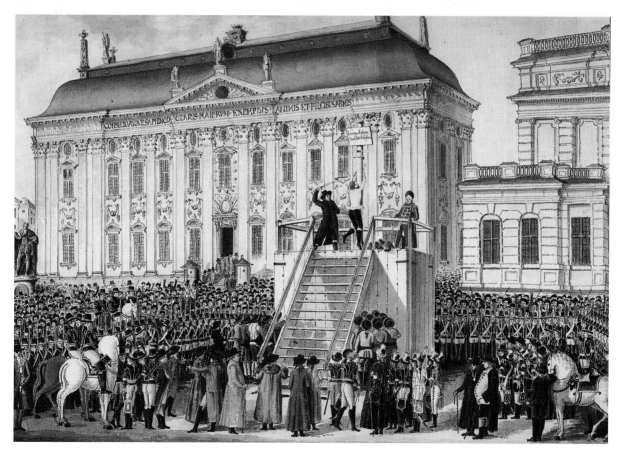

to shout: "Aïe, je suis blessé, arrêtez-le!" ("Ah, I'm wounded, arrest him!"). Gustav was taken aside, the doors were shut and those present had to give their names and addresses. The king was gravely wounded, but was still alive and the coup had thereby failed. No steps were taken to seize power, while the king's men acted rapidly and effectively. Anckarström was arrested the very next day, after being identified by the weapon he had cast aside, and subsequently the whole conspiracy was unravelled.

The king, who died a little less than a fortnight later from complications caused by the wound, had the satisfaction of receiving visits from many of his former opponents who were now full of repugnance at the atrocity. On the death of Gustav a great many plans both great and small had to be put on hold. Nothing came of the great crusade against the French Revolution, just as nothing came of the planned palace in the royal park at Haga at the northern approaches to Stockholm. Cultural activities were put on a starvation diet and new men were appointed to serve in the regency government. As the Swedish historian Erik Lönnroth writes in his biography of Gustav III, life in Sweden became much calmer, but a lot less interesting.

THE REGENCY GOVERNMENT OF 1792–96
∾ The assassination of Gustav III in March 1792, when his son Gustav Adolf was in his early teens, affected the boy for the rest of his life. A regency government was immediately appointed and was led by Gustav Adolf's uncle, duke Karl of Södermanland. The most forceful and decisive individual in the government was the duke's friend and fellow freemason, Gustaf

Adolf Reuterholm. By this time, the assassin and the conspirators had been punished. Anckarström alone was executed, the rest were shown leniency by the court and sentenced to prison or exile.

The duke had never been close to his brother or his advisers, and Reuterholm had belonged to the opposition during the parliament of 1789. The so-called Gustavians were accordingly removed from all leading posts in the capital. Gustaf Mauritz Armfelt became a minister at the Italian courts with a residence in Naples. Reuterholm was to all intents and purposes a prime minister. The duke, who lacked stamina and diligence and had no interest in the personal exercise of power, was like putty in the hands of his industrious friend. Unfortunately, this friend was a narrow-minded and envious character who never forgot a grudge, and these traits were to suffocate his enthusiasm for the great ideas of the eighteenth century and turn him into a despot. The execution of Louis XVI in 1793 put a definite end to his flirtation with liberalism. A rather ineffective conspiracy against the government was exposed in 1793. It originated with dissatisfied Gustavians and was planned by Armfelt, who was in Italy. The trial of the conspirators revealed that on one occasion they had established relations with the empress of Russia. Armfelt fled from Naples to Russia, and the other conspirators were arrested. The sentences handed down in the summer of 1794 were harsh. Armfelt's mistress, for instance, Malin Rudenschöld, a lady-in-waiting, was compelled to stand in the pillory before she was put in the spinning-house, a female prison for beggars and prostitutes.

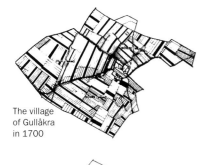

The village
of Gullåkra
in 1700

The village
of Gullåkra
in 1812

Starting in the early nineteenth century, the earlier redistribution of landholdings was followed by farm unification reforms, in which holdings were redistributed and the traditional tightly-knit villages became unravelled – a precondition for efficient agriculture. The maps show the village of Gullåkra in Skåne before and after the reforms. The land of the peasant who owned the narrow black strips was collected into the black patch to the west. Right, a photo from the large, unified holdings of our own day.

Reuterholm's foreign policy was officially neutral, but lengthy negotiations were carried on with revolutionary France, which tempted Sweden with huge subsidies. In the end Reuterholm didn't dare authorize a treaty with France, as Russia had openly shown its displeasure. Instead an alliance of neutrality was concluded with Denmark in 1794, providing a first premonition of later policies of Scandinavianism. In 1795, however, negotiations with France were renewed and in the autumn the French republic was recognized. A treaty was concluded which gave Sweden large subsidies.

Various negotiations were carried out during the regency to arrange an advantageous marriage between the young king and a suitable foreign princess. He was betrothed to Louise Charlotte of Mecklenburg-Schwerin, but Russian threats led to the engagement being broken off in 1796, when the French alliance was also dissolved. The king, the duke and Reuterholm now travelled to St Petersburg where they were received by Catharine the Great. The intention was for the young king to be betrothed to her niece, the grand princess Alexandra. Just as the tie was to be officially announced, Gustav Adolf refused to give a written pledge that his bride-to-be would be allowed to practise her Russian Orthodox religion. All attempts at persuasion were in vain – the king cited the Swedish Constitution which stated that the archbishop had to be consulted in such a matter. The royal party sailed back to Stockholm with its business incomplete, and shortly afterwards the duke abdicated the regency. Reuterholm was dismissed and fell from grace, and the Russian alliance and betrothal were finally struck from the agenda. The policies of the regency had failed. The death of Catharine in November 1796, however, meant that Sweden needed fear no reprisals on account of the embarrassing events in St Petersburg.

THE REIGN OF GUSTAV IV ADOLF, 1796-1809

With respect to both character and honesty the young king was very different from both his father and his uncle, but he utterly lacked Gustav III's political instincts and negotiating abilities. He concealed his flawed mental stability behind a stiff, self-aware presence. He was convinced of his divine right to the throne, but didn't regard himself as an absolute monarch. He had no favourites, and his thrift made a good impression. But he had an excessively bureaucratic character which made him ill-suited for governing a nation in crisis.

The year after he came of age, Gustav Adolf married Fredrika Dorotea Wilhelmina of Baden, but the marriage ended in divorce in 1812 after the king was deposed. They had several children, and Gustav, the successor to the throne, was born in 1799.

The only parliament summoned by Gustav Adolf was held in Norrköping in the spring of 1800. The main issues were as usual the finances of the nation, and a new coinage sale was enacted. It was not carried out until 1803, however, in a modified form. Above all the National Debt Office's notes of exchange had to be redeemed in silver. Radical currents of opinion had already irritated the king – there had been student demonstrations in Uppsala in 1799 – and during the life of the parliament there was vociferous opposition from the nobility. It led to no tangible results, but gave offence to the conservatives. A number of members of Parliament renounced their noble titles. Gustav Adolf was unable to forget these demonstrations, and summoned no more parliaments.

The coinage sale of 1803 improved the nation's finances considerably. To obtain the almost 2 million silver *riksdaler* guaranteed for distribution by the Bank of Sweden, the king pawned Wismar to Mecklenburg-Schwerin. Sweden had the right to redeem the city after 100 years, but wisely refrained from doing so in a treaty signed in 1903.

Of other important domestic matters the great land reform known as the *enskifte* (farm unification) demands attention. Ordinances relating to this reform were promulgated between 1803 and 1807. It was a continuation of the land reform initiated in 1757 with the *storskifte* (the great redistribution). Even if the implementation of the reform took time, it started the reshaping of rural Sweden. The close-knit village communities were dissolved and previously divided and subdivided fields were amalgamated into single units under one and the same owner. This entailed the disruption of the mediaeval village communities and marked the beginning of a movement away from the traditional settlements to outlying and often isolated individual farms.

FOREIGN POLICY AND WAR. THE KING IS DEPOSED

It would be foreign policy that finally brought the king down. Wiser and more supple men than Gustav IV Adolf would fail in their attempts to tack between the Great

Powers in the wars and revolutions that followed in the wake of the French Revolution and during Napoleon's struggle to conquer Europe. Initially Gustav Adolf maintained good relations with France and in 1800 he concluded an alliance of neutrality with other Baltic states against England, which had violated freedoms of trade. In 1801, however, the English destroyed the Danish fleet at Copenhagen – while the Swedish king watched the bombardment on the other side of the Sound from the Scanian coast. Tsar Paul of Russia was assassinated, which forced a reorientation of Swedish policy. In 1803, Sweden concluded a commercial treaty with England, and in 1805 war was declared on France. In 1803-05 the king had resided in Germany and Swedish Pomerania. While there he had been seized by revulsion at the brutality of Napoleon's policies. Some years later he would identify Bonaparte with the beast of the Apocalypse and regard any accommodation as unthinkable. War was conducted in Pomerania in 1805-07 with some success, but when Napoleon had reconciled himself with tsar Alexander of Russia at Tilsit in 1807, Sweden's position became extremely vulnerable. French troops invaded Pomerania and Gustav Adolf returned to Sweden with his army.

In February 1808, Russian troops invaded Finland and in March Denmark, which had long been an ally of France, also declared war on Sweden. The Swedes abandoned Finland the same year. Field marshal Wilhelm Mauritz Klingspor proved to be a very ineffective commander-in-chief, and despite sporadic successes under generals like Georg Carl von Döbeln and Johan August Sandels the general

The deposed Gustav IV Adolf, alias "colonel Gustafsson", drawn by Emil Rittmeyer in St Gallen ca 1835.

picture is one of an utter rout. The situation was catastrophic for Sweden.

The king had no support in the military or among his state officials, who realized better than he did himself how inadequate the nation's resources were. The only alternatives available were seen to be assassination or removal from the throne, and the latter course was chosen. In early March 1809, Georg Adlersparre occupied Karlstad in the province of Värmland and marched on Stockholm with the western army. When the king heard this, he decided to leave for Skåne to get the support of the southern army. A civil war was prevented, however, by the resolute intervention of major-general Carl Adlercreutz and leading state officials. Adlercreutz and six officers entered the royal palace in Stockholm on 13 March 1809 and arrested the king. A bloodless revolution "from the top" had been consummated, without popular support, granted, but also with no opposition worth mentioning. The king was forced to abdicate and was deposed by the Estates together with his heirs and expelled from the country. At the end of the year he left Sweden to live in exile.

The Gustavian Age was over. Its fall was mainly the work of high state officials and the generals ("the men of 1809"). It remained for them to give Sweden a new and more harmonious form of government.

FROM A LAND OF PEASANT FARMERS TO AN INDUSTRIAL NATION

THE CONSTITUTION OF 1809 ∾ The person closest to the throne was the uncle of the deposed king, duke Karl, who had, of course, been in the regency government.

Karl was probably aware of the crisis and the conspiracies in early 1809, but took no active part in them. He was persuaded to become Protector of the Realm on condition that his nephew was spared.

What changes now took place in Sweden after the bloodless coup of March 1809? We saw above that it was carried out by aristocratic officials and military officers as a reaction to royal absolutism, and they were now faced with the problem of providing Sweden with a new Constitution. The election of a monarch was left to Parliament, which was summoned to Stockholm in May 1809. In the meanwhile the war continued with little success for Sweden. Those responsible for the coup saw their hopes dashed for an immediate peace with Denmark, Russia and France, and a note they received from Napoleon gave them little

consolation: "Tsar Alexander is great and magnanimous. Turn to him!" Thus, in the midst of a serious war, Parliament had to confirm the removal of Gustav IV Adolf and his heirs, adopt a new Constitution and elect a new king.

The new Constitution was prepared in record time, and after just a few weeks the draft proposals could be submitted to the Estates. Once they had been adopted, duke Karl was offered the crown. On 6 June 1809 he accepted in accordance with the new Constitution, and came to the throne as Karl XIII.

The Constitution of 1809 laid down for the first time what exactly were the constitutional laws of Sweden. These were, in addition to the laws pertaining to the form of government itself, the Riksdag Act (adopted in 1810), the Freedom of the Press Act (adopted in 1810, subsequently revised in 1812 and 1949), and the Act of Succession, regulating the succession to the throne, which was adopted in 1809, but was replaced by a new act in 1810 in conjunction with the election of Jean Baptiste Bernadotte as the successor to the throne.

The Constitution laid down that the king was to govern the realm, but established at his side a Council of State with nine members, whose opinion the king was compelled to hear and who were responsible before Parliament for the advice they gave the king. The Council consisted of two ministers of state, one of them a minister of state for justice and one a minister of state for foreign affairs, a court chancellor and six other Councillors of State. It was further stipulated that Parliament should assemble every five years. The old provisions protecting the rights of citizens were also written into the Constitution.

The Constitution was an example of the principle of the division of powers between the king, Parliament and the courts, and it presupposed a powerful but not absolute monarchy. No votes were taken at the meetings of the Council of State, nor was the king compelled to follow the advice he received. The responsibility of the Councillors of State to Parliament, however, showed the adaptability and modernity of the new Constitution, and, mutatis mutandis, it was able to work in the conditions of a parliamentary monarchy. It remained in force until 1975.

THE ELECTION OF A SUCCESSOR. THE PEACES ∾ Since Karl XIII was old and childless, the succession became an urgent question. The "men of 1809" who held power feared that the son of the deposed Gustav IV Adolf would become an attractive alternative as crown prince, as there were those who desired this, including the Marshal of the Realm Axel von Fersen the Younger. To complicate matters, the Council of State was by no means sufficiently united to pursue vigorous and consistent policies. In hopes of gaining a rapid peace, Parliament elected the Danish prince Christian August of Augustenborg as crown prince. But Christian August refused to accept the nomination until the war was over. In September 1809 the harsh peace of Fredrikshamn was concluded with Russia, by whose terms Sweden ceded the whole of Finland and the eastern part of Västerbotten together with the Åland islands. At a stroke Sweden had lost one third of its territory. Peace was made with Denmark in December 1809, retaining the status quo, and with France in Paris in January 1810. Sweden was compelled to join the French Continental System, that is to say, it had to take part in the commercial blockade of England, but it regained Swedish Pomerania.

The long-lasting parliament – it continued until May 1810 – had to devote a great deal of time to financial matters, principally the war debt and the greatly reduced state revenues, due partly of course to the loss of Finland. Notes of exchange had once again been irredeemable, for over a year, and Sweden would retain its paper standard until 1834. Taxation was simplified by the removal of the many charges that had been levied for "luxury goods". A progressive scale of income tax was introduced (from 1/4 per cent to 10 per cent). The Estates were particularly keen on the extension of the Göta Canal, work on which was being led by Baltzar von Platen. State subven-

tions were allocated to the project along with labour power from the army.

In early 1810, the newly elected crown prince finally came to Sweden. He took the name Karl August, and was adopted by Karl XIII. The new successor to the throne quickly became popular. It has been doubted, however, that he really possessed the vigour needed to deal with the troublesome state of Sweden's foreign affairs and that the Constitution presupposed. He did not enjoy robust health, and during manoeuvres in Skåne in May 1810 he had a stroke and fell from his horse. Half an hour later, he was dead.

THE MURDER OF AXEL VON FERSEN ∾ Although the post mortem showed that the death was natural, a rumour rapidly spread that it was really due to poisoning – malicious tongues had previously been trying to make people believe that the Gustavians, who wished to see the son of Gustav IV Adolf on the throne, intended to murder Karl August. There is no doubt that the "men of 1809" were now planning to intimidate the Gustavian party into remaining silent in the run-up to the inevitable election of a new successor to the throne, in which their own candidate would be duke Frederik Christian, the brother of the deceased. It is, naturally, not at all certain that they foresaw the terrifying consequences of the campaign of slander they were conducting. At any rate, the manufactured rumours were soon pointing insistently at Axel von Fersen, the Marshal of the Realm, who was also a tempting target, since he was wealthy, aristocratic and loved pomp and finery.

The murder of Axel von Fersen in 1810. There was a great scandal when von Fersen was beaten to death and the troops failed to intervene. This picture shows the naked victim in the yard of the Bonde palace, then a courthouse and now the Supreme Court. Soon afterwards he was trampled to death. The House of Nobility is seen in the background. Contemporary washed india ink drawing.

When the funeral procession reached Stockholm, with the gilded coach of the Marshal of the Realm preceding the dusty hearse, the responsible authorities were well aware of what was likely to happen. Fired by agitators, the massed crowds started hurling stones at the marshal's coach. When, bleeding, he sought shelter in a house, he was lured into the street again, where the assault continued. The troops did nothing, but eventually some helpful officers rescued von Fersen and got him into the courthouse, next to the House of Nobility. The enraged crowd, however, soon dragged him back out into the street again, half-dead, stripped him, knocked him to the ground and finally killed him after an ordeal that lasted an hour. The troops didn't intervene until the afternoon, and the city was restless for days afterwards. We now know the names of a number of those who took part in the attack, and there is no doubt that the king, too, had been forewarned that something was being planned to silence the Gustavians. This repugnant murder, carried out in full view of a drawn-up regiment of guards, will always be a stain on the reputation of the high officials who planned to "frighten" their opponents and who, when the incident got out of hand, failed to restrain their hired assassins. The trial that followed carefully concealed the identities of the real instigators.

THE ÖREBRO PARLIAMENT OF 1810. THE ELECTION OF BERNADOTTE ∾ To avoid the seething capital, it was decided to hold the election for the successor to the throne in Örebro, where the parliamentary session commenced in July 1810. It had been preceded by intrigues and diplomatic correspondence, and the principal candidate was still Frederik Christian of Augustenborg. The intervention of a private individual gave a surprising twist to the election of the successor to the throne, however. Lieutenant Carl Otto Mörner, who was in Paris in the capacity of government courier, was convinced that Sweden needed a French marshal. Having been recommended a certain Jean Baptiste Bernadotte, he persuaded the Swedish consul-general in Paris that a Frenchman would quite certainly be elected in Örebro, and thus gained an audience with the marshal, who had become the prince of Ponte Corvo in Italy, although he had begun his career as a private

soldier in pre-revolutionary days. Space does not permit us to go into all the complicated but short-lived intrigues and negotiations that preceded the election of Bernadotte, but some of the more important elements of the process should be mentioned.

Mörner was given a cold reception on his return – after all, he had acted without instructions from the government – and he was not even allowed to participate in the parliamentary proceedings. But the kite had been flown and things also started happening in Paris. After some initial hesitation, Bernadotte had accepted the idea of becoming the crown prince of Sweden, and had turned to Napoleon for advice. Napoleon, who had once been engaged to

Désirée Clary, who was now married to Bernadotte, and whose brother was married to Désirée's sister, had promoted the career of the skilled general, partly for family reasons, but had long regarded him with some distrust. The French emperor tried to persuade his stepson, Eugène de Beauharnais, to accept the Swedish offer instead, but was met with a clear refusal and so gave his consent to Bernadotte.

In Sweden, the government had just decided to propose the duke of Augustenborg as its candidate in the election. Two days later, a French agent called Fournier arrived with oral greetings from Bernadotte and portraits of his wife and only son. Since Fournier's passport was signed by the French foreign minister, it was be-

Karl XIV Johan inspecting work on the Göta Canal. The builder of the Canal, Baltzar von Platen, holding his hat, is seen to the left of the king. Water colour by A. C. Wetterling, 1856.

lieved that he was acting on Napoleon's instructions. The government now changed its position and proposed Bernadotte as its candidate instead. On 21 August 1810, Bernadotte was accordingly elected crown prince of Sweden to the cheers of the Estates. It was an unprecedented event in the history of Sweden. It is very likely that the symptoms of social breakdown throughout the country reinforced the feeling that Sweden needed a "strong man".

A lot of hopes were pinned on the new crown prince, two of which he would never fulfil. He was not to reconquer Finland, and he failed to improve Sweden's relations with Napoleon. The mutual suspicion between the emperor and Bernadotte was unknown in Sweden, and in fact friendly relations with tsar Alexander would soon be a cornerstone of the crown prince's new foreign policy. Bernadotte arrived in Sweden in October 1810. The previous day he had converted to Protestantism in the Danish town of Helsingør, since the Constitution required this. Soon afterwards he was adopted by the aging Karl XIII, and took the name of Karl Johan. The crown prince immediately assumed the direct responsibilities of government.

ONE-MAN RULE (1810-59) ∽ Crown Prince Karl Johan quickly familiarized himself with Sweden, its circumstances and affairs. Thanks to his personality and charm he became well-liked, and was forgiven his occasional flashes of temper and his sometimes obtrusively suspicious demeanour, although this was to some extent understandable in a person who had been transplanted to a distant country where a king had been assassinated less than twenty

years previously, the king's son had been deposed and the Marshal of the Realm had recently been beaten to death in the street. It would not be until the 1830s that his regime would be subject to any real critical scrutiny.

The authority of the government was strengthened and the firm grip the crown prince had on the helm of state did not pass unnoticed in either the administration or the army. Fortunately, at this time almost all high state officials and officers spoke French, as Karl Johan never learned Swedish. All his life he remained a stranger to many facets of Swedish national life. He was a hard worker, and had soon mastered the intricacies of the administration. He exploited to the full the stipulations in the Constitution that "the king possesses the right to govern the realm alone", and towards the end of his reign he was being met by growing opposition.

Karl Johan soon undertook a complete change of course in his foreign policy. Napoleon did indeed force Sweden to declare war on England in November 1810, but the government secretly informed that country that it had no intention of mounting an offensive and no acts of war took place. Eventually the French emperor lost patience, and in January 1812 he arranged for Swedish Pomerania to be occupied anew. This, however, was an ideal turn of events for Karl Johan – he was now able to demonstrate to Swedish public opinion how little benefit it might expect to gain from Napoleon. Instead he drew closer to Sweden's traditional enemy Russia and in April 1812 he concluded a treaty in St Petersburg by which Sweden was to receive Norway and all thoughts of reconquering Finland were abandoned. In the summer, Karl Johan and tsar Alexander met in Åbo and ratified the arrangement. A little earlier, Sweden had withdrawn from the Continental blockade. This was a bold step, since Napoleon's defeat at the hands of Russia did not become general knowledge until late in the autumn. Ever since the previous year, Sweden had been strengthening its army. In Skåne in 1811 the levies even led to a peasant revolt which had to be put down by force. In August 1812, Parliament passed a law which introduced compulsory military service for all men between the ages of 20 and 25. The period during which exercises were to be held for the conscripts was a modest twelve days, however!

SWEDEN'S LAST WARS. THE UNION WITH NORWAY ❧ In March 1813, Sweden joined the coalition against Napoleon by signing a treaty with the English. Generous subsidies were paid out and England even ceded the island of Guadeloupe in the West Indies and promised its assistance in the conquest of Norway. An alliance was also concluded with Prussia. During the spring, the Swedish army was ferried over to Pomerania and placed under the command of the crown prince. Disputes with respect to the interpretation of the treaties, especially those with Russia, led to the army remaining inactive for several months on the orders of Karl Johan. In mid-July he met the tsar, Friedrich Wilhelm III of Prussia and representatives of Austria and England at Trachenberg palace in Silesia. It has been said that this was the last time Sweden played a crucial role in European affairs. The disagreements were smoothed over, and the autumn's campaigns were planned. Sweden was to participate in them with 30,000 men. The northern army with its 160,000 troops was to be under the command of Karl Johan.

The campaign ended with Napoleon's defeat at Leipzig in October 1813. In the run-up to this battle, the northern army had been deployed with caution, but had won a couple of minor skirmishes. Finally it took part in the last two days of the great battle of Leipzig. In all these encounters Karl Johan only used his Swedish troops to a very limited extent, which angered both the allies and many of the Swedish officers. The most likely explanation is that the crown prince partly wished to save the army it cost so much effort to levy for the war with Denmark that he considered would be inevitable for the annexation of Norway, and partly that he did not consider the Swedish soldiers to be as fit for battle as a former French marshal would require.

After the victory of Leipzig, Karl Johan obtained leave of his allies to march on northern Germany. Here he split the French from the Danes and conquered Lübeck, Kiel, Holstein and parts of Slesvig. In January 1814, the peace of Kiel was concluded, which put an end to Sweden's last war with Denmark. Norway was ceded to Sweden, or more correctly to "the king of Sweden and his successors", as a united kingdom. The old Norwegian territories of Iceland,

The escutcheon of Sweden's greater coat of arms displays the symbols of her royal dynasties. The lion with the three streams represents the Folkungs. The sheaf of grain in the centre represents the Vasas, with the arms of the Bernadottes, Ponte Corvo (a bridge with an eagle above it), beside it.

Greenland and the Faeroes remained Danish, and Sweden ceded Rügen and what remained of Swedish Pomerania to Denmark. The stipulations concerning Pomerania were never fulfilled, since Sweden later claimed that Denmark had failed to hand over Norway. In 1815, therefore, Pomerania was ceded to Prussia instead, which in return handed over Lauenburg to Denmark. A large sum of money was paid to the Swedish state and a smaller sum to Karl Johan personally. With this, Sweden had lost its last possession on the opposite shores of the Baltic. In this connection it may be mentioned that the island of Guadeloupe reverted to France, and that England paid the 24 million francs involved in this transaction. This compensation was considered to belong to the royal house, a view that was confirmed by the parliament of 1815. Most of the sum went towards paying off Sweden's foreign debt.

In the winter of 1814, the Swedish army advanced to Liège in Belgium, but then remained inactive. Karl Johan was attracted by the idea of playing a leading role in post-Napoleonic France, and if the conditions for this had materialized he would probably have been ready to abdicate his Swedish title. His ambitions were only supported by tsar Alexander, however, and thus he remained in Belgium, ill-pleased with his allies.

In the spring Karl Johan learned that the Norwegians had revolted against the peace of Kiel and that Louis XVIII had ascended the French throne. He now laid aside his French plans and paid his last visit to Paris, where the allies promised him their support against Norway.

The Norwegian independence movement was led by the country's last governor, Prince Christian Frederik of Denmark. A national constituent assembly convened at Eidsvold on 17 May, adopted a liberal Constitution and proclaimed Christian Frederik the king of Norway. Karl Johan now gathered a considerable army of 45,000 men at Norway's southern frontier and also mobilized the Swedish fleet. After some initial Swedish successes, negotiations were begun, which led to certain Swedish concessions. Karl Johan wished to end the war as rapidly as possible and demonstrate his magnanimity so as to impress above all French public opinion. By the terms of the convention of Moss of 14 August 1814, Christian Frederik abdicated the Norwegian crown, while the Swedish king promised to accept the Norwegian Constitution. The Storting, the Norwegian parliament, would meet to approve the convention. In November 1814, after lengthy discussions, the convention was approved and the Norwegians finally "elected and acknowledged" Karl XIII as the king of Norway. The Union was supplemented in 1815 by what was known as the Act of State, which was drawn up by the Swedish parliament and approved by the Storting. Numerous unclear points remained, however. In hindsight, it may be noted that a union between two states on such a flimsy basis – and in the century of nationalism into the bargain – was bound to be a failure in the long run.

Swedish neutrality ∾ In 1814, Sweden concluded its last wars and embarked on a period of peace that has held ever since. Karl Johan, who in reality acted as his own foreign minister, wished to avoid all conflicts in the future. He

pursued a pro-Russian foreign policy with a high degree of consistency, even though it ran into turbulence on one or two occasions. For natural reasons he found it hard to share the despair of his subjects at the loss of Finland or the repugnance they felt towards their traditional enemy.

The greatest risk faced by Sweden in the period between 1815 and 1890 was to be drawn into a war between England and Russia. In the mid-1820s, relations between Sweden and Rus-

sia became rather tense, but when Nicholas I became tsar, good relations were once more established. The fortification of the Åland islands at Bomarsund in the 1830s was viewed with displeasure by Sweden, and the feeling was reciprocated by Russia in relation to Swedish plans to establish a free port at Slite in Gotland.

The movement known as Scandinavianism that emerged in the Nordic countries during the first half of the nineteenth century was thoroughly peaceful in character. It appealed

Karl XIV Johan is crowned king of Norway in Nidaros Cathedral, Trondheim, in 1818. Painting by J. Munch.

The Bernadotte family in the late 1830s. On the far left, Prince Oscar (II), Queen Desideria, Crown Princess Josefina, Prince August, Princess Eugénie, Crown Prince Oscar (I), Prince Karl (XV), Karl XIV Johan and Prince Gustav. The bust on the right shows the king's adoptive father, Karl XIII. Painting by F. Westin.

particularly to the intellectuals, but the Danes also viewed these pan-Nordic attitudes with political hopes of gaining Swedish support in their struggle with "Germanism" in the Danish province of Slesvig (now Schleswig and part of Germany). Karl Johan kept his distance from Scandinavianism, however, as it displeased Russia.

The union with Norway was never to be revised, although Karl Johan had originally envis-

aged this. In the end he accepted the decisions of the Norwegian parliament, even when they went against his wishes, and finally even gave up his opposition to the celebration of 17 May as the Norwegian national day (a tradition as powerful in Norway today as Bastille Day in France). It was possible for Karl Johan to feel himself a union monarch in a way none of his successors could, as he was neither a Norwegian nor a Swede. His successors did however follow him in rarely capitulating to purely nationalistic Swedish public opinion, and the royal family was educated in a spirit of bilingualism.

Karl XIII, who reigned in a purely nominal capacity, died in February 1818. The real ruler of the country then quite uneventfully ascended the throne as Karl XIV Johan.

"No one has had a career like mine"

ᖚ The above words are from a statement dictated by Karl XIV Johan on his deathbed in 1844. It may serve as an appropriate motto for an extraordinarily remarkable career which would have been unthinkable without the French revolution and the turbulent reshaping of Europe that took place in the Napoleonic era – and, not least, without the desire of the Swedish establishment to avoid the return of the old dynasty at any cost.

During the years immediately preceding the death of Karl XIII, Karl Johan was very concerned about his position. Reaction had won the day in Europe, and all the newly-created kings and reigning princes who had temporarily occupied so many of the thrones of the Continent had been deposed. Napoleon languished on the island of St Helena as the prisoner of the English. The only surviving new monarch of this generation was marshal Bernadotte. But his concerns were baseless. The most prominent men in Sweden supported him, and his neighbours did not want to shoulder the difficulties involved in restoring the old dynasty. The only sensational aspects of this succession were that it established a new dynasty on the throne and that this dynasty had such an unusual origin compared with other European royal houses. Some months later the one-time professional soldier from Pau was confirmed in his title and crowned, first in Stockholm and then in Trondheim in Norway.

Defence, the national finances and domestic policy

ᖚ In addition to foreign policy, the king was naturally enough very interested in questions of national defence, the shortcomings of which he saw clearly, and in the nation's finances, which also needed to be refurbished. Karl Johan was an enthusiastic supporter of the Distributive System of military service described above, and he also promoted the idea of a centralized defensive system for the whole nation, that is to say, the view that it was impossible to defend the whole country and that a fortified complex should be created far from the coast to which both the national administration and the army could be concentrated in the event of war. It is still possible to see an embodiment of this theory by visiting Lake Vättern and the now long obsolete fortress of Karlsborg, whose interior was so capacious that it would have been possible to rule Sweden from it.

Karl Johan believed himself to be a financial prodigy, but seems to have overestimated his own abilities in this respect. From 1812 onwards, the country was shaken by great monetary and commercial crises, initially affecting agriculture. In opposition to the government, Parliament recommended protectionism and higher customs duties – provoking Karl Johan to make his notorious remark that "opposition means conspiracy!". During the years that followed, the cultivation of new agricultural land was encouraged, however, and the number of people engaged in agriculture and related occupations rose somewhat to culminate around 80 per cent of the population in 1840, after which it began to fall. During Karl Johan's reign the population grew by about one million people, and the reasons were generally said to be "peace, vaccinations and potatoes". This great increase could not be absorbed by either the towns or Sweden's still insignificant industries, however, and the rural proletariat increased by leaps and bounds.

Karl Johan inherited the weakened finances caused by the wars of 1808-09, and further crises erupted in the wake of the Napoleonic wars. Denmark fell into national bankruptcy, Norway faced severe difficulties and Sweden, which had paid off its foreign debts with a weakened currency, was not a country which inspired confidence in foreign markets. But it would also be many years before Sweden was of any interest to international financiers. The king and his minister of finance thought themselves wiser than they were in these matters, and speculated in the currency markets behind the back of the government and Parliament with the intention of keeping up the value of the *riksdaler*. They failed.

The monetary situation gradually improved, however, thanks in particular to a massive coinage sale in 1834. Notes once more became redeemable in silver and a fixed rate of exchange was established. The first savings bank was opened in Gothenburg in 1820, and at the end of Karl XIV Johan's reign the first private banks were authorized to issue their own notes.

Mining long remained Sweden's most important industry. In the 1830s, what was known as the Lancashire method of forging was introduced, a cheaper process that simultaneously improved the quality of the iron produced. The forges had to be expanded, and many small metallurgical works were squeezed out of business by the large ones. The historical model for the villainous Sintram in Nobel laureate Selma Lagerlöf's novel *The Story of Gösta Berling* was in fact just such a ruthless buyer-out of small works in Värmland.

Investments in which the government placed great hopes included the canals, of which the most important was the Göta Canal, the waterway which would link the North Sea with the Baltic. This last was a vast project that swallowed enormous sums of money and required enormous amounts of labour. It was inaugurated in 1832, by which time its creator, Baltzar von Platen, had died. The Göta Canal did not come to have the great importance that had been envisaged for it, however, as the railways that were built just a few decades later offered a cheaper and faster way of carrying freight. What's more, the canal was too narrow to permit the passage of modern cargo vessels.

Swedish popular education had many glaring shortcomings, and neither the ordinance of Karl XI's reign concerning the obligation of priests to instruct children in reading and Christianity, nor certain reforms introduced in the reign of Gustav IV Adolf had led to any substantial improvement. In Parliament, farsighted individuals in all the Estates agitated vigorously for the establishment of a national school

Parliament enacted legislation on compulsory elementary schooling in 1842. The law could only be implemented in stages, however, and the earliest schools were often rudimentary – as in this picture, from the Stockholm archipelago in 1843. Oil painting by Julius Ringdahl.

system for all children, but it was many years before their efforts bore fruit. The first elementary school ordinance did not come into force until 1842, and even then the general poverty of the country meant that it would be a long time before every child was able to receive schooling.

THE OPPOSITION ✎ Karl XIV Johan appointed most of his Councillors of State from the ranks of the high state officials. Recruitment to the Cabinet was sluggish in the 1830s, partly as a result of the king's growing conservatism and an irritability which tolerated no contradiction, but partly because many people were reluctant to expose themselves to the vigorous opposition being voiced in Parliament

and the constant sniping and slander in the press. The liberal opposition, which grew stronger and stronger in the 1830s, argued that the king also had advisers outside the circle of Councillors of State, and made particular reference to Marshal of the Realm count Magnus Brahe. The criticisms levelled at Brahe were exaggerated – his influence seems on the whole to have been limited to appointments and the armed forces.

Opposition to the king and the government gathered momentum in the parliament of 1834-35, and also made itself felt in the press. When the government began to make use of the power of suppression that had been included in the Freedom of the Press Act of 1812,

The "bedchamber regime". During the morning, the increasingly conservative Karl XIV Johan ruled Sweden from his bed. After twelve he dressed, and council business did not take place until three o'clock or later. Painting by C. F. Bennet, 1843.

which made it possible to prohibit the publication of "libellous" journals, this only made matters worse. It proved to be an ineffective weapon, as the newspapers merely changed their legally responsible editor and modified the name slightly. A leading opposition newspaper was *Aftonbladet*, Sweden's first modern newspaper, which used a series of different names including *Aftonbladet 11, Aftonbladet 12*, etc., up to *Aftonbladet 23*! Among the most prominent publicists of the period were the wealthy businessman Lars Johan Hierta, the founder of *Aftonbladet*, and Magnus Crusenstolpe. Initially a supporter of the king Crusenstolpe turned dramatically against him and spoke in Parliament as a member of the oppo-

sition, but he is best remembered as a vitriolic historical-political pamphleteer. When Crusenstolpe was charged with "seditious speech" against the king and sentenced to three years penal servitude, he was regarded as a martyr by the liberal opposition and riots broke out in Stockholm.

The circle surrounding Lars Johan Hierta nurtured the idea of creating so much trouble for the king that he would abdicate in favour of the "future", that is to say Crown Prince Oscar. In the 1840-41 parliament the opposition was strong and controlled by the burgher and the peasant Estates. It also succeeded in carrying the House of Nobility and thus gained the majority in the parliamentary committees. The

Council offered to resign, but initially their offer was rejected by the king. An important reform in the functions of the Councillors of State, known as the ministerial reform, was now undertaken. From now on the Cabinet was to consist of seven heads of ministries and three consultant members. In the long term, this gave the individual Councillor of State a stronger position. Eventually Karl Johan replaced several of his advisers with more independent individuals, but he didn't appoint them from the opposition. The latter nonetheless considered itself to have won a victory, and Parliament had indubitably demonstrated its power. The burgher Estate was increased by making representatives of industrial mills – at this time usually radical in their views – eligible for election.

Other attacks on the king failed, however, and various proposals for a reform of the rules of parliamentary representation came to nothing.

LIBERALISM ✺ Karl XIV Johan died in 1844 and was succeeded by his son Oscar. The mere existence of Oscar had indirectly influenced the election of his father as successor to the throne, since an heir was necessary. Oscar received a Swedish education and unlike his father soon learned Swedish.

Oscar had artistic talents and was also active as an author. Nowadays he is perhaps best remembered for his work *Om straff och straff-anstalter*, 1840 (*On Punishments and Prisons*, 1842), which was translated into a number of languages and in which he advocated modern penal practices.

His clashes with his father concerned politics. Oscar was a liberal. Particularly during the later parliaments of his father's reign, the opposition tried to exploit the crown prince, but outwardly Oscar always remained loyal to Karl Johan. He was biding his time.

The liberals had great expectations of the new king. Now the conservatives formed the opposition. Oscar had never actively opposed his father, but people sensed – or thought they sensed – his pro-reforming views. With his accession to the throne, the moment of truth had arrived! The work of getting the legislation drafted and passed was led by the prominent liberal Johan Gabriel Richert, and included such matters as equal inheritance rights for men and women. The hated power of suppression was removed from the Freedom of the Press Act soon after Oscar became king. The obligation for craftsmen to belong to a guild disappeared, as did the commercial monopoly of chartered towns. The payment of taxes was simplified. The king, who almost never drank alcohol, was also interested in the temperance movement, and at the parliament of 1853-54 home distillation was forbidden despite the lively protests of the peasant Estate.

In the political sphere Oscar disappointed the liberals. He was never willing to hand over the real power of government, even though he proceeded with greater caution than his father and bowed to parliamentary pressure if this proved necessary.

When riots broke out in Stockholm in March 1848 in the wake of the February Revolution in Paris, the troops intervened and at least 18 people were killed. After this experience, the king

In 1848, almost all the capitals of Europe were shaken by rebellion and massive demonstrations. The signal was given by the February revolution in Paris. There was great unrest in Stockholm in March, and the troops were sent in. In the picture "an inquisitive house-maid gets a bullet in her stomach". Drawing by F. von Dardel.

became more and more conservative, even though much practical reform work continued. The fate of parliamentary reform is typical. For many years now it had been discussed at each new parliament, since most people were well aware of the shortcomings of the old system with its four Estates, but after yet another proposal had been rejected in 1850-51, the government let the issue rest. A number of minor improvements were introduced, however. Parliament was to meet every three years and the burgher and peasant Estates had new categories of electors added to their ranks.

EMIGRATION AND GRADUAL INDUSTRIALIZATION ❧

The familiar, modern Sweden of the twentieth century now gradually began to take shape, but social inequalities were still enormous and the continued population growth was still not being absorbed by the industrial centres that were slowly forming or by the areas of new cultivation in the countryside. In the 1850s, emigration from Sweden got under way in earnest, and between 1850 and 1914 around one million Swedes emigrated, most of them to the USA. The decision of the parliament of 1853-54 to start building railways created one of the preconditions for the coming rise in production, and facilitated the movement of freight around the country. The Post Office was modernized with coach routes, with the introduction of postage stamps in 1855 and with the use of the railways a little later. The electric telegraph system was set up in 1853.

FOREIGN POLICY ❧

In relation to foreign policy, the king was even more a one-man ruler than he was in domestic matters. He was without question well acquainted with the issues and is generally considered by later historians to have handled them with skill. Scandinavianism grew in strength, and was given cautious encouragement by the new king. His words to a meeting of students from the Nordic countries in 1856 are well-known: "From now on, war between Scandinavian brothers is an impossibility." In many quarters there was talk of a new union under the Bernadotte dynasty, as King Frederik VII of Denmark was childless.

During the turbulent year of 1848, Scandinavianism was put to the test. The ethnic Germans living in the Danish provinces of Slesvig and Holstein rebelled against Denmark and were helped by Prussia. Sweden came to Denmark's assistance with a volunteer corps and a body of troops stationed on the island of Funen. But the diplomatic efforts being carried out were perhaps of greater significance, and they were given extra weight by a threatening Russian declaration against Prussia. The peace of 1849 failed to resolve the question of the duchies, however, and merely put it on hold.

The conflict that erupted in 1853 between Russia and Turkey came to involve other countries in the following year. England and France took Turkey's part and declared war on Russia and its absolute monarch, Nicholas I. The Crimean War is named for its principal theatre of war on the northern coast of the Black Sea.

Both Denmark and Sweden declared themselves neutral. This soured relations with the government in St Petersburg, which had previously been very satisfied with the Swedish contribution in the conflict between Denmark and Prussia. A reorientation of Swedish policy was about to take place. The liberal press in particular thought the time had come for Sweden to press back its traditional enemy, but the conservatives were more cautious.

The king pursued a policy of remarkable duplicity. His government officially adopted a

In massive waves of emigration between 1850 and 1914, almost a million Swedes left their homeland. Painting by G. Saloman entitled "Emigrants on their way to Gothenburg", 1868.

neutral stance, but during the summer of 1854 negotiations were taking place concerning an alliance with England and France, which had a fleet stationed in the Baltic. Once the important fortress of Bomarsund on the Åland islands had been destroyed, however, the allied fleet left Nordic waters, and from September 1854 the Crimea became the principal arena of battle. An alliance was now out of the question, since Oscar had no wish to confront Russia alone in the Baltic. During the war, in conditions of great secrecy, he wrote anonymous articles for publication in the western European press, including *The Times*. These were then taken up by a Swedish press that knew nothing of their origin. In these articles he stressed the importance of Sweden regaining Finland as a bulwark against Russia. In other words, Swedish neutrality was not the "sacred cow" it later came to be. Oscar was very cautious, however, and the sole result of his negotiations was the November treaty of 1855 with England and France, in which Sweden promised not to cede any territory to Russia or to make any other concessions. In return, Sweden and Norway would be given all possible help in any future conflict with the tsar. The negotiations concerning war preparations that were being carried out at the same time fizzled out, however, despite the visit of the French marshal Canrobert to Sweden and the enthusiastic reception he was given. Early the following year, Russia sued for peace, and negotiations led to the peace of Paris in 1856 that resulted in a minor gain for Sweden. The Åland islands were to be demilitarized, and no fortifications were to be permitted there. This obligation was taken over by Finland after the First World War and is still in force.

THE GOVERNMENT TAKES CHARGE

In 1857 illness made it impossible for Oscar I to perform his duties. Crown Prince Karl took his place as regent, and on his father's death in 1859 he succeeded to the throne as Karl XV.

Karl XV was unlike his father in almost every respect. He was extravert and had the common touch, and won a popularity that probably no other Swedish king has enjoyed. Despite his popularity, however, he failed completely in his attempts at asserting personal royal power. His government instead initiated the processes that were to lead to parliamentarism, and none of his successors were to be able to regain the influence wielded by Karl XIV Johan or Oscar I. This was not only due to the tide of liberalism, which would prove impossible to resist in the long run, but also to the king's lack of stamina and determination. As he rarely bothered to master the essentials of the complicated issues that arose, he was unable to counter the arguments of his advisers when they proposed measures for which he felt an instinctive repugnance.

REFORMS

Karl had already changed the composition of the Cabinet during the regency. His appointments included Louis De Geer as minister of state for justice, but he kept the landowner Johan August Gripenstedt as his minister of finance. The period of reform that now got under way was led by Councillors of State, principally De Geer and Gripenstedt, and not the king. Long before the post of prime

minister was introduced in 1876, De Geer was playing a prime minister's role. He and the Councillors of State constituted a ruling government, and the king was rarely able to assert his will against them.

Collaborating smoothly with Parliament and with the backing of the press, the moderately liberal Cabinet began to implement its programme. During the regency, the requirement for an unmarried woman to have a legal guardian was abolished, and an employer's right to inflict corporal punishment on employees was restricted to apply to minors only. The hated Conventicle Proclamation, by which private religious meetings were forbidden, was abolished despite the opposition of the clergy, and in 1860 the freedom of religion was extended to make it no longer a punishable offence to leave the state church. Local self-

government was introduced in 1862 for both urban and rural areas, and at the same time the county councils were instituted. The administration of the Church was also reorganized, so that civil and ecclesiastical local government became separated. In 1863, the ecclesiastical assembly was instituted, and after the parliamentary reform of 1866 this assembly replaced the clerical Estate as the forum for debating ecclesiastical affairs, although it had no powers of decision.

The work of modernizing the laws, which had been led by Richert (see p. 141) and resulted in a penal reform and less severe punishments, was continued energetically and presented in the early 1860s. Sweden obtained new maritime laws, new bankruptcy laws and a new penal code.

The 1842 law on elementary schools had only

The southern main line is inaugurated with royal pomp by Karl XV. *Ny Illustrerad Tidning*, January 1865.

The four Estates – depicted as a four-headed dragon – being fought by St George/Louis De Geer. The heads of the nobility and the clergy remain to be cut off. In the background the princess/Mother Svea. Cartoon, *Ny Illustrerad Tidning*, December 1865.

been observed in a desultory fashion. Now it was implemented with great energy.

The minister of finance – like so many of his successors a strong-willed individual – pushed through measures reflecting liberal principles in a number of spheres. The freedom to conduct business was extended further, a number of customs duties were reduced or abolished, including the duty on grain, a step that provoked great opposition in Parliament. The railways were further extended under the almost dictatorial leadership of colonel Nils Ericson, the brother of the famous inventor John Ericsson. Free trade was almost completely established.

Swedish military readiness was still in a state of neglect, despite certain efforts during the Crimean War. In this sphere the king showed a personal interest that he lacked in relation to other reforms. The parliament of 1861 presented proposals for reform which were worked into a government Bill. This was defeated during the parliament of 1865-66, to be sure, but

the defeat failed to remove the defence issue from the agenda – quite the opposite in fact, as it was to occupy successive Cabinets until the end of the century.

THE PARLIAMENTARY REFORM OF 1866

The question of reforming the antiquated system of a parliament of the Estates had long been a matter of urgency – it had been raised as early as 1809. At the parliament of 1859-60 the burgher and peasant Estates asked the government itself to prepare a Bill on the matter. In 1863, once the king's opposition had been overcome, De Geer presented a proposal for a new parliamentary organization and it was provisionally adopted by the Estates. The interval until the next parliament, due in 1865-66, was filled with an extremely lively public debate on the question, during which the conservatives tried to paint the proposals as a crime against historical development. From the left there were criticisms of the grading of the franchise as "plutocratic", since certain categories of voters would have more than one vote. The pressure of public opinion was growing rapidly, however, and men like Lars Johan Hierta and the celebrated author August Blanche, a key figure in early Swedish liberalism, formed part of a national committee that organized a great petition on behalf of the reform. The newspapers also made a significant contribution. No previous political question had aroused such popular interest in Sweden. The only later comparison is with the feverish months of 1917-18 when the universal franchise was pushed through Parliament. The Bill was rapidly approved by the peasant and burgher Estates, but the clergy waited to see how the nobility would vote. The magnificent debate in the House of Nobility took place on 4-7 December 1865, and the Bill was approved by 361 votes to 194. One of the reasons for its approval was the fact that the king himself supported the Bill. On the following day the clergy approved the new parliamentary order, which, with significant subsequent modifications, remained in force until 1971. The middle class and the rich peasants had won the day, and they were to dominate the second chamber of the new Parliament.

Parliament now consisted of two chambers.

The members of the first chamber were elected for nine years by the county councils and the largest towns and renewed successively by one-ninth annually. These electoral colleges were in their turn chosen on the basis of a fairly extensive municipal franchise, which was graded by income, however. In certain municipalities it was possible for a single individual to have more than half of the votes in the elections to the county council, but in the towns, a limit of 100 votes was soon introduced. To be eligible for election to the first chamber you had to be a man of at least 35 years of age, with an income

The nobility won a victory over itself when the proposal for a new parliamentary constitution was adopted. The people outside the House of Nobility were jubilant, with only a priest looking dubious. Drawing by the pseudonym Konrad, *Ny Illustrerad Tidning*, 7 December 1865.

of at least 4,000 kronor or a fortune of at least 80,000 kronor. These restrictions meant that not more than 7,000 men in the whole country were eligible.

The second chamber was elected directly. Those eligible to vote were men owning real estate valued at at least 1,000 kronor or leasing real estate worth at least 6,000 kronor, or who had a taxable income of at least 800 kronor. The voting age was 21, and elections were to be held at least every three years, later four. Since most workers earned less than 800 kronor a year, very few of them had the vote, whereas peasants usually did, as the qualifying limit for property was set so low. All in all just under 22 per cent of all men over 21 were now eligible to vote for the second chamber. Democracy was still far in the future.

More than half the members of the first two-chamber parliament, which met in 1867, had been members of the old parliament of the Estates. The first chamber was dominated by the nobility, but the peasantry had a strong position in the second chamber. Intractable financial problems confronted the members of the new Parliament, and the situation in the country was made worse by the bad harvest of 1867-68 and the subsequent famine. This was the last time barkbread (bread baked using ground bark to supplement scarce flour) was generally consumed in Sweden, and these years remained branded in the popular memory for a long time to come. Emigration increased markedly, and in 1869 almost 40,000 people left Sweden, most of them from rural areas.

Now there were real political parties in the Swedish parliament again for the first time since the Age of Freedom. The most important of these was the Rural Party, which had the majority in the second chamber between 1868 and 1887 and whose members were from the peasantry. They soon came into conflict with the "masters", a term used to refer not just to the old nobility but also to landowners, high officials, manufacturers, town dwellers and the intelligentsia. Since these "masters" had a crushing majority in the first chamber and not a few members in the second (the "Centre"), the work of Parliament was far from smooth. The chambers reached different decisions, which meant that government Bills and motions failed to pass. The wave of reforms ground to a halt and great issues like the reorganization and modernization of the armed forces, which was stubbornly linked by the peasants with the issue of the abolition of land taxes, came to be the subject of perpetual debate and brought down a number of governments.

The economy began to pick up from the early 1870s, and living conditions improved for many people, which meant that few radical currents emerged. The last government of Karl XV's reign was led by A. Adlercreutz – De Geer had resigned in 1870 – and was mainly composed of high public officials. It twice failed to assert its will in the question of defence, but nevertheless remained in office – parliamentarism had still not struck very deep roots in the public mind and least of all among the members of the government itself.

FOREIGN POLICY. THE BANKRUPTCY OF SCANDINAVIANISM ∾ Relations with Russia had been strained since the Crimean War of 1853-56, and were not improved by vigorous demonstrations in Sweden supporting Poland during the Polish rebellion against Russia in 1863. Karl XV himself had an emotional commitment to Scandinavianism, and was in addition a personal friend of the Danish king Frederik VII. Among the Great Powers, his preference lay with France. In 1861 he visited both Napoleon III and Queen Victoria, and spoke with leading politicians, who listened to his grandiose plans with some astonishment. The difficult question of the status of the Danish provinces of Slesvig and Holstein became acute after the Danish government accorded special status to Holstein in 1863. The German federal Parliament in Frankfurt threatened to occupy the duchy. In this situation Karl XV made bold promises to Denmark without the

knowledge of his ministers, which he was later unable to keep. In September 1863, a conference was organized, hosted by the king, and it became clear that the government didn't consider it feasible to help the Danes, since the Great Powers intended to remain neutral. In November 1863, the Danish government adopted a new constitutional law which was considered to conflict with previous agreements. Some days after this, Frederik VII died and was succeeded by his distant relative Christian IX of the house of Glücksburg, whose right of succession in Slesvig and Holstein was disputed.

War broke out in December, when federal German troops marched into Holstein, and in February 1864 Slesvig was attacked by Prussia and Austria, who were temporarily

Carl Jonas Love Almqvist (1793-1866). Painting by C. P. Mazer. No Swedish writer of the nineteenth century is able to match him for intellectual range or originality, except Strindberg. The novel *Sara Videbeck* (*Det går an*) created a sensation in 1839 when it was published –

and long afterwards – by polemicizing against marriage and for a woman's right to support herself. The picture is from a dramatization of the work at the Royal Dramatic Theatre in 1972. Almqvist's fate was tragic – he fled the country in 1851 under suspicion of forgery and attempting to poison a usurer.

in agreement on this question. Denmark had to fight alone – those Swedes who took part were volunteers.

The peace at the end of the summer compelled Denmark to cede Slesvig, Holstein and Lauenburg. It was not until after the Treaty of Versailles in 1919 that part of what was now Schleswig was returned to Denmark, with the new boundary following the language frontier. Karl XV's Nordic policy had failed, and Scandinavianism had not stood up to the test of reality. As it happened, De Geer's refusal to yield to the king's will was well justified, as it would have taken Sweden several months to mobilize even 20,000 troops, and their equipment was extremely antiquated.

During the remainder of his reign the king grew more and more hostile towards Germany, and in particular Prussia, which in 1871 had established the German Reich with Wilhelm I of Prussia as German emperor. On the whole, Swedish public opinion was francophile, too, and remained so during the Franco-Prussian war of 1870-71, but a reorientation was to take place during the 1870s. On the death of Karl XV in 1872, the foreign policy situation was not particularly auspicious. Relations with Sweden's powerful Baltic neighbours (Russia, Germany and Prussia) were poor, friendly France had been defeated and England was led by W. E. Gladstone, who detested becoming involved in Continental affairs.

MONETARY POLICY ∽ The 1860s and 1870s were the years in which Sweden prepared itself for industrialism. The banking and credit systems gradually expanded, the savings bank movement was extended, commercial banks increased their capital, railways were established and foreign capital began to show an interest in Sweden. The great financial dynasties which came to dominate Swedish economic life were founded by such people as A. O. Wallenberg, who established and led *Stockholms Enskilda Bank*. But at the same time, wages remained low, emigration accelerated and the overcrowded living conditions in the towns, and especially in Stockholm, were atrocious.

I INDUSTRIALIZATION AND SLOW PROGRESS

A NEW KING AND THE GOLD STANDARD ∿ Karl XV's brother and successor, Oscar II, was a stickler for tradition and, despite some grumbling about extravagance from certain quarters, had himself and Queen Sofia crowned in 1873, first in Stockholm Cathedral and then in Trondheim. He is the last Swedish king to have undergone this ceremony. There was no question of any return to a personal exercise of royal power, however, and the king respected popular opinion as expressed in Parliament and mainly occupied himself with performing a mediating role. At the same time he was opposed to the parliamentary rule he was compelled to apply in practice. Recent research has shown unequivocally that Oscar II exerted no decisive influence on developments in Sweden, not even in the sphere of foreign policy to which he devoted a lot of attention. He often appeared irresolute, which gave an opening to the will of others, including the less con-

servative queen, whose ideas on child-rearing and other matters were put into practice and who gained a certain degree of political influence.

Oscar II took over his brother's Cabinet. The reforms carried out by this government and Parliament included the adoption of the gold standard in 1873, along with the *krona* as the unit of currency, and the creation of a Scandinavian currency union. The king backed the government in a new attempt to solve the defence question, but his support made little difference and the attempt failed. In 1875, Louis De Geer returned to government and formed a new Cabinet with a view to obtaining smoother cooperation with Parliament. He had a free hand in the selection of his ministers, a harbinger of parliamentary democracy. An amendment to the Constitution in 1876 introduced the post of prime minister, to which De Geer was duly appointed.

Sawmill workers and a marking-girl. Child labour was long used in the sawmills. Photo from the 1890s.

PARLIAMENT AND THE MILITARY QUESTION

ண The initial antagonism between the first and second chambers of Parliament had not diminished. The "Upper House" was still dominated by landowners, nobles and many business magnates. A fundamentally conservative attitude was combined with a certain readiness for reform in relation to defence, taxation and cultural affairs. The second chamber was controlled by the Rural Party, which was dominated by peasant farmers. This party included in its programme demands for the repeal of the land taxes and an equal sharing of the costs of the Distributive System by all citizens. In addition it was adamantly thrifty and rejected many proposals for reform because they were considered too expensive. The loose grouping known as the Centre was far too fragmented to have any real influence, and a number of members of Parliament refused to associate themselves with any of the parties.

In 1880, De Geer attempted to initiate a solution of the defence question by way of a partial reform relating to a new method of military conscription, but the proposal was defeated in Parliament as usual, inducing De Geer to tender his resignation. It was not until 1885 that partial reforms of defence and the land taxes succeeded in gaining the approval of Parliament. Twelve year-groups were now eligible for military service and the period of training was raised to 42 days. At the same time, 30 per cent of the land taxes were repealed and central government assumed responsibility for the corresponding amount previously paid by the peasantry for the Distributive System.

FINANCIAL CRISIS AND PROTECTIONISM

ண Towards the end of the 1870s, the economic boom ended and the corn trade was hit by a crisis. American, and to a certain extent Russian, exports of grain, in conjunction with more efficient means of transportation, caused prices to fall dramatically. The recession also affected the saw mills and wages were cut by 20 per cent, a step that provoked the first great labour stoppage in Sweden, the saw-mill workers' strike of 1879 in the town of Sundsvall in which 4,000 men took part. At the time, those in power regarded a strike as a violation of the rule of law, and troops were sent in to force the strikers back to work. The working class was defeated, but had learned an important lesson – it had to get organized.

During the 1880s, the crisis led to sharp disputes between free traders and protectionists,

who were calling for protective tariffs. England stood by its liberal system of trade and the result was a new flight from the countryside, as grain producers were unable to compete with duty-free imports. A corollary of this was a further expansion of industry, however, as it was able to turn an influx of cheap labour-power to its advantage. Germany and France opted for protectionism, while Denmark changed the orientation of its agricultural production and began to export pork, eggs and butter.

Emigration from Sweden increased because it was not possible to carry out any large-scale restructuring of agriculture. Bread became cheaper, and from this time on almost everybody was able to afford to eat bread made from wheat as part of their everyday diet. Motions were submitted to Parliament for the introduc-

tion of corn tariffs. There were, of course, two sides to this question. The steadily growing, unenfranchised industrial working population of the towns naturally wanted cheap bread, and the free traders in the press wrote of "starvation tariffs", while most farmers saw their standard of living falling and joined forces with the manufacturers. In the autumn of 1887, the protectionists obtained a majority and a relatively moderate system of protective tariffs was introduced.

The Rural Party was now decisively split. The free traders became the "Old Rural Party", which glided more and more to the left, whereas the opponents of free trade, including the landowner Emil Gustaf Boström, formed the "New Rural Party" which gradually developed in a conservative direction. Towards the end of

In its early years in the nineteenth century, the sawmill and paper industry was often responsible for a regime of reckless profiteering, frequently cheating the peasants of Norrland into selling their timber at giveaway prices and ruthlessly exploiting its workers. This led to the first modern strike in Swedish history, by the sawmill workers of Sundsvall in 1879. The picture shows the Strömnäs sawmill ca 1910.

the 1880s it is possible to speak of the beginnings of a division between "right" and "left" in Parliament. A modern political consciousness was stirring.

State revenues increased as a result of the new tariffs, and Oscar II made a statement for the records of the Council of State in which he recommended that the money should be used for tax relief and to help the poor by introducing an old age insurance scheme. His declaration had no immediate effect, however.

Military reform and the franchise

In 1891, the above-mentioned E. G. Boström became prime minister, after having moderated his once fanatical protectionism. He would prove to be a man capable of manoeuvring Parliament in any direction he wished. Granted, he relied for his support on pro-tariff groups who had a majority if they voted together, but he was skilled at playing the parties off against one another or getting them to vote across party lines. In addition, he enjoyed the confidence of the king more than any other politician. The prime minister now took up the whole complex issue of military reform and the land taxes, and in 1892 a new army organization was finally adopted. Military service was extended to all men between 21 and 40 years of age and the training period was set at 90 days. The Distributive System was retained for a time as the core of the army, but its costs were gradually assumed by central government over a period of twelve years. During the same period the land taxes were to be abolished, and with them the last reminders of Sweden's traditional subsistence farming disappeared.

After his victory in Parliament Boström's position was very strong. Oscar II came to repose great trust in his prime minister. This hastened constitutional developments, as many matters could now be decided without the king trying to influence the result.

At this time the question of the franchise was assuming greater urgency, and many voices were demanding reform. The previous decade had seen the start of popular agitation for the universal franchise on the part of both Liberals and the Social-Democratic Party, which had been founded in 1889 and was led by Hjalmar Branting. The National Association for the Universal Franchise was founded in 1890 and compulsory general military service gave rise to the slogan "one man, one rifle, one vote". Parliament remained cool to the idea, however, and developed along conservative rather than radical lines.

The reforms accomplished by Boström included the Bank Act of 1897, which gave the Bank of Sweden the exclusive right to issue banknotes. The government obtained the right of appointing the chairman of the Board of Governors of the Bank of Sweden, a right it retained until 1989. The whole of this period was characterized by long-submerged social, political and economic problems rising to the surface – workers developed political awareness and demanded the transformation of society in a radical programme, and many Liberals moved leftwards, without going so far as to demand socialism, however. Inspiration came from developments in Europe and from the breakthrough of parliamentary rule in the more democratically managed Norway, which

A peasant-farmer's family around the porridge dish. The bread is sliced and every head is bowed in prayer. Photo from the village of Västra Klagstorp in Skåne, 1902.

Oscar II had been compelled to accept. Conservative currents were also strong, however, as is reflected in the literature of the 1890s, and the right was heavily influenced by foreign examples, particularly Germany, where Bismarck had developed social legislation as a way of calming the radical opposition. More and more people supported popular grassroots movements based on issues like temperance and non-conformist religious practice, and before very long their influence was making itself felt in Swedish politics.

Emigration from Sweden continued undiminished and in some years totalled more than 50,000 people. Contemporary theories that the exodus was due to a fear of conscription and a loathing of those in power scarcely hold water, as the main reasons were economic in nature.

This is clear from the fall in emigration in the late 1890s, which saw better times and brought notable economic progress. Not a few emigrants returned home and played an important part in reshaping Sweden. Real wages began to improve and practically doubled during the reign of Oscar II – although it should not be forgotten that the starting point was fearfully low.

Boström resigned in the autumn of 1900, due in part to the Norwegian question, and was succeeded by admiral Fredrik von Otter, a member of Parliament. His government carried out the great military reform of 1901, whose passage through Parliament was far from smooth. The Distributive System was finally phased out by natural attrition and was replaced by universal military service of 240 days for the infantry and twelve months for other branches of the armed forces.

The attempts at linking these military reforms with the question of the franchise, on the other hand failed. A new government Bill on the matter was rejected in the following year. In 1902, Boström formed his second Cabinet and included a number of ministers from the centre and right of the Liberal Party. Demands for universal franchise became louder throughout the country, demonstrations were held and a three-day general strike was proclaimed. The new proposals of the government were defeated in both 1904 and 1905. Boström, who had to wrestle with the Norwegian question at the same time, resigned in 1905. A short-lived caretaker Cabinet was succeeded by what has been called Sweden's first parliamentary government, led by a right-wing conservative from the first chamber, Christian Lundeberg. This was soon followed by a Liberal Cabinet. The king had played no active part in the change of government, but this was far from representing a final acceptance of parliamentary government on the part of the monarchy – that would only come in 1917.

A NEW FOREIGN POLICY ∾ After the Franco-Prussian war of 1870-71, the traditional orientation towards France that Sweden had had since the seventeenth century had begun to change. After the Danish war of 1863-64, relations with the German Empire long remained cool, but both the king and political leaders thought that Sweden should break out of its isolation. In the spring of 1875, Oscar II paid an official visit to Berlin to visit the old emperor Wilhelm I and had several conversations with Bismarck. In the summer, he travelled to St Petersburg and met tsar Alexander II. There was a certain amount of criticism of this in the press, but the king and his foreign minister continued to follow the path they had mapped out and drew closer to Germany. This began to have an effect not just in the armed forces, which were more and more following the example set by the admired German military machine, but also in the world of business and in education, where German took the place of French as the most important foreign language. When Crown Prince Gustaf married Viktoria of Baden, a granddaughter of the German emperor, in 1881, the royal house also found itself with closer ties to Sweden's powerful southern neighbour. Before the First World War, the monarchs of Sweden and Germany paid many visits to each other, both official and unofficial. Despite trips to both England and France, these countries remained less important. When Prince Gustaf (VI) Adolf became engaged to an English princess in 1905, such a dynastic alliance no longer had any political impact. Official relations with Russia were good, but were distorted during the 1890s by the Russification of Finland and later by the fear of espionage entertained by right-wing groups.

In 1844, the single Union flag of Sweden and Norway was replaced by separate flags with a common Union emblem (the Norwegian flag below).

NORWAY'S SECESSION FROM THE UNION

The Union with Norway was the major foreign policy issue of Oscar II's reign. He did his level best to put an end to the innumerable disputes between the nations and the causes underlying them, but failed miserably. His measures were regarded with suspicion in Norway – and sometimes in Sweden, too – and all the while Norwegian left Liberals were actively working for the dissolution of the Union. In the 1880s the veto controversy erupted in relation to the king's right to veto decisions taken by the Norwegian parliament, the Storting. In 1884, the right-wing Cabinet of Stang was forced to resign, and Oscar had to accept a new government under the left Liberal Johan Sverdrup, a step which marked the introduction of parliamentary democracy in Norway. After this year, no viceroy was appointed, and the post was formally abolished in 1891.

The next conflict was about Norway's desire to have its own representatives abroad. A law authorizing a system of its own consulates for Norway was passed by the Storting in 1892, but the king refused to approve it. The following years were very trying, with demonstrations on the part of the Storting using such measures as reduced budgetary allocations. In 1898, a committee for the revision of the Union presented four proposals (which were mutually incompatible) and in the same year the Storting removed the Union emblem of 1844 from the Norwegian merchant flag, creating what became known as the "clean flag". In 1903, the last Union Committee recommended separate consular systems for Sweden and Norway, but the Hagerup Cabinet, which had only recently come into office, was unable to find any common ground with Boström in Stockholm. Negotiations were broken off in February 1905, and the Storting appointed a committee with representatives from all the parliamentary parties. Hagerup resigned and was replaced by Christian Michelsen, who worked very energetically for the immediate introduction of an independent Norwegian consular system.

During the spring, Crown Prince Gustaf, who was regent in 1905 during Oscar II's illness, made a final attempt at initiating serious negotiations, but reached the conclusion that the Union was beyond rescue. When the Storting's decision to establish a separate consular system was presented to the king to be signed into law, he refused to approve it. Michelsen's government resigned immediately and the king was forced to concede that he could find nobody to form a new Cabinet. The Storting now took the crucial step of declaring that the royal power was no longer effective and that as a result the Union with Sweden had ceased to exist. In international law this was actually an untenable measure, and the decision aroused great bitterness in Sweden, particularly in chauvinist circles. Both the king and the crown prince desired a peaceful resolution, however, and in the summer of 1905 an extraordinary session of Parliament presented a report that conceded the dissolution of the Union on certain conditions. Negotiations were begun in Karlstad, on Lake Vänern, but before they got under way a plebiscite on the question that had been demanded by the Swedes showed that almost 100 per cent of Norwegian voters supported the decision of their parliament.

The Conventions of Karlstad of September 1905 stipulated steps like the abolition of border fortresses, the setting up of a neutral zone, and the regulation of the reindeer pasture for the nomadic Sami. The agreement was approved by the Swedish and Norwegian parliaments and then Oscar II officially abdicated his Norwegian crown. He rejected a Norwegian proposal that his younger son Prince Carl should become the king of Norway. After a plebiscite had shown that a great majority was in favour of retaining the monarchy, the Storting elected a younger son of Crown Prince Frederik (VIII) of Denmark. At the end of October 1905 he came to Norway, changed his name from Carl to Haakon VII. The end of the Union marked the end of what became known as the Oscarian age in Sweden. With the Union question resolved, Swedish life over the next fifteen years would be dominated by issues concerning the armed forces and the implementation of parliamentary democracy and the universal franchise.

Preparing for parliamentary democracy ⮯ In the autumn of 1905, elections to the second chamber produced a left-wing majority, and the liberal lawyer Karl Staaff formed his first Cabinet. Staaff was a convinced supporter of the English parliamentary system of the House of Commons. He was an energetic and skilful party leader, but had an authoritarian style and lacked flexibility. His government remained in office until 1906, when it was defeated in relation to the long-drawn-out struggle for the franchise. The right-wing, led by Arvid Lindman, took over and managed to pass a programme of reforms through Parliament. The Reform Bill finally became law in 1909. The process of democratization took a great step forward. The graded franchise was admittedly retained in local elections, but nobody was allowed more than 40 votes. In elections to the second chamber all men above the age of 24 obtained the vote, and elections became proportional.

When Oscar II died in 1907, Gustaf V succeeded him. During his last two years as crown prince, he had been the real king, due to his father's illness. Thus Gustaf V was well prepared for his occupation. He fully realized the restricted potential of a monarch in the twentieth century, but was not prepared to accept all the consequences of the new order.

Reforms and the military question

∾ Both Staaff's short-lived government at the end of Oscar II's reign and Lindman's government (up to 1911) carried through significant reforms in the fields of public management, administration and legislation. On the other hand, however, there was considerable unrest in the labour market, where the trade union movement had grown in strength. It found itself confronted by the Employers' Federation. In the summer of 1909 a general strike broke out. The strike funds ran dry after a month or two, and the trade union movement was subsequently more cautious. It was never again to attempt a lengthy and ruinous strike of this kind.

The years immediately preceding 1914 were turbulent throughout Europe. The Great Powers were arming and a number of minor wars

took place. Russian spies were feared in "little" Sweden. Despite the Baltic treaties and other agreements it was considered necessary to speed up the re-equipping of the armed forces, but the left objected to this. In the autumn of 1911, the first elections to the second chamber to be held on the basis of universal suffrage for men took place. Under Staaff's leadership the Liberals mounted a powerful campaign. Their programme included parliamentary democracy, a reduction in armaments and a solution to the temperance question, possibly by way of a prohibition on strong spirits. Left of the Liberals were the Social-Democrats. The elections of 1911 resulted in defeat for the right-wing, success for the workers' party and no change for the Liberals. In October 1911, Karl Staaff formed his second government and prepared for democratic parliamentary rule and the democratization of Sweden.

In Parliament, the government succeeded in postponing the building of a battleship. Pro-military forces in the country took the initiative in a large-scale fundraising drive to obtain the necessary finance by voluntary means. The sums collected grew very rapidly and soon amounted to more than the actual cost of the battleship. The government was less than enthusiastic about this. New military commissions reached the conclusion, however, that the situation required stronger defences. Meanwhile, the government continued to implement its reform programme, including Sweden's first

FÖRSVARET·FRÄMST

A poster for the elections of 1914, in which the Right points to the threat from abroad and agitates for a strong national defence.

Gustaf V addressing the Farmers' Rally in the inner courtyard of the royal palace in 1914. Beside him are members of the royal family. This was the last occasion on which a Swedish monarch acted against the wishes of the government. Inset, a memorial plate commemorating the Farmers' Rally.

the so-called Farmers' Rally. On 6 February, 30,000 peasant farmers came to Stockholm from around the country and presented both the king and the prime minister with demands that the armed forces should be strengthened immediately. Gustaf V took the opportunity to deliver what became known as the Courtyard Speech – most of which had been written by the famous explorer, Sven Hedin – at the royal palace. In the speech he came out against his own government and declared that in his view the military question should be resolved "at once and comprehensively". On 10 February the government resigned.

After the king had failed to persuade the Right to form a minority government, he gave the task to the county governor Hjalmar Hammarskjöld, whose Cabinet was mainly made up of senior public officials. The government immediately called new elections, and an embittered campaign followed, in which there were offensive personal attacks on Staaff. Seventy per cent of those eligible to vote took part, which was a very high proportion for the time. Admittedly, the right now made gains, and the Liberals lost ground, but together with the relatively successful Social-Democratic Party the left still retained its majority. It appeared to be impossible for the government to get its Defence Bill adopted in the summer of 1914, but at that moment the First World War broke out and saved both the king and the Hammarskjöld government. Domestic disputes were immediately put on the back burner.

The growth of swedish industry ∞

The transformation of Sweden from an agri-

law on a universal retirement pension (which was far from providing everybody with a minimum subsistence income, however).

In the autumn of 1913, the military question provoked a crisis. The king found it difficult to cooperate with Staaff, and the conflicts between them now grew more inflamed. In the early months of 1914, a lively campaign of extra-parliamentary agitation was conducted throughout the country, and eventually led to cultural country to a modern industrial nation accelerated dramatically in the last few decades of the nineteenth century. At the beginning of this period, the process of industrialization had gone much further in England and most of the powers of continental Europe than in Sweden. Three-quarters of Sweden's population were still dependent on agriculture for their subsistence in the 1860s, and many of them lived in great poverty – only some fifty per cent were peasant farmers who owned their own land. The ongoing "flight from the countryside" provided labour-power for industry and was the most important single reason for the large-scale emigration that took place in the nineteenth and early twentieth centuries, mainly to North America. By the outbreak of the First World War, the agricultural population had diminished markedly, to just half of the total population of the country, and the process has continued ever since, with the corresponding figure today being less than 3 per cent. The international economic boom in the final decades of the nineteenth century led to a huge demand for exports from which the Swedish timber industry benefited enormously. Many new sawmills were established, especially along the coast of Norrland, and the forests were plundered so recklessly that in 1903 Parliament felt compelled to pass legislation for their proper care and conservation.

The iron and steel industry also boomed in the final decades of the nineteenth century thanks to the introduction of new methods such as the bessemer, martin and thomas processes, which produced steel of excellent quality for which there was an insatiable demand on foreign markets. Old, small-scale works were forced to close down, one after the other, and were replaced by large, powerfully capitalized companies. More than a third of Swedish iron and steel went for export at the turn of the century. Important Swedish inventions had a great impact on the expansion of the engineering industry. The centrifugal separator, designed by Gustaf de Laval, and the many inventions of Gustaf Dalén, including the acetylene lamp and the sun valve (the Aga beacon), gave rise to great industrial enterprises, as did L. M. Ericsson's improved telephone technology. Sven Wingquist's ball bearings were another world-famous product that gave rise to the giant SKF company. Safety matches were invented in Sweden, and dynamite was invented by Alfred Nobel, who left his fortune to a foundation which was to distribute its earnings in the form of annual awards to those who had "made the greatest contribution to humanity" in a number of fields. It is probable that the Nobel Prizes more than any other single factor have helped establish Sweden's current international reputation.

Electricity was introduced at the end of the nineteenth century and slowly began to replace kerosene and gas for lighting purposes, and eventually

Like many other ingenious Swedish ideas, the separator, invented by Gustaf de Laval, was to prove of decisive significance for the development of industry in the country. A poster shows the ease with which cream is separated from the milk. Almost every peasant-farmer in the country bought a separator – but large-scale dairies were soon to make many of them redundant!

The products of the match factory in Jönköping made Sweden internationally known in the nineteenth century. For many years they ranked among Sweden's leading exports. Inset, matchbox labels for the world market.

coal too as a fuel. Europe's first electric railway was opened in Sweden in 1895 in Djursholm, a suburb of Stockholm, and hydroelectric power came into more and more general use. The railway system was extended with extreme rapidity. New land was still being brought under cultivation, and the area of land under the plough peaked just before and during the Second World War. The introduction of agricultural machinery further contributed to the ongoing reduction in the rural population.

From Karl XV's accession to the throne in 1859 to the First World War, the proportion of industrial workers in the population increased from nine to more than thirty per cent. The rural population moved into the towns, whose share of the population rose from ten to almost twenty-five per cent in the same period. The

population of the capital, Stockholm, almost tripled to some 275,000 people.

LIVING STANDARDS ∾ During the greater part of the nineteenth century Sweden developed slowly, and industrialization only gathered speed in the last few decades. The nation was one of the poorest in Europe, with poor public hygiene – for a long time Stockholm was one of the filthiest capitals of Europe – and a huge gulf between the few rich people and the rural and urban poor, who owned nothing at all. Craftsmen and peasant farmers were never far from starvation, either, and poor harvests affected them catastrophically. The loss of Finland in 1809 had reduced both the territory and the population of Sweden, turning it into a minor nation, and the Union which was forced upon Norway in 1814 completely failed to compensate for this development.

After the loss of Finland, Sweden remained a peasant nation, even though the urban population was slowly growing due to the migration of the landless poor to the towns. As late as the 1860s, three-quarters of all Swedes lived by agriculture or related occupations (particularly forestry). In most places, the traditional villages had been blown apart by the land reforms of the late eighteenth and early nineteenth centuries, with the farms moving away from the village centres to be closer to their now unified fields. The three factors of progress named by the author Esias Tegnér – "peace, the [small-pox] vaccine, and the potato" – had contributed to a rapid growth in the number of Swedes who lived beyond early childhood, but the families of peasant farmers who owned their own land only made up some half of the rural population. Although agriculture was modernized using such techniques as the scientific cultivation of pasture-land with fodder crops, pipe-drainage, artificial fertilizers and new breeds of cattle, and this increased the production of food, it was still insufficient to feed the growing population, and initially there were not enough jobs in the emerging industrial centres for the people who had moved there from the countryside, either. One of the solutions which provided a safety-valve in this situation was large-scale emigration to North America.

For many centuries the growth of the largest towns had been dependent on migration. Mortality rates were high, due mainly to inadequate public hygiene and almost unimaginable overcrowding. Cholera was a recurrent terror, with the most devastating epidemic taking place in 1834. From the 1860s onwards, drains became common, and water-pipes followed soon afterwards. These improvements, in conjunction with the advances of medical science, reduced mortality rates, although the national scourge of tuberculosis remained a mass killer until well into the twentieth century, particularly in the poor rural north. The middle classes – primarily urban business and professional groups – made up a growing proportion of the population. Living standards gradually improved, although they were exceedingly low to start with. Child mortality fell continuously and average life expectancy rose.

A large proportion of the population eked out a very meagre living until well into the twentieth century. Photo of a farming family in Uppland, 1924.

The greatest problems were faced by the poorest layers of the population. Their predicament was made worse by the laws against vagrancy. After the war of 1809, more than ten per cent of Stockholm's population was living on poor relief. With the Poor Relief Ordinance of 1847, Sweden finally obtained uniform national legislation covering all those who were incapable of working. After the catastrophic harvest of 1868 (the last "bark-bread" year), a new ordinance was enacted, which made things worse for those unable to keep themselves – maintenance was set as low as possible as the general rule, and the right of appeal was abolished. It would not be until 1918 that a new Poor Law would mark the first (small) step towards a modern welfare state.

THE POPULAR MASS MOVEMENTS ∾ The nineteenth century saw the rise of the great popular mass movements which were to have such an impact on the shape of modern Sweden. The free churches formed the oldest of these movements. These non-conformist organizations were long opposed by the Church of Sweden and the authorities, who justified their hostility by referring to the Conventicle Proclamation forbidding private religious meetings unless they were organized by the state church. Some of these movements remained within the state church, however, as was the case with the severe northern sect of Læstadianism, named after Lars Levi Læstadius, a vicar in Norrland, whereas Baptists, Pietists and the later Pentecostal movement preferred to stay outside. The Dissenters Act of 1873 made it possible to leave the state church, but by then the Conventicle Proclamation was already a dead letter. A contributory factor in the earliest emigration to America was the desire to exercise religion without the interference of the authorities.

There is nothing quintessentially Swedish about alcoholism, but at times it reached epidemic proportions in the country, culminating in quite immoderate levels of consumption of akvavit at the end of the eighteenth and during much of the nineteenth century. Sweden had an annual consumption of forty to fifty litres of akvavit per person. In the nineteenth century, the correlation between drunkenness and crimes of violence was already established. Concern at the effects of such high levels of alcohol consumption led to the rise of the temperance movement. The imposition of high charges brought the end of home-distilling in the 1850s, and the practice was later forbidden completely. The Order of Good Templars and the Swedish Blue Ribbon Society (a free church organization) were founded and became increasingly influential. People were attracted to the organizations by the lodges, the hierarchical setup with its various ranks, the impressive ceremonial rites and (innocent) amusements.

The popular sports movements should not be forgotten in this connection. Sport became the biggest popular movement of all. It originated in the nineteenth century with the "father of Swedish gymnastics" Per Henrik Ling. Sport in the modern sense came to Sweden later, in the 1880s, and was strongly influenced by British models. Associations were set up with both summer and winter sports on their programmes. The Swedish Sports Confederation

A painting by Hildur Hult-Wåhlin, entitled "Agitation", 1899. Towards the end of the nineteenth century, employers tried to prevent the spread of socialism among the workers. Enthusiastic agitators won the ear of the workers, however, and the first trade unions were formed.

was founded in 1903. Sweden participated in the modern Olympic Games from the very start and actually arranged the Games in 1912.

THE LABOUR MOVEMENT ❧ Changes in agriculture and industrialization led to many people who had no property of their own being absorbed in the new labour market – in the timber and manufacturing industries, food factories, mines, shipyards and many other sectors, where Swedish inventions had been a major factor in creating work. The working class appeared on the scene, but this "fifth estate", which had had no representation in the old parliament of the Estates, also lacked representation in the new system, since generally speaking the income restrictions limited the franchise to

bourgeois groups such as businessmen and professionals or peasants who owned their own farms (and of these only the men, of course). Gradually the first tentative steps towards organization were taken, in the form of trade unions, the earliest of which were liberal in character. The great sawmill strike of 1879 in Sundsvall served to rouse the class. Two years later, workers in Stockholm and Skåne formed trade unions in the modern sense. At the same time August Palm, a tailor, had returned to Sweden from Germany and initiated a campaign of popular, socialist agitation. Newspapers were founded with the universal franchise on their programme. An individual who came to be more important than Palm was Hjalmar Branting, who despite his bourgeois background be-

8 TIMMARS ARBETE
8 TIMMARS FRIHE
8 TIMMARS HVI

The May Day demonstration became an important tradition in the labour movement – the first nation-wide demonstration took place in 1890. The picture shows May Day in Sundsvall. The main demand was still for the 8-hour day.

came a convinced socialist of the reformist persuasion, that is to say he did not advocate revolution. The Swedish Social-Democratic Party, the first political party in the country in the modern sense, was founded in 1889, with Branting as its leader. Much later he would become Sweden's first Social-Democratic prime minister. In a few decades the Social-Democrats grew to be Sweden's largest political party, which they have remained despite a certain decline in support since their peak. The party adopted a programme demanding the eight-hour day, the right to hold demonstrations, minimum wages, compulsory retirement insurance, compensa-

tory damages for accidents at work, arbitration in labour disputes, the prohibition of undue violence against strikes and a republic. All the demands in this programme except the last have been met. In 1898, the trade unions joined forces to form the Swedish Trade Union Confederation (LO). At the time there were 60,000 unionized workers in Sweden – today there are over two million. LO helped workers when they were refused the right of forming associations or in the event of such actions as lock-outs or wage cuts. Some years later, in 1902, a corresponding organization for employers, the Swedish Employers' Confederation (SAF), was founded, which would have a central role in such matters as wage negotiations.

THE WOMEN'S MOVEMENT ❧ The growth of industrialism together with the need for labour in such occupations as elementary school teachers, telegraphists and telephonists had brought women into gainful employment, although their wages were always lower than the men's, of course. This did not just affect the working class – where it was rarely possible to support a family on a single (male) wage – but also women from other social groups who found themselves working in education, the care sector or in offices. It also became possible for women to pursue higher education (from the 1870s) or to obtain positions in the civil service.

Among the pioneers of the women's movement in Sweden the most prominent, and the first, was Fredrika Bremer. Her weapon was the pen. In her famous novel, *Hertha* (1856), she argues for the right of single women to be given responsibility for managing their own affairs. Soon afterwards, this right was passed into law. She also travelled widely and in one of her books reported on a trip to the "New World" of America.

Organizations like the Fredrika Bremer Society, which still exists, put forward demands for equality with men. This period, too, saw the beginnings of the struggle for female suffrage, which was met by a torrent of abuse and scorn from innumerable vocal defenders of vested male interests. A special association with female suffrage on its programme was founded in 1903, but women did not actually get the vote

until after the First World War. Two of the most prominent figures in the struggle for women's rights at the turn of the century were Ellen Key and Anna Whitlock.

THE FIRST WORLD WAR AND THE VICTORY OF PARLIAMENTARY DEMOCRACY ❧ At the outbreak of the First World War on 1 August 1914, church bells were rung throughout Sweden to summon both regular soldiers and the veteran reserve to duty, a party truce was agreed and Sweden declared itself neutral. The Hammarskjöld Cabinet was able to settle in comfortably for a long period of government.

Fredrika Bremer (1801-65), who pioneered the movement for women's emancipation in Sweden. After her death, the vigorous and influential Fredrika Bremer Society was formed. Inset, the title page of the society's journal *Hertha*, named after Fredrika Bremer's best-known novel.

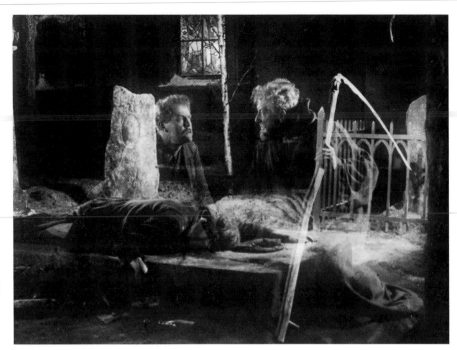

Selma Lagerlöf (1858-1940), who won the Nobel Prize for Literature in 1909, became an internationally renowned author. Her dramatic novel, *Thy Soul shall Bear Witness (Körkarlen)*, 1912, was soon made into a film. This still is from Victor Sjöström's 1921 classic. After modest beginnings in 1897, motion pictures soon swept the world.

Denmark and Norway were also able to keep out of the fighting, and the cooperation that was now initiated between the Scandinavian states was first expressed in the meeting of the three kings in Malmö in December 1914. Three years later a second meeting took place in Kristiania (now Oslo) and assumed the character of a reconciliation between fraternal nations.

The government faced no great problems in the early years of the war. The Swedish bourgeoisie of the time generally favoured Germany, an attitude encouraged by the widespread chauvinist view of Russia as Sweden's traditional enemy. Liberals and Social-Democrats advocated a regime of strict neutrality. In the royal family, Queen Viktoria, who had been born in Baden, openly supported the Germans, while the crown prince and his consort Mar-

garet, who was from Great Britain, found it natural to support the English. King Gustaf sympathized with the Central Powers Germany and Austria-Hungary, but in public he maintained an attitude of neutrality. As during the Union crisis and later during the Second World War, he worked hard to keep Sweden out of the conflicts that were raging in the world beyond its borders.

The trade blockades maintained by the belligerents caused great problems, however. In retrospect it is possible to argue that the neutrality observed by the Hammarskjöld government was more advantageous to Germany than to the Entente countries of Britain and France. The embargo and the import difficulties it created led to severe shortages of food and other essentials in Sweden, but a Committee of Supply was not set up until 1916, with rationing being introduced in early 1917. By then, however, the lack of food was acute. Rich people had hoarded large stocks and unscrupulous small traders suddenly became rich by dealing in desirable goods in short supply. Prices rose sharply and were accompanied by mounting discontent. Attacks on the government gave rise to a number of prosecutions and prison sentences.

All the discontent focused on Hammarskjöld, who was mocked with the nickname "Hunger-skjöld". The news of the fall of the tsar in Russia in March 1917 and the proclamation of a republic there contributed to clashes between the left-wing and right-wing par-

ties. The party truce was over and Hammarskjöld's Cabinet resigned. The new right-wing Cabinet that replaced it was mainly made up of civil servants, with the exception of the prime minister Carl Swartz and the foreign minister Arvid Lindman. The government was weak, as the Liberals and the Social-Democrats joined forces against it. During the spring, the government was faced by generalized opposition. There were louder and louder demands for a revision of the Constitution. In June, violent demonstrations took place in Stockholm. In the midst of this unrest, a rationing system for wines and spirits was introduced for reasons which had nothing to do with ideals of temperance. This "Bratt system", with its noto-

On 5 June 1917, Parliament debated a revision of the Constitution. Violent demonstrations took place outside. In the picture, Hjalmar Branting is seen, stick in hand, calming the demonstrators. A resolution was finally adopted and the debate was concluded peacefully – the rebellious crowd neither breaking into Parliament nor getting beaten up outside.

rious ration book, was finally abolished in 1955.

In the elections to the second chamber in September 1917, the Right lost support, with the Liberals polling more votes than them and the Social-Democrats becoming the largest party. A new party, the Agrarian Party, entered Parliament, as did a left-wing socialist party (later to become the Communist Party, now the Left Party), formed by a faction of the Social-Democrats who split on questions of the war and the revolution in Russia. The king was unable to form a coalition government and gave the task of forming a new government to the Liberals and the Social-Democrats. Nils Edén became prime minister and the Cabinet included four Social-Democrats, among them Hjalmar Branting. With this government, parliamen-

tary democracy may be considered as finally established in Sweden. After this the king was no more to intervene in the political life of the country, except on a few rare occasions. In the late autumn of 1917, the Bolsheviks took power in Russia, and in November 1918 the World War ended. Great changes took place and in many countries monarchy was swept away. Agitation for universal suffrage was linked with powerful republican demands and in many places a revolutionary mood was in the air.

During this period, with little fanfare, Sweden paid back the money it had borrowed to finance its modernization. A high rate of inflation devalued many currencies and meant that it became advantageous for Sweden to pay off loans taken in these currencies.

Propaganda for female suffrage took many different forms, such as this Christmas card. In Finland and Norway, women already had the vote.

DEMOCRACY AND THE "PEOPLE'S HOME"

At the extraordinary session of Parliament in the autumn of 1918, an important reform was approved abolishing taxation requirements in relation to the franchise for local government elections. The great constitutional reform was passed during the normal parliamentary session of 1919. Universal suffrage was introduced giving both men and women the right to vote in elections for the second chamber. Since these changes involved constitutional laws, a second session of Parliament had to approve the reform, and it finally became law in 1921. Sweden was now a true democracy. The left-wing obtained a majority in both chambers of Parliament. In this connection it should be noted that although electoral procedures were now completely democratic, the members of the first chamber were elected for a period of eight years, half of them being elected every four years, while the members of the second chamber were elected for four years. This led to a parliamentary lag in relation to electoral opinion, as this could not

stamp its character on a new parliament completely after an election, since half of the members of the first chamber retained their seats for another four years and were able to vote against majority decisions from the newly elected second chamber in joint votes. The difference between the conservative, "bourgeois" group in Parliament and the socialist group was often no more than a few seats, a circumstance which lent itself to behind-the-scenes compromises.

In the spring of 1920, Sweden joined the newly formed League of Nations. That autumn the Eight Hour Day was enacted, entailing a forty-eight hour Monday to Saturday working week. In the following year, the death penalty was abolished.

THE ÅLAND QUESTION ❧ Nordic cooperation had continued during the final stages of the war. The situation in Finland constituted a special problem, however. After the Russian revolution of 1917, Finland, which had been a

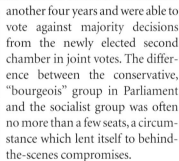

Grand Duchy in a personal union with the tsar since 1809, declared its independence. Social and political antagonisms led to a bloody civil war between Reds and Whites, in which the Reds sympathized with the newly established Soviet state and the Whites (mainly the bourgeoisie and better-off peasant farmers and, it goes without saying, bitter anti-socialists) wanted complete independence but at the same time were not shy about asking Germany for assistance. Volunteers from Sweden fought with the Whites, who were led by the Finnish-born former tsarist general Gustaf Mannerheim. After the White victory, Finland became a non-socialist republic. A dispute blew up in relation to the Åland islands, whose Swedish-speaking people wished to be reunited with Sweden. The question was finally arbitrated in 1921 at the League of Nations. Åland remained Finnish, but obtained a high degree of autonomy and constitutional guarantees for the protection of its Swedish language. The islands would continue to be demilitarized.

A PERIOD OF WEAK GOVERNMENTS ∽

The coalition between the Liberals and the Social-Democrats fell apart in early 1920 and Hjalmar Branting formed a minority government which remained in office until the autumn. It fell when the parliamentary elections – the last to be held according to the old rules – gave a majority to the Right and the Agrarian Party. Two caretaker governments held office until the elections of 1921. During the next ten years Sweden had no less than eight governments, which found it difficult to carry out their party programmes. The difficulties of

forming a stable government were partly due to disunity in the parties, and partly to the fact that the left-wing had no majority, while the bourgeoisie and its allies were very fragmented. So as soon as the opposition was able to find common ground on some matter of importance, the minority governments in power were defeated. It was possible for the Social-Democrats to carry out a drastic programme of disarmament in 1925, however, with the support of the left-leaning faction of the non-socialist parties. But it proved impossible to reach unanimity on unemployment policy or on raising certain taxes.

The high levels of inflation during and after the First World War were followed by a period of deflation, with money rising in value and prices falling. An unwelcome corollary to this was high unemployment, which fell somewhat during the boom of the 1920s, however. In 1924, Sweden was able to return to the gold standard, which had been abandoned in the whole of Europe during the war. Swedish industry expanded strongly, subsidiaries were set up abroad and exports grew. This was partly linked with the bold operations of Ivar Kreuger, the "Match King", which were reputed to be giving Sweden "a new age of greatness".

The temperance issue became the focus of intense controversy. A consultative referendum was held in 1922, in which a proposal to introduce complete prohibition was rejected by a slender majority. The question split the Liberal coalition party into liberal and dissenting (free-church temperance) factions, although they reunited in 1934 to form the still active Liberal Party. The leader of the dissenters was Carl

Gustaf Ekman. During the whole of this period the Social-Democrats remained the largest party in Parliament. Hjalmar Branting participated in the formation of two minority governments before his death in 1925. Per Albin Hansson was a member of these Cabinets. Implementing socialist policies was out of the question, as the parliamentary support for this was too weak. In January 1925, Branting passed the post of prime minister to Rickard Sandler, and shortly afterwards the admired leader of reformist Swedish Social-Democracy died. The government finally resolved the military question in collaboration with the dissenting Liberals. The Right was angered by the decommissioning of a number of regiments, but it was powerless to prevent it.

The Sandler government never got the chance to implement its programme of social insurance, but fell in the spring of 1926 on the intractable question of unemployment. Carl Gustaf Ekman then assumed the role of national "tightrope walker", controlling the balance of parliamentary power. Together with the liberal faction, the dissenters only had 64 votes in the two chambers, but they were able to remain in government until the autumn of 1928 with the alternate support of the Right and the Social-Democrats. This apparently weak and much-criticized government was able to carry through a number of important measures, however, including an educational reform, laws on collective bargaining and the institution of a court of labour arbitration (1928). In 1928, the

The funeral following the Ådalen riots of 1931. 12,000 workers took part, and observed perfect discipline. The impressive solemnities were organized by the Communists, and red banners waved over the whole procession.

173

The great Stockholm exhibition of 1930 marked the breakthrough of functionalism in Sweden.

Right formed a government under Arvid Lindman, which was to be its last until 1991, when (under its new name, the Moderates) it participated in a coalition government.

The Great Depression which began with the stock exchange crash in New York in 1929, soon spread to Europe. Agriculture was particularly vulnerable, and Lindman proposed support measures to Parliament in 1930, including higher customs duties, but this split the government. Carl Gustaf Ekman returned with a Cabinet composed entirely of dissenting Liberals, with only the most minimal parliamentary support. The depression caused unemployment to rise and labour disputes once more became common. At one demonstration against strike-breakers during a conflict in the northern region of Ådalen in 1931, five people were killed when the troops who had been called in opened fire on the crowds of people. The government rode out the violent political storm that ensued, but the military has never

again been used in Sweden in this kind of situation.

THE SOCIAL-DEMOCRATS IN GOVERNMENT ❧ In March 1932, the country was shocked by the news that Ivar Kreuger had shot himself in Paris, and details of the case that subsequently came to light led to a deepening of the depression. Many companies were affected and had to receive government aid. Others went bankrupt and wealthy individuals were ruined. Serious strikes broke out and gave rise to vigorous polemics against the "murderous government". When it emerged that the dissenting Liberals had been receiving secret subsidies from Kreuger, and the prime minister went as far as to attempt to deny his own signature, the Cabinet fell. Ekman was also compelled to resign as party leader. Following Social-Democrat gains in the elections of September 1932, Per Albin Hansson formed a new Cabinet, which included Rickard Sandler as foreign minister, Ernst Wigforss as finance minister and Gustav Möller as minister of social affairs. From now until 1976, there would be a Social-Democrat prime minister in power for more than forty years without a break, apart from a three-month interregnum in 1936. The severe financial situation, in which a surplus of imports put pressure on the currency reserves, had led to the abandonment of the gold standard in 1931. As a result, the krona fell, boosting Swedish industrial exports.

The first priority of the new government was to tackle unemployment. The prime minister spoke of his desire to create a "home of the people" – *folkhemmet* – the Swedish version of the welfare state. This concept covers so many aspects of modern Sweden that it is almost magical to many Swedes of most political persuasions, especially those of older generations. No one would suffer deprivation any more, unemployment would disappear, class divisions would be reduced and eventually disappear completely, but above all, the whole people would feel a sense of security as it faced the future. There was no attempt to conceal that this would mean higher taxes for the rich and also involve the socialization of certain industries and businesses in the future. By cooperating with the Agrarian Party in Parliament the government was able to carry into law measures mitigating the effects of the economic crisis, such as relief work, at the same time as agriculture was given substantial subsidies. There is still no consensus as to whether or not these policies materially affected the ensuing economic boom. The government resigned in the early summer of 1936 after suffering some defeats in Parliament, and the leader of the Agrarian Party, Axel Pehrsson from Bramstorp, formed a short-lived government (popularly known as the "holiday government"), which was to be the last purely non-socialist government in Sweden for decades. It was replaced in September 1936 by a coalition of the Social-Democrats and the Agrarian Party. Per Albin Hansson was once more prime minister and Rickard Sandler foreign minister.

In 1932, the "march to the welfare state" was begun, a period of social reforms unprecedented in the history of Sweden that was only interrupted by the onerous demands of military preparations in connection with the Second World War. An important principle in the "home of the people" welfare state was that social benefits should be universal rights untainted by the least suggestion of charity.

A significant event in this process was the signing of the extremely important Saltsjöbaden Agreement in 1938. It had been negotiated by the Swedish Confederation of Trade Unions (LO) and the Swedish Employers' Confederation (SAF) over a period of two years. The agreement contained clearcut rules for the labour market, covering such matters as notice of strike action, compulsory negotiations before a strike could be undertaken, dismissals and redundancies. Employers also agreed not to make use of strikebreakers. The agreement marked a significant step towards détente in the labour market, even if large-scale conflicts such as the great metalworkers' strike of 1945 could not be completely prevented. This new situation gave rise to the "Swedish model" so admired abroad. It was to dominate the labour market and its centrally negotiated collective agreements, and it became normal to see the Employers' Confederation representative and the general secretary of the Confederation of Trade Unions cordially shaking hands after successfully concluded negotiations.

FOREIGN POLICY ∾ The threatening situation in Europe, especially since the Nazis had taken power in Germany in 1933, was attracting more and more attention in Sweden. After the resolution of the Åland question, foreign relations in the years immediately following the First World War had not been of any acute concern to policy-makers. The optimism felt in relation to the League of Nations and its potential for solving international disputes would prove to be misplaced, however. When Japan conquered Manchuria in the early 1930s, the League was unable to do anything about it. Mussolini's fascist Italy attacked Abyssinia in 1935 and the sanctions decreed by the League of Nations proved toothless. The only effect they had was to drive Italy closer to Germany. The dictatorship of Adolf Hitler and the acts of violence it perpetrated both in Germany itself and against Germany's neighbours led the Swedish government to reassess its defence policies. From 1934 to the outbreak of hostilities in 1939, the prime ministers of the Nordic states met annually and in 1938 they issued a joint declaration of neutrality. No real political unity of action was achieved, however, and none of these declarations – or the celebration of Nordic Day and the institution of a committee for Nordic cooperation – would prove to have any deterrent effect whatsoever on future aggressors.

In the 1930s, the Nazis and their ideology of violence gained some adherents in Sweden, but they were never represented in Parliament.

In 1936, the bloody Spanish Civil War broke out. It was to last three years and has been called a dress rehearsal for the Second World War. Italy and Germany gave open support to the rebels led by general Francisco Franco, while the government forces were supported by volunteers from throughout the world and by the Soviet Union. The government was defeated in 1939 in a civil war that was conducted with repugnant cruelty.

Great Britain and France long pursued a policy of preserving peace at almost any price. After the Munich agreement of 1938 between Hitler, Mussolini, Britain's prime minister Neville Chamberlain and the head of the French government Edouard Daladier, most people were still hoping against hope that peace would be able to be maintained. Appeasement policies long enjoyed majority support. In 1939, after the German invasion of what was left of Czechoslovakia after Munich, and the Easter annexation of Albania by Italy, it was clear to the allies that a war was inevitable. Many years neglect of the armed forces now had to be made good. Shortly before war broke out, the two mortal enemies Germany and the Soviet Union concluded a non-aggression pact known as the Molotov-Ribbentrop pact. Its immediate effect was to enable Hitler to attack Poland without risking a war on two fronts. On 1 September 1939 the German army and air force invaded Poland. Two days later France and England declared war on Germany and the Second World War had started.

SWEDEN DURING THE SECOND WORLD WAR ∾ In a speech shortly before the outbreak of war, prime minister Per Albin Hansson assured the Swedish people that "Sweden is fully prepared". This white lie concealed the real situation, which was that Sweden, despite the military policy adopted in 1936, was very ill-pre-

EN SVENSK TIGER

A famous poster enjoining silence to foil spies. *En svensk tiger* is a pun on the double meaning of the word 'tiger' in Swedish: on the one hand it means 'stays silent', so the text means 'A Swede stays silent', while on the other it means 'tiger': 'A Swedish tiger'. The poster hammers home the first meaning by illustrating the second. Bertil Almqvist, 1941.

pared for war. In the years that followed there was a frenetic process of rearmament, in which the military industries that already existed – cannons from Bofors were justifiably renowned – were greatly expanded and large orders were placed abroad. The strengthening of the armed forces was made possible by big loans raised on the money market and by extra taxes, but it was not until 1943 that the Swedish armed forces are considered to have been in a position to offer efficient resistance and deter would-be aggressors. Sweden's ability to pursue a strong and credible policy of neutrality was consequently very limited.

After the rapid defeat of Poland by the Germans and the division of its territory between Germany and the Soviet Union, the latter conquered the Baltic states under the pretence of concluding pacts of friendship and assistance. This was followed by a Soviet demand for certain Finnish territories, partly with a view to reducing the vulnerability of Leningrad given its geographical situation. While these negotiations were in progress, the Nordic heads of state and foreign ministers met in Stockholm in October. The public demonstrations of sympathy for the Finnish cause obscured the fact that the meeting produced no concrete results what-

During the Second World War it was necessary to mobilize every available resource for the homeland. The picture shows prime minister Per Albin Hansson and Gustaf V opening an exhibition: "The people and the defence effort".

ever. Finland's refusal to cede the territories demanded by the Soviet Union provoked a Soviet bombing raid on Helsinki on 30 November 1939.

Sweden found itself in an extremely difficult position during the Finnish-Soviet war, which became generally known as the Winter War. There was great popular sympathy for Finland, but the government didn't dare take any measures that might lead to war.

In mid-December the government was reshaped, becoming a coalition government led by Per Albin Hansson and including the four major democratic parties, the Social-Democrats, the Agrarian Party, the Liberals and the Right. The former foreign minister, Rickard Sandler, who wished to see more active support for a country which had belonged to Sweden for so many years, had to leave the government. A professional diplomat, Christian Günther, who was not tied to any political party replaced him as foreign minister.

The new government gave Finland as much support as it dared, approving munitions and other military supplies, food and large-scale loans. At the same time great voluntary aid operations were undertaken (in conformance with the popular slogan *Finlands sak är vår* – "Finland's cause is our own"). Great Britain and France requested permission to send troops through northern Sweden to relieve Finland, but the government refused, as such a step

The transit of German troops via Sweden took place between 1940 and 1943, and ostensibly involved German troops travelling to and from occupied Norway "on leave". However, the trains also carried guns and ammunition. Here some German soldiers are seen walking along the tracks under the supervision of Swedish conscripts.

was considered to violate Sweden's neutrality. There was also a suspicion that the main objective of the allies' plan was not to support the Finns – a difficult task given the nature of the communications routes involved – but to block or destroy the iron mines of Swedish Lapland in the Arctic north. With the release of British documents dealing with this period it became clear that these suspicions were in fact well-founded. Sweden mediated the Russian offers of peace, which were accepted by the Finns in March 1940.

Swedish concessions to germany ❧

The allies were greatly preoccupied by Swedish exports of iron ore to Germany at this time. They were considering such steps as a landing in Norwegian ports. The greater part of Swedish exports passed throught the Arctic but ice-free Norwegian port of Narvik after being taken there by rail. In Narvik the iron ore was loaded into German ore ships. This iron ore was absolutely vital for the German war industry. Then on 9 April 1940 Germany suddenly invaded Denmark and Norway. The occupation of Denmark took place without fighting, but Norway resisted and was helped, ineffectively, by England and France. It was not until June that the Norwegian royal family and government left their country for London. The Norwegian army capitulated and with this the German occupation was accomplished.

Sweden mounted a full-scale mobilization of its forces in the face of the German threat in the spring of 1940, but at the same time it assured the German government in a note of its intention to remain neutral. Sweden became more

and more dependent on Germany, and this led to a number of vigorously criticized deviations from its principles of neutrality. One of these was the transit of German troops through Sweden – on the pretext that they were on leave – a traffic that was at its height during the spring of 1941 and included the transport of munitions. In the spring of 1940 the Germans also mounted their rapid and successful invasions of Holland, Belgium and France. After this Great Britain remained alone in resisting Germany, and it is understandable that Swedish politicians and generals considered a German victory to be the most likely outcome of the war, with the only choice being the degree of independence that Sweden might be able to attain.

German pressures were not restricted just to Sweden's trade or the transit traffic. Its free press was a thorn in the side of the Germans and on several occasions the government saw itself compelled to intervene against newspapers that attacked Germany. In the autumn of 1940, the government was concerned about Finland's situation and negotiations were undertaken in relation to such extreme steps as a possible union with Sweden. Russian opposition ruled this out, however. After Hitler's invasion of the Soviet Union on 22 June 1941 and Finland's alliance with Germany, the situation took a turn for the better as far as Sweden was concerned, although the changes were not immediately visible. During the summer the government was compelled to permit yet another large-scale transit of German troops, involving 15,000 German soldiers of the Engelbrecht division who were moved from Norway to Finland. On this occasion the government was not unanimous. The prime minister, who wished to yield to German pressure, was supported by Gustaf V. It was argued that it was a one-off event. In the spring of 1942, relations between Sweden and the Nazi regime were so strained that a German invasion was feared. It later emerged that an invasion plan had in fact been prepared, but the severe German defeats of the autumn and winter of 1942-43, most notably at Stalingrad, made it possible for Sweden to defend its interests in a new and more assertive fashion. What is more, in the late autumn of 1941 the USA entered the war. After the Japanese attack on Pearl Harbour in December 1941, both Germany and Italy declared war on the USA.

THE FINAL STAGES OF THE WAR ∾ During the summer of 1943, the agreement allowing the transit of troops to and from Norway was revoked, and other concessions were subsequently withdrawn, too. In the following year exports (mainly of iron ore and ball bearings) to Germany were restricted, and they were stopped altogether in the autumn of 1944. At the same time the allied invasion of France in June 1944 had led to further German setbacks. Thanks to Swedish mediation, separate peace negotiations were initiated between the Soviet Union and Finland in December 1943, but it was not until September 1944 and the appointment of marshal Mannerheim to the presidency that the capitulation, with severe conditions attached, was finally arranged. Leaving a trail of extreme destruction German forces withdrew from Finland to Norway via Finnish Lapland. Sweden was inundated by large waves of

Finnish refugees fleeing from the Germans over the northern Finnish border.

The violence of the Nazi occupation in Denmark and Norway aroused great indignation in Sweden, and voluntary aid efforts were organized. Towards the end of the war the government gave open support to these, including the organization of military training for refugees. Thanks to advance warning of a planned wave of mass arrests, most of the Jewish population of Denmark fled across the Sound in small boats and was given a humane and efficient reception in Sweden. Pressure on the German government in the final stages of the war led to Scandinavian (and later other) prisoners being released from concentration camps and sent to Sweden. Count Folke Bernadotte acted as a legate of the Swedish government. Raoul Wallenberg, who was later seized by Soviet troops, saved tens of thousands of Jews from death in Nazi concentration camps using the Swedish legation in Budapest as his base. He provided Jews with Swedish "protective passports", which placed them under the protection of the Swedish government.

At the end of the war there were some 400,000 refugees in Sweden, including many from the Baltic states of Estonia, Latvia and Lithuania. Despite very critical public opinion and internal dissension, the Swedish government submitted to Soviet demands for the extradition of Baltic soldiers in German service who had fled to Sweden at the end of the war. In January 1946, 146 Balts were extradited, and many people considered the measure a disgrace.

When Germany capitulated on 7 May 1945, shortly after Hitler's suicide, scenes of wild re-

Raoul Wallenberg at the Swedish legation in Budapest in 1944. By issuing "protective passports" he saved tens of thousands of Jews from Nazi extermination camps. After the Soviet army of occupation marched into the city, Wallenberg was taken into "protective custody" and vanished without trace. Many years later, Russian officials claimed that he died in the Lubyanka prison in Moscow in 1947. In 2000, official Russian sources declared that Wallenberg had fallen victim to the terror of the Soviet regime during the 1940s.

joicing took place in Sweden – the nation's sympathies had long been with the allies. Europe was at peace, but in ruins. In neutral Sweden the task of building the modern welfare state got under way.

DOMESTIC POLICY 1939-45 ✿ In general, problems of supply were managed much better during the Second World War than during the First. No one was at risk of starvation and the restrictions on consumption led to an actual improvement in public health. There was a comprehensive rationing system. Motor traffic was restricted and the main fuels used were producer-gas and carbide. For the last time, horses were used on a large scale, particularly in agriculture and forestry. Vast stores of firewood were laid up in the towns. During the war, the severe winters occasionally led to the closure of schools and churches, as it was impossible to heat them adequately.

The planning of production and the control of the labour market necessary during the war prepared the people for the "strong society" that was to come after the war. Even if active reform policies had to be put on hold during the war, one or two important domestic events deserve mention. In the spring of 1941, Parliament decided to lower the voting age to 21. In the following year, an education commission was appointed, whose report was to signal the start of the post-war reforms. In 1942, a general price-freeze was implemented. Labour and the employers also agreed on a wage-freeze. The labour market truce was not broken until February 1945, when the great metal-workers' strike broke out, affecting some 125,000 employees.

THE IMMEDIATE POSTWAR PERIOD ∞ In July 1945, the coalition government resigned and was replaced by a Social-Democratic government led by Per Albin Hansson. When he died in 1946 he was succeeded as prime minister by Tage Erlander. The agenda of the new government was to carry out the reforms that had been held up by the war, and to raise the standard of living and housing. An intense struggle broke out between the government party and the non-socialist opposition in relation to the new proposals, which entailed heavier taxation of companies and those with high incomes – higher government revenues were necessary for the welfare state envisaged by the Social-Democrats. The proposals were approved by Parliament in 1947. Dissension was also generated by the great trade agreement concluded with the Soviet Union in 1946 – it was negotiated because there was a general apprehension that the postwar period would bring a severe depression. This did not happen, however, and as a result the trade agreement lost much of its significance.

The rapidity of the recovery in Western Europe after the Second World War must at least in part be attributed to the plan of economic stabilization approved by the US Congress and known as the Marshall Plan after its originator, US Secretary of State George Marshall. The Cold War between the Soviet Union and the other states of Eastern Europe on the one hand, and the Western Powers on the other, then gave rise to two systems of alliances, the North Atlantic Treaty Organization (NATO) and the Warsaw Pact. The Swedish government initiated negotiations for Scandinavian collaboration in defence policy, but they ran aground in 1949. Denmark and Norway joined NATO, while Sweden remained non-aligned. There was a high level of domestic agreement in relation to Sweden's neutrality doctrine: non-alignment in peace with the objective of neutrality in war. Sweden's foreign minister for seventeen years (1945-62), Östen Undén, became a symbol for the Swedish rejection of power bloc policies. There was also a high level of agreement that powerful armed forces were a prerequisite for a non-aligned policy. Sweden's position was reinforced by its geographical and strategic location near the Soviet Union. It later emerged that Sweden, despite its non-aligned policies, was for decades actively but clandestinely collaborating with NATO in military and technological matters. Very few people knew about this collaboration, which was routinely denied if the matter was ever publicly raised. The revelations did not give rise to any great public debate, however.

Although Sweden was officially neutral, most newspapers supported the USA during the Cold War, which was perhaps at its most intense until 1963 (although it revived to a certain extent during the Brezhnev era). In public debate, however, a group emerged which wished to adopt a critical attitude to the Western Powers, too – the "third standpoint". While the Cold War was at its most threatening, a strong Swedish defence was considered indispensable, and vigorous rearmament continued. Since the 1970s, however, most political parties have agreed (with the exception of the Moderates) that a policy of cautious disarmament – or at least a reduction in the armed forces – is ap-

During the Vietnam war, many Swedes were fiercely critical of the USA. The picture shows Olof Palme in the celebrated demonstration in Stockholm in 1968, accompanying the North Vietnamese ambassador to Moscow. For a number of years after this, Swedish-US relations were quite frosty.

propriate. It has been many decades since Sweden had any great navy to speak of. In the 1990s, the diminished risk of war led to proposals for a very vigorous reduction in the armed forces – as in 1925, some people spoke of regimental extermination. At the same time it is emphasized that a certain degree of military preparedness is necessary for Sweden to be able to participate in international observation, surveillance and aid efforts.

INTERNATIONAL UNDERTAKINGS ∽ Neutrality did not prevent Sweden committing itself to international undertakings, as long as these had no links with the Great Powers. Sweden and the Swedes emerged from the enforced isolation of the war years with a powerful sense of com-

mitment to the wartorn nations and subsequently also to more distant, poor and "underdeveloped" countries in what became known as the third world, most of which had recently freed themselves from colonial dependence. From the moment of its election in 1946 to the United Nations – which had been founded by the victorious powers shortly before the end of the Second World War – Sweden became one of the most enthusiastic members of that body. It has always given whole-hearted support to the UN. In 1953, Dag Hammarskjöld, a Swede, was elected General Secretary of the UN. He died in 1961 in a plane accident in Ndola while on a peace mission.

Sweden and individual Swedes have given a great deal of support particularly to countries

The arrival of television in the 1950s brought great changes both in social behaviour and home furnishing.

The introduction of a universal child allowance in 1948 was a major step towards the welfare state.

Below, the most celebrated poster of the national supplementary pensions battle of 1959. The Social-Democrats won by one vote (a member of the opposition Liberals defected on this issue). The poster says: "A medal's fine, but first a proper pension".

gärna medalj men först REJÄL PENSION socialdemokraterna

in the third world – the doctrine of neutrality gave rise to few problems in this connection. This support developed into the relatively open backing given to a number of national liberation movements. Leading politicians – notably Olof Palme – were highly critical of the USA for its war in Vietnam, and of the Soviet Union for its invasion of Czechoslovakia to crush the "Prague spring" of 1968. Sweden's current, very active support for the Baltic states did not materialize until after the fall of the Berlin wall in 1989, however.

The official policy of neutrality not only made it impossible for Sweden to join NATO, but it also prevented Swedish membership of the emerging European economic community (the EEC, later to become the EU). To compensate for this, Sweden was very active in setting up the European Free Trade Organization (EFTA) in

1959 together with Great Britain, Norway, Denmark, Austria and Switzerland. These countries were later joined by Finland. EFTA later lost much of its significance when most of its member states joined the EEC.

Nordic collaboration recommenced as soon as it became possible. (Some dissonance with respect to the initial strictness of Swedish neutrality after 9 April 1940 was muted at least in part by the help Sweden gave towards the end of the war and later.) The forum for this collaboration is the Nordic Council, whose members are Denmark, Finland, Iceland, Norway and Sweden. The fields in which the Nordic countries have collaborated have been wide-ranging, but have not included military matters since three of the member states are long-standing members of NATO. The countries share a joint labour market and a passport union.

MODERN SWEDEN ∾ From the end of the war in 1945 until 1976 the Social-Democrats enjoyed uninterrupted power. Between 1951 and 1956 they were in a coalition with the Agrarian Party, and occasionally they had to rely on voting support from the Communists, as they had no outright majority. Tage Erlander was prime minister until 1969, when he was succeeded by Olof Palme. The important reforms of the immediate postwar years, such as the introduction of a universal child allowance and improvements in the basic retirement pension – were only a prelude to the intense socio-political activity of the 1950s and 1960s which resulted in, among other things, the introduction of a general health insurance system. A particularly important reform was the national supplementary pension scheme (ATP), which was approved by Parliament in 1959 by a majority of

Swedes have become accustomed to immigrants in the community – not just from the neighbouring Nordic countries but from Asia and Africa, too.

Parliament flanked by the royal palace and the City Hall.

one vote after a long and acrimonious debate and a consultative referendum. This created a system of retirement pensions which survived unchanged until the 1990s, when its assumptions of unbroken growth necessitated radical modification. Housing construction had never been as comprehensive or intensive as it was after 1945 and it continued with unabated vigour practically up to the recession of the 1990s.

This long period of social reforms was made possible by Sweden's impressive industrial growth. It was not until the 1970s that the Swedish welfare state began to feel the pinch of encroaching economic problems, including the inability of the Swedish krona to maintain its value against most other European currencies and the dollar, a state of affairs which led to a number of devaluations.

For many years during the postwar period Sweden suffered from a shortage of labour in its manufacturing industries. Central government actively promoted large-scale migration

from rural areas into the towns, and women entered the labour market in ever greater numbers. This development was made possible by the ongoing expansion of day care facilities and a switch to individual taxation as opposed to joint taxation of married couples. But these national sources of labour-power were insufficient, and more workers had to be imported from abroad, mainly from Sweden's Nordic neighbours, especially Finland, but also from countries in southern Europe like Yugoslavia and Italy.

A second great wave of immigration began in the 1970s, however, including people from outside Europe, and had less to do with labour-power seeking work than with asylum-seeking refugees and their families. An early and typical example involved young people fleeing the military dictatorship in Chile after the bloody right-wing coup against the constitutional government of Salvador Allende in 1973. During the 1980s and the early 1990s immigration reached very high levels, but in the late 1990s, Swedish immigration policies, which had long been generous, became somewhat more restrictive. Today a full fifth of Sweden's population of just under 9 million people consists of first or second generation immigrants. From having been an ethnically homogeneous nation with the Sami as the only sizable, clearly delimited minority, Sweden is on its way to becoming a multi-cultural society.

A NEW CONSTITUTION ∾ Until 1970, Sweden's constitutional laws consisted of the Instrument of Government of 1809, the Riksdag Act of 1866, the Act of Succession of 1810 and the Freedom of the Press Act of 1949 which had replaced that of 1812. After a number of commissions had studied the subject, new constitu-

tional laws were prepared. A new Riksdag Act was approved in 1970 whereby the two chambers of Parliament were replaced by a single chamber. General elections to this single chamber were to be accompanied by simultaneous elections to municipal and county council assemblies and the electoral period was reduced to three years (although this was raised to four years as of 1994). When Gustaf VI Adolf died in 1973 and was succeeded by Carl XVI Gustaf, Parliament had approved a new Constitution, but all modifications to the Swedish Constitution require two parliamentary decisions separated by a general election. The new Constitution finally came into force in 1974. According to the new Constitution "all public power emanates from the people". The king retains his position as head of state, but his remaining

King Carl XVI Gustaf, Queen Silvia, and their three children: Crown Princess Victoria, Prince Carl Philip and Princess Madeleine.

Opponents of nuclear power outside Barsebäck nuclear power plant in 1982. Nuclear power remains a highly controversial subject. In 1999, the first reactor at Barsebäck was shut down, but the decommissioning of other reactors is still an open question.

powers – which had long been merely formal in nature – have now been assumed by the government, and his role in the formation of governments has been taken over by the Speaker. In place of the weekly meetings of the royal council, "information councils" are held when deemed necessary. The decisions of the government are taken under the leadership of the prime minister. In 1972 the voting age was lowered to 18. To win a seat in Parliament, parties must obtain either 4 per cent of the votes cast nationally, or 12 per cent of the votes cast in any single constituency.

In the summer of 1976, Carl XVI Gustaf married Silvia Sommerlath from Germany. The royal couple have three children. A new Act of Succession was approved in 1979 by which Sweden also adopted the principle of female succession, which means that Princess Victoria (b.1977), not her younger brother Carl Philip (b. 1979), will succeed to the throne.

ALTERNATING GOVERNMENTS ✆ The era of great successes and "permanent" growth ceased in the 1970s, although it would be many years before the people of Sweden realized this had happened. In 1973 the first international oil crisis exploded and Sweden's balance of trade was overturned. The trade union movement agitated stubbornly for legislation to take the place of some of the voluntary arrangements originating with the Saltsjöbaden Agreement. People still referred to the spirit of Saltsjöbaden, but it was evaporating rapidly. Wildcat strikes became commonplace and one of the earliest and most dramatic took place in the iron ore mines of Arctic Sweden in December and January 1969-70. As a component of its reform policies, the government of Olof Palme enacted legislation on increased trade union influence and security of employment. These laws stipulated that the highly controversial principle of "last in, first out" should apply whenever a company needed to dismiss employees.

For many years and with great singleness of purpose the Swedish Confederation of Trade Unions agitated for the creation of wage-earner funds. The idea behind this policy was that all large companies should annually place a portion of their profits in collective funds which would then purchase shares in Swedish companies. In this way the influence of wage-earners over these companies would gradually be strengthened. The proposal was energetically opposed by the private sector and by the non-socialist parties, but it was approved by Parliament in modified form and the funds were in operation between 1984 and 1992. In this year they were abolished by the non-socialist government then in power. At the time their holdings amounted to more than 23 billion kronor. Some of this money has been set aside for funds to promote such objectives as the development of knowledge and the improvement of the environment.

Alfred Nobel (1833-96).

The Polish poet Wis≥awa Szymborska receiving the Nobel Prize for Literature at the Stockholm Concert Hall in 1996. Except during the two World Wars Nobel Prizes have been presented annually since 1901.

The free trade agreement covering industrial goods concluded between Sweden and the EEC in 1972 would eventually prove to be a very significant step. Cooperation between the EEC and the countries that remained in EFTA developed even more in subsequent years.

In the mid-1970s the powerful position of Swedish industry was weakened when important sectors such as shipbuilding, textiles and sections of the steel and forestry industries encountered new and tough competition from low-wage countries. Production costs in Sweden were too high, and in part this was due to rapidly rising wage costs.

After an intensive election campaign full of

With its revolutionary packaging system for liquid foodstuffs, Tetra Pak has been a postwar success story in Swedish industry.

Sweden has a large, research-intensive pharmaceutical industry. Losec, a stomach ulcer medicine, has been an important product for Astra (now AstraZeneca), a pharmaceuticals giant.

Thousands of Russians queue at the opening of Ikea's furniture superstore in Moscow in March, 2000.

controversy, including the major issue of the future of nuclear power in Sweden, the autumn elections of 1976 removed the Social-Democrats from office and weakened their powerful electoral base. The first purely non-socialist government in 44 years took office, in the form of a coalition between the Moderates (the renamed Right), the Centre Party (the renamed Agrarian Party) and the Liberals. The prime minister was the Centre Party leader, Thorbjörn Fälldin. Six years of non-socialist governments ensued, in which they had to administer a severe recession, support many companies which found themselves in difficulties and cope with internal dissension and conflict – not least in relation to the issue of nuclear power in which some of the non-socialist parties held diametrically opposed views. The incompatibility of these views split the government after only two years. The leader of the Liberals, Ola Ullsten, then formed a short-lived minority government that fell from office after the September elections of 1979. Fälldin returned to office leading a coalition government that remained in power with a narrow majority for another three years.

Nuclear power remained a highly controversial issue. The nuclear accident at Three Mile Island in Harrisburg, USA, in 1979 provided additional fuel to the anti-nuclear campaign. After a consultative referendum in 1980, Parliament decided that all twelve reactors which were then in use or under construction would be decommissioned by 2010. In 1988 the timetable was made more explicit and it was specified that two reactors would be phased out in 1995-96. This move was prompted by the serious nuclear accident at Chernobyl in the Ukraine in 1986, after which dangerous nuclear fallout contaminated areas of northern Sweden. The original decision was rescinded in 1991, after it was realized that the closure of all reactors by 2010 was probably not feasible. Today three parties – the Centre Party, the Greens and the Left Party – are in favour of phasing out nuclear power and frequently appeal to the referendum. The Social-Democrats are more hesitant, but in principle favour decommissioning. After a deal between the Social-Democrats, the Centre Party and the Left, Parliament decided in 1997 that the phasing-out process should start at Barsebäck, located on the south-western coast of Sweden and within sight of the Danish capital, Copenhagen. In the autumn of 1999 one of Barsebäck's two reactors was shut down. No firm date for the closure of further reactors has

Sweden's EU commissioner in Brussels, Margot Wallström, is responsible for environmental matters, a field given high priority in Swedish EU activities.

yet been specified, and the previous objective of phasing out all the existing nuclear plants by 2010 has been abandoned.

The repeated oil crises, together with a growing awareness of environmental issues led to the red wave resulting from the events of 1968 and its student revolt being succeeded by a green wave, and a new party, the Green Party, was launched following the lead of German environmentalists. Gradually all the political parties have become more inclined to devote greater attention to environmental issues.

In the elections of 1982 the Social-Democrats were returned to office with Olof Palme as prime minister. They got off to a flying start thanks to a bold devaluation and a marked boom in the economy. The government failed to take full advantage of the situation, however, and found it hard to innovate in matters of political strategy. A few years later, the murder of Olof Palme shocked the entire nation. He was

gunned down in central Stockholm on 28 February 1986. The murder has still not been solved despite the deployment of extraordinary police resources. It has been said that Sweden lost its innocence with this, its first political murder since 1792. The new prime minister was Ingvar Carlsson, who had participated in Social-Democrat Cabinets since 1969.

The Social-Democrats remained in government until 1991. By then an unusually deep recession was under way, with unemployment figures not seen in Sweden since the 1930s. At the same time the expansion of the public sector and the growing cost of the welfare state were making great demands on the nation's finances.

THE EU, THE EMU AND THE EURO ∾ The final act of the Carlsson government was a U-turn on the EU – in 1991 it submitted Sweden's application for full membership. After the fall of the Berlin wall in 1989 and the dissolution of the Soviet Union, the political map had changed and the government no longer considered that Sweden's traditional neutrality constituted an obstacle to full membership in the European Community. On 1 January 1995 Sweden became a member of the EU after a narrow majority had voted Yes in a referendum a few months earlier. Sweden chose to remain outside when the common currency the euro – the third stage of EMU – was introduced in 1999, but kept the door open for entry later.

It should be noted that until the first few decades of the nineteenth century Europe used common currencies that were valid everywhere. They did not disappear until the "century of nationalism" was well under way. A typical currency of this kind was the *taler banco*, which was a pure accounting currency with no physical manifestation. Gold ducats could also be used for payment anywhere regardless of their place of production. And the world has long made use of reserve currencies, primarily the US dollar, which are preferred in countries with a weak currency of their own.

Sweden has retained its military stance of non-alignment, but as mentioned above, the capacity of the armed forces to participate in humanitarian and peace-keeping efforts is to be enhanced. Since the dissolution of the

Sweden has a wealth of new museums, such as the Museum of Labour in Norrköping, housed in a disused textile factory in the river Motala ström. The museum does not collect objects, but puts on thematic exhibitions.

The Öresund bridge opened in 2000. For the first time since it was a hunting and gathering society, Sweden once again has a land link with Denmark and Continental Europe.

Soviet Union, Sweden has considerably increased its commitments in the Baltic region – a peaceful version of its policies of the seventeenth century.

Embarking on a new millennium ∞

The elections of 1991 were contested by an unusually large number of parties. The Greens, who had been in Parliament since 1988, had a poor election and lost their seats, while the rather older Christian Democratic Party easily exceeded the 4 per cent limit. The Left Party (renamed from the Left Party Communists) lost votes but beat the cut-off. A new party, New Democracy, with a right-wing populist message, made a dramatic entrance on the parliamentary scene, but broke up shortly before the next elections and lost all its seats.

A minority government was formed by Carl Bildt, the leader of the Moderates, in the autumn of 1991. He was the first right-wing head of government since 1929. The Cabinet included ministers from the Liberals, the Centre Party and the Christian Democrats. At the same time an international recession once more had the world in its grip and unemployment rose sharply. The non-socialist government faced a worsening budget deficit that finally reached catastrophic dimensions. In the autumn of 1992 the Swedish krona was exposed to a giant wave of speculation and currency poured out of the country. The government and the Bank of Sweden held out as long as they could against freeing the exchange rate but the continued pressure finally broke their resistance, and as a result the krona weakened dramatically in value. The government managed to carry out a number of conservative reforms, however, including the privatization of certain state activities, and it also initiated cutbacks in the public sector.

In September 1994 new elections were held for the new constitutional period of four years instead of three. They showed great gains for Social-Democracy, which won some 46 per cent of the votes. The Greens returned to Parliament and the Left Party grew, while all the non-socialist parties except the Moderates fell back. The Liberals had now largely lost their former significance in Swedish politics. Ingvar Carlsson was once again prime minister and showed little hesitation in ruling alone with the support of various *ad hoc* parliamentary majorities, mainly relying on the support of the Centre Party. As mentioned above, on 1 January 1995 Sweden joined the EU. In the spring of 1996 Ingvar Carlsson resigned as prime minister and was succeeded by Göran Persson, who had been Carlsson's finance minister. In the elections of 1998, the Social-Democrats lost many votes and the Left Party made big gains. The Social-Democrats managed to remain in power, however, primarily with the support of the Greens and the Left. The most pressing task of these Social-Democratic governments was to balance public finances by a combination of tax increases and a major programme of public savings, viewed by many as a dismantling of the welfare state. The result of the 2002 elections confirmed the dominant position of the Social-Democrats, while the balance between the socialist and non-socialist blocks in Parliament remained substantially the same.

In the wake of an accelerating boom towards the end of the 1990s, the previously high unemployment figures began to fall and a shortage of skilled labour began to make itself felt in certain sectors. Swedish industry has become more and more internationalized, and many large Swedish companies have long had more employees in other countries than in Sweden itself. Other important Swedish companies which had been a source of national pride for much of the nineteenth century, such as Saab and Volvo, were bought up by even larger foreign companies, such as General Motors and Ford. Vast mergers in key sectors such as banking, forestry, chemicals and pharmaceuticals became commonplace. At the same time, Sweden has won a place at the forefront of developments in telephony and telecommunications, and is an acknowledged leader in the use and technology of the Internet.

SWEDEN'S KINGS AND REGENTS FROM AD 1000

(All datings up to the end of the twelfth century are uncertain and only approximate.)

Olof Skötkonung	ca 995-1022
Anund Jakob	1022-1050
Emund the Old	1050-1060
Stenkil	1060-1066
Halsten	1066-1080s
Inge the Elder	1080s-ca 1105
Filip	ca 1105-1118
Inge the Younger	1118-1120s
Ragnvald Knaphövde	ca 1125
Magnus Nilsson (Götaland)	ca 1125-1130

The Sverker and Erik Clans

Sverker the Elder	ca 1130-1156
Saint Erik	1156-1160
Karl Sverkersson	1160-1167
Knut Eriksson	1167-1195 (1196)
Sverker the Younger Karlsson	1196-1208
Erik Knutsson	1208-1216
Johan Sverkersson	1216-1222
Erik Eriksson (a minor)	1222-1229
Knut Holmgersson (the Tall)	1229-1234
Erik Eriksson (the Lisping and Lame)	1234-1250

The Folkunga Dynasty

Birger Jarl, royal guardian and *jarl*	1250-1266
Valdemar Birgersson	(1250) 1266-1275
Magnus Birgersson (Barn-Lock)	1275-1290
Birger Magnusson's regency	1290-1298
Birger Magnusson	(1290) 1298-1318
Magnus Eriksson's regency	1319-ca 1332
Magnus Eriksson	(1319) ca 1332-1364

The Mecklenburg Dynasty

Albrekt of Mecklenburg	1364-1389

Union Regents and Protectors of the Realm

Margrete, union queen	1389-1412
Erik of Pomerania, union king	(1397) 1412-1434 (1439)
Karl Knutsson, protector	1438-1440
Kristoffer of Bavaria, union king	1441-1448
Karl (VIII) Knutsson, Swedish king	1448-1457
Christian I, union king	1457-1464
Karl Knutsson, Swedish king	1464-1465, 1467-1470
Sten Sture the Elder, protector	1470-1497
Hans, union king	1497-1501
Sten Sture the Elder, protector	1501-1503
Svante Nilsson Sture, protector	1504-1511
Sten Sture the Younger, protector	1512-1520
Christian II, union king	1520-1521

The Vasa Dynasty

Gustav Eriksson Vasa, protector	1521-1523
king (Gustav I)	1523-1560
Erik XIV	1560-1568
Johan III	1568-1592
Sigismund	1592-1599
Karl IX, protector,	1599-1604
king	1604-1611

Gustav II Adolf	1611-1632
Kristina's regency	1632-1644
Kristina	(1632) 1644-1654

The Palatine Dynasty

Karl X Gustav	1654-1660
Karl XI's regency	1660-1672
Karl XI	(1660) 1672-1697
Karl XII's regency	1697
Karl XII	1697-1718
Ulrika Eleonora	1719-1720

The Hessian Dynasty

Fredrik I	1720-1751

The Holstein-Gottorp Dynasty

Adolf Fredrik	1751-1771
Gustav III	1771-1792
Gustav IV Adolf's regency	1792-1796
Gustav IV Adolf	(1792) 1796-1809
Karl XIII	1809-1818

The Bernadotte Dynasty

Karl XIV Johan	1818-1844
Oscar I	1844-1859
Karl XV	1859-1872
Oscar II	1872-1907
Gustaf V	1907-1950
Gustaf VI Adolf	1950-1973
Carl XVI Gustaf	1973-

SWEDEN'S WARS AND PEACE TREATIES AFTER THE DISSOLUTION OF THE KALMAR UNION IN 1523

1534–36 • Sweden intervenes in the Count's Feud, in which Christian II, who is supported by Lübeck, is prevented from regaining the Danish crown.

1563–70 • The Nordic Seven Years War with Denmark. Peace of Stettin: the Älvsborg ransom.

1570–83 • War with Russia for control of Estonia.

1590–95 • War with Russia. Peace of Teusina: Narva and Estonia become Swedish.

1611–13 • The Kalmar War with Denmark. Peace of Knäred: second Älvsborg ransom.

1617 • Peace of Stolbova: Russia cedes Keksholm province and Ingria.

1621–29 • War with Poland – for Livonia in 1621–26 and for the Prussian harbours in 1626–29. Armistice of Altmark, 1629: Livonia and a number of Prussian harbours become Swedish for six years.

1630–48 • Sweden a belligerent in the Thirty Years War. The Heilbronn league, 1633.

1643–45 • War with Denmark – Lennart Torstensson invades Holstein in 1643. Peace of Brömsebro, 1645: Sweden obtains Ösel, Gotland, Jämtland, Härjedalen, as well as Halland for 30 years and exemption of tolls in the Sound.

1648 • Peace of Westphalia signed in Osnabrück and Münster: Sweden obtains part of Pomerania including the islands of Rügen, Usedom and Wollin, territories on the Oder including Stettin, together with Wismar and the duchies of Bremen and Verden.

1655–60 • War with Poland: Karl X Gustav seizes Cracow in 1655. Denmark declares war in 1657.

1656–61 • War with Russia. Peace of Kardis: no territorial concessions.

1657–58 • War with Denmark. Peace of Roskilde, 1658: Sweden obtains Skåne, Blekinge, Halland, Bohuslän, Trondheim province and Bornholm.

1658–60 • War with Denmark. Peace of Copenhagen, 1660: Trondheim province and Bornholm returned to Denmark.

1660 • Peace of Oliva with Poland: Livonia becomes Swedish.

1674–75 • Brandenburg War. Sweden defeated at Fehrbellin in 1675. Denmark declares war.

1675–79 • The Skåne War with Denmark. Treaty of Lund: no territorial concessions.

1679 • Peace of Fontainebleau: Sweden regains most of Pomerania after France imposes a settlement on Brandenburg and its allies.

1700–21 • The Great Northern War.

1719 • Peace of Stockholm with Hanover: Bremen and Verden ceded.

1720 • Peace with Prussia: Sweden cedes Western Pomerania as far as the river Peene, Usedom and Wollin. Peace of Fredriksborg with Denmark: Sweden agrees to pay tolls in the Sound again.

1721 • Peace of Nystad with Russia: Livonia, Estonia, Ingria and part of Karelia ceded.

1741–43 • The "Hats' War" with Russia. Peace of Åbo: territory east of the Kymmene River ceded.

1757–63 • The Pomeranian War, the Seven Years War. Peace of Hamburg: no territorial concessions.

1788–90 • Gustav III's Russian war. Peace with Denmark, 1789. Peace of Värälä with Russia, 1790: no territorial concessions.

1805–07 • War in Pomerania. Sweden joins Britain, Hanover and Russia against Napoleon. French troops attack Swedish Pomerania in 1807. Treaty of Tilsit between France and Russia.

1808–09 • The Finnish War. Russia attacks in February, Denmark in March. Peace of Fredrikshamn: all Finland, including the Åland islands, ceded. Peace of Jönköping with Denmark: no territorial concessions.

1810 • Treaty of Paris with France: Sweden regains Pomerania, but is forced to join the Continental System and declare war on Britain.

1812 • Napoleon occupies Swedish Pomerania. Sweden signs a treaty with Russia.

1813 • Sweden joins attack on Napoleon in Germany. Karl Johan attacks Napoleon's ally Denmark.

1814 • Treaty of Kiel: the Swedish king obtains Norway, which is forced into a union with Sweden. Denmark receives Swedish Pomerania in exchange.

1814 • War with Norway ends with the Convention of Moss. Norway is compelled to accept the union, but keeps the Eidsvoll Constitution.

PRIME MINISTERS AND PARTIES IN POWER FROM 1876

Louis De Geer	1876-1880	Ernst Trygger, *Right*	1923-1924	Tage Erlander,	1957-1969
Arvid Posse	1880-1883	Hjalmar Branting,	1924-1925	*Social-Democrat*	
Carl Johan Thyselius	1883-1884	*Social-Democrat*		Olof Palme,	1969-1976
Oscar Robert Themptander	1884-1888	Rickard Sandler,	1925-1926	*Social-Democrat*	
Gillis Bildt	1888-1889	*Social-Democrat*		Thorbjörn Fälldin,	1976-1978
Gustaf Åkerhielm	1889-1891	Carl Gustaf Ekman,	1926-1928	*Centre-Moderate-Liberal*	
Erik Gustaf Boström	1891-1900	*Liberal (dissenters)*		*coalition*	
Fredrik von Otter	1900-1902	Arvid Lindman, *Right*	1928-1930	Ola Ullsten, *Liberal*	1978-1979
Erik Gustaf Boström	1902-1905	Carl Gustaf Ekman,	1930-1932	Thorbjörn Fälldin,	1979-1981
Johan Ramstedt	1905	*Liberal (dissenters)*		*Centre-Moderate-Liberal*	
Christian Lundeberg	1905	Felix Hamrin,	1932	*coalition*	
Karl Staaff,	1905-1906	*Liberal (dissenters)*		Thorbjörn Fälldin,	1981-1982
Liberal		Per Albin Hansson,	1932-1936	*Centre-Liberal coalition*	
Arvid Lindman, *Right*	1906-1911	*Social-Democrat*		Olof Palme,	1982-1986
Karl Staaff,	1911-1914	Axel Pehrsson-Bramstorp,	1936	*Social-Democrat*	
Liberal		*Agrarian*		Ingvar Carlsson,	1986-1991
Hjalmar Hammarskjöld,	1914-1917	Per Albin Hansson,	1936-1939	*Social-Democrat*	
Civil servant ministry		*Social-Democrat-*		Carl Bildt,	1991-1994
Carl Swartz, *Right*	1917	*Agrarian coalition*		*Moderate-Centre-*	
Nils Edén,	1917-1920	Per Albin Hansson,	1939-1945	*Liberal-Christian-*	
Liberal-Social-Democrat		*National coalition*		*Democratic coalition*	
coalition		Per Albin Hansson,	1945-1946	Ingvar Carlsson,	1994-1996
Hjalmar Branting,	1920	*Social-Democrat*		*Social-Democrat*	
Social-Democrat		Tage Erlander,	1946-1951	Göran Persson,	1996-
Louis De Geer, *Non-party*	1920-1921	*Social-Democrat*		*Social-Democrat*	
Oscar von Sydow, *Non-party*	1921	Tage Erlander,	1951-1957		
Hjalmar Branting,	1921-1923	*Social-Democrat-*			
Social-Democrat		*Agrarian coalition*			

Note: Names of parties are only given from the 1905 Staaff government onwards, as it was not until then that political parties in the modern sense of the word began to exert a decisive influence on the composition of Cabinets.

POLITICAL PARTIES (seats in Parliament)

FIRST CHAMBER

Year	Conservative, from 1969 Moderate Party	Agrarian, from 1958 Centre Party	Liberals	Social-Democrats	Communists	Total
1912	86	-	52	12	-	150
1914	88	-	49	13	-	150
1915	89	-	47	14	-	150
1918	88	-	45	17	-	150
1921	37	19	40	51	3	150
1922	41	18	38	52	1	150
1925	44	18	35	52	1	150
1929	49	17	31	52	1	150
1933	50	18	23	58	1	150
1937	45	22	16	66	1	150
1941	35	24	15	75	1	150
1945	30	21	14	83	2	150
1949	24	21	18	84	3	150
1953	20	25	22	79	4	150
1957	13	25	30	79	3	150
1958	16	24	29	79	3	151
1961	19	20	33	77	2	151
1965	26	19	26	78	2	151
1969	25	20	26	79	1	151

SECOND CHAMBER

Year	Conservative, from 1969 Moderate Party	Agrarian, from 1958 Centre Party	Liberals	Social-Democrats	Communists	Total
1912	64	-	102	64	-	230
1914	86	-	70	74	-	230
1915	86	-	57	87	-	230
1918	57	14	62	97	-	230
1921	71	30	47	80	2	230
1922	62	21	41	99	7	230
1925	65	23	33	104	5	230
1929	73	27	32	90	8	230
1933	58	36	24	104	8	230
1937	44	36	27	112	11	230
1941	42	28	23	134	3	230
1945	39	35	26	115	15	230
1949	23	30	57	112	8	230
1953	31	26	58	110	5	230
1957	42	19	58	106	6	231
1958	45	32	38	111	5	231
1961	39	34	40	114	5	232
1965	33	36	43	113	8	233
1969	32	39	34	125	3	233

SINGLE-CHAMBER PARLIAMENT (number of seats and proportion of votes)

Year	Moderate Party	%	Centre Party	%	Liberals	%	Christian Democrats	%	Social-Democrats	%	Communists, from 1990 Left Party	%	Green Party	%	New Democracy	%	Total
1970	41	11.5	71	19.9	58	16.2			163	45.3	17	4.8					350
1973	51	14.3	90	25.1	34	9.4			156	43.6	19	5.3					350
1976	55	15.6	86	24.1	39	11.1			152	42.7	17	4.8					349
1979	73	20.3	64	18.1	38	10.6			154	43.2	20	5.6					349
1982	86	23.6	56	15.5	21	5.9			166	45.6	20	5.6					349
1985	76	21.3	44	12.4*	51	14.2			159	44.7	19	5.4	-				349
1988	66	18.3	42	11.3	44	12.2			156	43.2	21	5.8	20	5.5			349
1991	80	21.9	31	8.5	33	9.1	26	7.1	138	37.7	16	4.5	0	3.4	25	6.7	349
1994	80	22.4	27	7.7	26	7.2	15	4.1	161	45.3	22	6.2	18	5.0	0	1.2	349
1998	82	22.9	18	5.1	17	4.7	42	11.8	131	36.4	43	12	16	4.5			349
2002	55	15.2	22	6.1	48	13.3	33	9.1	144	39.8	30	8.3	17	4.6			349

Independent members and also minor parties have been added to the major party they stood closest to. *Together with the Christian Democrats.

INDEX

Act of Union and Security 118
Adam of Bremen 17, 22
Adolf Fredrik 97 ff.
Aftonbladet 140
Age of Freedom 87–106, 109, 110,
 148
Agrarian Party 170, 175, 178,
 185, 191
Albrekt of Mecklenburg 32
Almquist, Carl Jonas Love 149
Alsnö Diet 27
Alströmer, Jonas 93
Altmark, armistice of 62
Anckarström, Jacob Johan 120,
 121, 122
Anjala league 117
Ansgar 17, 22
Anund Jakob 17
Armfelt, Gustaf Mauritz 116, 122
Articles of Arboga 46
ATP 185

Balts, extradition of 180
basic retirement pension 160, 185
Bellman, Carl Michael 111
Belt, march across the 72
Bender, the kalabalik of 83
Bernadotte, Folke 180
Bernadotte, Jean Baptiste,
 see Karl XIV Johan
Bildt, Carl 195
Birger Jarl 25, 26
Birger Magnusson 28
Birgitta, Saint 30, 33
Birka 14, 16, 17, 22
Black Death 31, 55
Boström, Emil Gustaf 153, 154,
 156, 157
Branting, Hjalmar 154, 166, 169,
 170, 173

Breitenfeld, battle of 63
Bremer, Fredrika 167
Bronze Age 11 f.
Brunkeberg, battle of 38
Brömsebro, peace of 67

Cabo Corso 69
Caps, the 94, 99, 102, 103 f.
Carl XVI Gustaf 187, 188
Carlsson, Ingvar 192, 195
Celsius, Anders 103
Centre Party 191, 195
Christian Democrats 194, 195
Christian I 37, 38
Christian II ("the tyrant") 39 f., 41,
 44
Chronicle of Erik 25, 26, 28
Church, the 22, 24 f., 30, 32, 42, 45
Cistercians 25
Communists, see Left Party
Compulsory military service 133,
 152, 154, 155
Conventicle Proclamation 145,
 164
Count's Feud 44
Court Party 99, 101, 103, 105
Crimean War 144, 146, 149

Dacke, Nils 44
Dahlberg, Erik 68, 78
De Geer, Louis 69, 86
De Geer, Louis 144, 145, 146, 149,
 150, 151, 152
De la Gardie, Magnus Gabriel
 73, 74, 75, 77
defence 146, 149, 151, 152, 154, 159,
 182
Descartes, René 70
distributive system, the 78, 86,
 152, 154, 155

East India Company 92, 93
Edén, Nils 170
EEC/EU 184, 190, 191, 192 f.
Efta 184, 190
Ekman, Carl Gustaf 173, 174
elementary school ordinance
 139, 146
emigration 142, 143, 148, 150, 153,
 155, 161, 163, 164
EMU 192
Emund the Old 23
Engelbrekt Engelbrektsson 35 f.
Erik Eriksson (the Lisping and
 the Lame) 25
Erik Magnusson, duke 28, 29
Erik of Pomerania 34 ff.
Erik the Victorious 17
Erik XIV 34, 45 ff.
Erik, Saint 24, 26, 27, 37
eriksgata 17
Erlander, Tage 182, 185
Estonia 48, 60, 89

Farmers' Rally 160
Fersen, Axel von (the Younger)
 120, 128, 129, 130
Finland 26, 28, 45, 47, 53, 80,
 83, 89, 91, 96, 97, 125, 128, 132,
 133, 144, 171, 177, 178, 179, 180
First World War 161, 167 ff.
Fleming, Klas 53
folkhemmet, see people's home
Folkunga Dynasty 25, 28
Fredrikshamn, peace of 128
freedom of religion 112, 113, 145
Freedom of the Press Act 103, 113,
 116, 127, 140, 141, 187
Friedrich of Hesse (Fredrik I) 84,
 85, 87, 88, 89, 90 f.
Fälldin, Thorbjörn 191

Gotland 13, 15, 19, 20 , 23, 31, 32, 33
Great Northern War 78, 80 ff.
Green Party 191, 192, 194
Grip, Bo Jonsson 33
Gustaf V 158, 159, 160, 168, 177, 180
Gustaf VI Adolf 157, 187
Gustav II Adolf, Gustavus Adolphus 28, 42, 53, 54, 57 ff.
Gustav III 99, 100, 105, 106, 107, 108, 109, 110 ff., 124
Gustav IV Adolf 112, 122 ff., 127
Gustav Vasa 39, 41 ff.
Gyllenstierna, Kristina 40
Görtz 84, 85, 88

Hammarskjöld, Dag 183
Hammarskjöld, Hjalmar 160, 168, 169
Hanse, the 26, 35, 42
Hansson, Per Albin 173, 174, 175, 176, 177, 182
Hats, the 94, 96, 97, 98, 99, 100, 101, 102, 103, 105
Helgö 14
Hierta, Lars Johan 140, 146
Horn, Arvid 90, 91, 92, 94
House of Nobility 59, 103, 114, 147
hunter-gatherer cultures 7 f., 194
Håtuna, Games of 28

Ice Age 7 f.
immigration 185, 186
industrialization 150, 161, 162
Ingria 61, 80, 89
inventions 161, 190
Iron Age 12 f., 15

Johan III 34, 45, 46, 47, 48, 50 ff.

Kalmar Union 33 ff., 48
Kalmar, War of 55, 60
Karin Månsdotter 49, 50
Karl IX 45, 52 ff.
Karl Knutsson Bonde 36 ff.
Karl Sverkersson 24
Karl X Gustav 66, 68, 70 ff., 74
Karl XI 69, 71, 73 ff., 86
Karl XII 79 ff., 87, 88, 95
Karl XIII 122, 127, 128, 129, 132, 136, 137
Karl XIV Johan 130 ff., 144
Karl XV 136, 144 ff., 162
Katarina Jagellonica 48, 49
Key, Ellen 167
Kiel, peace of 134
Kreuger, Ivar 172, 174
Kristina 64, 66, 67 f., 69, 70
Kristoffer of Bavaria 37

Labour movement 165, 166
Lagerlöf, Selma 138, 168
land reforms (unification) 90, 123, 124
land taxes 149, 152, 154
Left Party 170, 185, 191, 194, 195
Leipzig, battle of 133
Lewenhaupt, Charles Emil 95, 97
Liberal Party 172, 178, 188, 191, 195
liberalism 106, 141
Liberals 141 f., 145, 146, 154, 156, 159, 160, 168, 169, 170, 172
Lindman, Arvid 158, 159, 169, 174
Linköping bloodbath 53, 54
Linné, Carl von 92, 100
Livonia 62, 71, 73
Lovisa Ulrika of Prussia 98, 99, 101, 102, 113
Lund, battle of 76
Lützen, battle of 64, 65

Magnus Eriksson 28, 29 f.
Magnus Eriksson's national code of laws 29
Magnus Ladulås (the Barn-Lock) 26, 27, 28
Margrete, union queen 30, 32 ff.
mendicant orders 25
Moderate Party 182, 191, 195
monasteries 25, 43
Möller, Gustav 174

Narva, battle of 80
neutrality policy 134, 144, 168, 176, 179, 182, 183, 193
New Democracy 194
New Sweden 69
Nobel, Alfred 161, 189
nobility 46, 59, 69, 112, 118
Nordic Seven Years War 48
nuclear power 188, 191
Nyköping, the Banquet of 29
Nystad, peace of 89

Olaus Magnus 42, 54, 55
Olaus Petri 43
Olof Skötkonung 17, 21, 22
Oscar I 136, 141 ff.
Oscar II 136, 151, 154, 155, 156, 157, 158, 159
Oxenstierna, Axel 42, 54, 57 f., 61, 62, 64, 65, 66, 67, 69

Palm, August 165
Palme, Olof 183, 184, 189, 192
parliamentarism 167, 170
parliament of the Estates 37, 58, 146
parliamentary reform 142, 146 ff.
passage graves 10
pastorate trade, the 114

Patkul, Johan Reinhold 78, 80, 81
peasant farmers 36, 55 f. 86, 91,
   109 f., 148
Pechlin, Carl Fredrik 100, 105,
   121
people's home 174 f.
Persson, Göran 46, 47, 49, 50
Persson, Göran, prime minister
   195
pictorial stones 15
Platen, Baltzar von 131, 138
Polhem, Christoffer 101
Poltava, battle of 82
Pomerania 63, 67, 71, 83, 88, 101,
   125, 128, 133, 134
popular mass movements 155,
   164

Reduction, the 73, 77, 78, 86
Reformation, the 42, 43
Reuterholm, Gustaf Adolf 122,
   123
Richelieu 63, 66
Right, the 159, 160, 169, 170, 173,
   178
Riksdag (Parliament) 32, 42
Rimbert 17, 22
rock carvings 11
Roskilde, peace of 72
Rudbeck, Olof 78
rune stones 15, 18, 23
Rural Party 148, 152, 153

S:t Barthélemy 115
Saltsjöbaden Agreement 175, 189
Sami 7, 10, 15 f., 55, 158, 187
Sandler, Richard 174, 175, 178
Scandinavianism 136, 142, 149, 150

Second World War 162, 175, 176 ff.
Sigismund 48, 52, 53, 59
Sinclair, Malcolm 95
snapphane guerillas 76
Social-Democratic Party 154,
   159, 160, 166, 168, 170, 172, 174,
   175, 178, 182, 185, 188, 189,
   191, 192, 195
Staaff, Karl 158, 159, 160
Stenkil 23
Stockholm bloodbath 39, 40, 41
Stolbova, peace of 61
Stone Age 9, 11
Strindberg, August 149, 192
Sture, Sten (d.ä.) 38, 39
Sture, Sten (d.y.) 39, 40, 41
Succession, Act of 127, 187
Svante Nilsson, Natt och Dag 39
Swedish Employers' Federation,
   SAF 166, 175
Swedish Trade Union Confed-
   eration, LO 166, 175, 189
Svensksund, battle of 119
Sverker 24
Synod of Uppsala 1593 52

Tacitus 13
temperance question 141, 155,
   159, 164, 172
Tessin, Carl Gustaf 94, 98, 99, 100
Thing 18, 27
Thirty Years War 62 ff., 86
Torgils Knutsson 28
trade union movement 159, 165,
   166, 188
Trolle, Gustav 39, 40
two-chamber parliament 148,
   187

Ullsten, Ola 191
Ulrika Eleonora the Younger 79,
   84, 87, 89, 90
Undén, Östen 182
Union with Norway 134, 137,
   156, 157 f.
United Nations, UN 183
universal suffrage 147, 154, 156,
   159, 165, 167, 170, 171, 181, 188

Wage-earner funds 189
Valdemar Atterdag 31, 32, 33
Valdemar Birgersson 25, 26, 27
Wallenberg, Raoul 180, 181
Vasa, Kettil Karlsson 38
Vasa Race 42
welfare state 181, 182, 185, 195
Vendel Period 14
Westphalia, peace of 67
Viborg 28, 95
Wigforss, Ernst 174
Viking Age 9, 16–22, 23
Viking expeditions 17 ff.
witch-hunts 85
women's movement, the 167

Åbo, peace of 96
Ådalen 173, 174
Åland 128, 135, 144, 171, 172, 175
Älvsborg 49, 51, 60
Älvsborg, first ransom 51
Älvsborg, second ranson 60, 85

Öresund bridge 9, 194

Illustrations:

Alfa Laval AB 161
Bertil Almqvist 176
Ingvar Andersson/PRESSENS BILD 188
Arbetets Museum, Norrköping 193
Archivo Fotografico dei Musei Vaticano 30
AstraZeneca AB 190 *(above right)*
Jens Astrup/SCANPIX 194
ATA 19, 26 *(centre)*, 27, 42 *(right)*
Beata Bergström/Drottningholms teatermuseum
    149 *(below)*
The British Museum 20 *(right)*
Lennart Broborn/N/Naturfotografernas Bildbyrå
    123 *(right)*
Francis Bruun/ Stockholms Stadsmuseum 104, 121
Frank Chmura/TIOFOTO 61
Erik Cornelius/Statens Konstmuseer 38 *(below)*
    45, 65
Chad Ehlers/TIOFOTO 186
Bengt Drobin/PRESSENS BILD 191
Jonas Ekströmer/PRESSENS BILD 189 *(left)*
Anders Engman 68
Eric Feferberg/EF/PRESSENS BILD 190 *(below)*
Finlands Nationalmuseum 129
Jenny Flensborg 37
Folkets Hus 165
Göteborgs Stadsmuseum 93, 143
Sören Hallgren 8, 10, 13, 14, 18, 24, 97
Raymond Hejdström/Gotlands Fornsal 31 *(below)*
Jernkontoret 116
Bodil Karlsson/Statens Konstmuseer 98
Lennart Karlsson 36
Det Kongelige Bibliotek, Copenhagen 39
Krigsarkivet 59
Kungl. Biblioteket 22, 42 *(left)*, 44, 49,
    54, 55, 82, 85, 90, 100, 111, 120, 145, 146, 147,
    148, 161, 162, 167, 168 *(left)*, 170, 173, 174
Kungl. Husgerådskammaren 46–47, 48 *(right)*
Kungl. Myntkabinettet 66, 69, 94–95
Kungl. Vitterhetsakademien 58
Kunstmuseum St. Gallen 125
Lantmäteriverket 96

Ola Lejonborn 34
Torbjörn Lilja/N/Naturfotografernas Bildbyrå 7
Håkan Lind/Kungl. Husgerådskammaren 140
Linnémuseet, Uppsala 92
Livrustkammarens arkiv 62
Denny Lorentzen 184 *(above)*
Bengt A Lundberg/Statens Historiska Museum 15
Åsa Lundén/Statens Konstmuseer 48 *(left)*
C. O Löfman/Promedia *(photo and model of Birka)* 16
Anders Mattsson 192 *(right)*
Malmö Museum 77
Nationalmuseet, Copenhagen 31 *(above)*
Nobelstiftelsen 189 *(right)*
Nils-Johan Norenlind/TIOFOTO 185
Ulf Nordh/Västergötlands Museum 12
Nordiska Museets Bildbyrå 21, 102, 139, 155, 163
Lennart Olsson 40
PRESSENS BILD 157, 166, 169, 173, 178
Rigsarkivet, Copenhagen 33
SCA Forest and Timber AB 152, 153
Toni Sica/PRESSENS BILD 187
Sven-Erik Sjöberg/PRESSENS BILD 183
Ulf Sjöstedt/TIOFOTO 38 *(above)*
St. Annen-Museum, Lübeck 35
Statens Historiska Museum 20 *(left)*
Statens Konstmuseer 50, 53, 67, 72, 73, 75, 76, 79,
    81, 89, 108, 110, 114, 115, 119, 130-131, 136, 149 *(above)*
Jan Svanberg 26 *(left and right)*
Svensk Filmindustri 168 *(right)*
SVT Bild 184 *(below right)*
Truls Teigen/Kungliga slottet, Oslo 135
Hans Thorwid/Statens Konstmuseer 43
Uppsala Universitetsbibliotek 29
Tetra Pak AB 190 *(above left)*
Bengt Wanselius 192 *(centre)*
Thomas Veres/The Holocaust Memorial Museum,
    Washington 181
Vitlycke Hällristningsmuseum 11
Östergötlands och Linköpings stads Museum 112

Maps: Stig Söderlind 17, 74

Swedish Institute

THE SWEDISH INSTITUTE (SI) is a public agency established to disseminate knowledge abroad about Sweden's social and cultural life, to promote cultural and informational exchange with other countries and to contribute to increased international cooperation in the fields of education and research. The Swedish Institute produces a wide range of publications on many aspects of Swedish society. These publications can be obtained directly from the Swedish Institute or from Swedish diplomatic missions abroad and many are available on Sweden's official website, www.sweden.se.

In the SWEDEN BOOKSHOP on Slottsbacken 10 in Stockholm as well as on the website www.swedenbookshop.com, you will find – in many languages – books, brochures, richly illustrated gift books on Sweden, a broad selection of Swedish fiction, children's books and Swedish language courses.

The Swedish Institute
Skeppsbron 2
Box 7434
SE-103 91 Stockholm

Phone: +46(0)8 453 78 00
Fax: +46(0)8 20 72 48
E-mail: si@si.se
Internet: www.si.se